Harry Dean Stanton

Harry Dean Stanton

✢

Hollywood's Zen Rebel

Joseph B. Atkins

UNIVERSITY PRESS OF KENTUCKY

The University Press of Kentucky,
scholarly publisher for the Commonwealth,
serving Bellarmine University, Berea College, Centre
College of Kentucky, Eastern Kentucky University,
The Filson Historical Society, Georgetown College,
Kentucky Historical Society, Kentucky State University,
Morehead State University, Murray State University,
Northern Kentucky University, Spalding University,
Transylvania University, University of Kentucky,
University of Louisville, University of Pikeville, and
Western Kentucky University.
All rights reserved.

Editorial and Sales Offices: The University Press of Kentucky
663 South Limestone Street, Lexington, Kentucky 40508-4008
www.kentuckypress.com

Frontispiece: Sketch of Harry Dean Stanton by Zack Wallenfang.
(Courtesy of Zack Wallenfang.)

The Library of Congress has cataloged the hardcover edition as follows:

Names: Atkins, Joseph B., author.
Title: Harry Dean Stanton : Hollywood's Zen rebel / Joseph B. Atkins.
Description: Lexington : The University Press of Kentucky, 2020. | Series:
    Screen classics | Includes index.
Identifiers: LCCN 2020032982 | ISBN 9780813180106 (hardcover) | ISBN
    9780813180120 (pdf) | ISBN 9780813180137 (epub)
Subjects: LCSH: Stanton, Harry Dean, 1926-2017. | Motion picture actors and
    actresses—United States—Biography.
Classification: LCC PN2287.S6688 A75 2020 | DDC 791.43/028092—dc23
LC record available at https://lccn.loc.gov/2020032982

ISBN 978-0-8131-9772-2 (paperback)

To Lucy Jones,
who more than anyone brought me
into the world of Harry Dean Stanton

Contents

Prologue

We were north of Bowling Green nearly a hundred miles from the Blue Grass Memorial Gardens outside Lexington, Kentucky, and the memorial service for Harry Dean Stanton was to start in an hour. My wife, Suzanne, and I had miscalculated the time. "We have to be there," I told her. I pressed the pedal on my Chevy Malibu, speeding eighty-five to ninety miles an hour through bluegrass country, never seeing a single cop the entire way. We arrived just as musician and close Harry Dean friend Jamie James began to sing "Canción Mixteca."

It's a lonely song, full of grief, sadness, and homesickness for the "land of sun" the singer had long left behind.

> Oh, land of sun
> I sigh to see you
> Now so far away
> I live without light, without love

Harry Dean loved "Canción Mixteca," and he sang it all the time. He sang it in *Paris, Texas*. He sang it to his friend Michelle Phillips as they sat on his couch at his home on Mulholland Drive. He sang it to the crowds at the Troubadour and the Mint in LA, and on *David Letterman* as Dave grinned and the crowd chuckled, not knowing whether he was serious or clowning.

He was serious, all right. Harry Dean rarely, if ever, sang a lyric or spoke a word of dialogue that he didn't mean.

Suzanne and I joined an intimate gathering of fewer than a dozen people around the small granite marker that contained Harry Dean's ashes. The inscription next to his photo included his name, his birth and death dates, and the words "Actor and Musician / Navy WWII" next to depictions of a musical note and the dual masks of comedy and tragedy.

James and actor-musician Dennis Quaid sang Quaid's "On My Way to Heaven" and "Montana Hills," which Quaid cowrote with Harry Dean. "That was Harry's spiritual side," Quaid said about a man famous for eschewing notions of God, heaven, and organized religion. "His music." Harry Dean's cousins, Jim Huggins Sr. and Jr., both FBI men, told stories, as did James and Quaid. Lucy Jones, founder of the annual Harry Dean Stanton Film Festival in Lexington, smiled and listened, remembering her own stories, maybe the time he came to the festival and asked the audience, "What happens when you die?" And then his answer: "I think it's black, right? You go to sleep, right?"

With the stories came tears, but maybe even more laughs. Jamie James told Harry Dean's favorite joke: "What did the skeleton ask the bartender? 'Give me a beer and a mop.'" Everyone looked at each other a moment, and then the laughter broke out. Harry Dean had told that joke during the card game scene with Willie Nelson, Morgan Freeman, and Owen Wilson in *The Big Bounce* (2004).

Near Harry Dean's marker was a bench honoring his niece Andrea Huggins, who was just nineteen when she died of cancer in 1990. Harry Dean called her "Princess Andrea." A dozen yards or so from the marker were the graves of Harry Dean's mother, Ersel, and his grandparents. "Mama Ersel," as she preferred to be called, and her oldest son had a tortured relationship. As cousin Joy Spicer described it, "She was a very free spirit. Harry Dean did what he wanted, and so did his mother." Another cousin, ninety-two-year-old Etta Clay Moberly Hamilton, put it this way: "He was just like her." The artist in him owed something to Mama Ersel. A beautician, cook, and hard drinker who also once worked in a bar and had to escape a handsy customer through the bathroom window, she played guitar, sang with a low voice, and loved to paint, sometimes scandalizing folks with her portrayals of nude women. She also loved to fish and to play the horses and the dogs, and she would disappear for days at a time, telling folks she was either fishing or at the track. Harry Dean stopped speaking to her for years and only reconciled shortly before she died, but he kept a framed photo of her in his bedroom at home, and there's a picture of the two of them hanging on a wall in *Paris, Texas*.

Like Harry Dean, I'm a Southerner who grew up working in tobacco fields and going to fundamentalist country churches on Sunday, learned to pick guitar and play the harmonica, and left my hometown as a young man, first to the military and then to follow my calling. I started working on this book a few months before he died, and I never got to meet him. I asked Jim Huggins Jr. once if Harry Dean knew someone out there was writing a book about him.

"Yes, he did," Jim said.

"What was his response?" I asked.

Jim smiled. "His response was, 'I don't give a fuck.'"

I love that story, but I don't believe Harry Dean. He gave a fuck. As I stood among his family and his friends at his final resting place, I studied the face on that granite marker. "I may never have met you," I told him, "but I saw you come home."

I left that service thinking about the Harry Dean Stanton I saw in *Paris, Texas,* his character Travis Henderson, and I remembered something director Wim Wenders once said. "He turned that part into his own story. It got more and more hard to say this is Travis and this is Harry Dean. . . . His whole person, his whole biography, everything he had . . . got into character."

The film begins with Travis Henderson wandering in the desert, where he has been for four years. This is no locust-eating, camel-hair–wearing John the Baptist crying in the wilderness. He's more like a desert monk with a vow of silence for the sins of his past: an abandoned wife and child. He wants to recover what he lost—his family, his innocence?—and his first word in the 1984 film is "Paris," the place where things made sense before he threw it all away.

Travis Henderson says nothing for the first twenty-six minutes of the film. Instead you see him walking against the background of Robbie Müller's brilliant cinematography. You listen to Ry Cooder perform Blind Willie Johnson's 1928 "Dark Was the Night," surely the loneliest, most woebegone gospel ever written. Johnson was a Texas street preacher who knew the miseries even a man of God can suffer. Harry Dean/Travis Henderson never talked much about his miseries. He was a man who knew and valued silence. "Silence is very powerful," the actor once said. "Just not saying anything is already a powerful statement."

Paris, Texas was Harry Dean's favorite film, the film in which he finally got to play the lead and get the girl. Director Wim Wenders wanted an actor who could capture the essence of a "stubborn, catatonic, strange man who came out of another world and seems to be going nowhere." He chose one who had spent decades playing small or supportive roles, a character actor with a face everyone knew but who, like most character actors, remained largely anonymous to the public.

Wenders had a penchant for character actors. His previous film, *Hammett* (1982), featured legends like Elisha Cook Jr., Royal Dano, R. G. Armstrong, and Mike Mazurki. In *Paris, Texas,* Wenders also cast Nastassja Kinski, the daughter of the late Klaus Kinski, Germany's greatest character actor before

3

another noted German director, Werner Herzog, turned him into a leading man in *Aguirre, the Wrath of God* (1972) and *Nosferatu* (1978).

"I have in fact loved to work with actors who have not been in the limelight for a long time but have been persistently convincing character actors," Wenders told me in an October 2019 interview. "Harry certainly was a prototype of those. . . . What I liked in those actors is their dedication to their craft, the modesty by which they often disappeared behind their roles and their unconditional support of the filmmakers they worked with. You can count on the fact that you won't run into any ego problems or have to face any eccentric behavior, which can possibly occur every now and then if you work with 'movie stars.'"

Character actors are the working stiffs of the big and small screen, the toiling thespians who always find work, if not a big salary. "Not gorgeous enough to be stars," wrote Melissa Holbrook Pierson and Luc Sante in their 1999 book *O.K. You Mugs: Writers on Movie Actors.* "Their noses have been broken one too many times. . . . In short, they are real."

Wenders, who like Werner Herzog came out of the German New Cinema film movement that was born in Munich in the 1970s, initially wanted actor-writer Sam Shepard to play the lead. Shepard, who had written the screenplay for *Paris, Texas,* wanted Harry Dean. Earlier that year, at a bar in Santa Fe, New Mexico, the two were drinking tequila shots when Harry Dean told Shepard he was sick of the kind of roles he'd been playing. "I told him I wanted to play something of some beauty or sensitivity." Shepard convinced Wenders this was Harry Dean's role. "Harry is an actor's actor," Shepard said. "You don't have to be a lead to be well thought-of. He's one of those actors who knows his face is a story."

Maybe it was no accident that it took a European to give Harry Dean his first big shot at a solo lead. Despite the fact that this iconic film could only take place in America, *Paris, Texas* is infused with European sensibilities— from Wenders's directing to Dutchman Robbie Müller's camera work to German Nastassja Kinski's portrayal of Travis Henderson's wife, Jane. Harry Dean got another top billing in 1984 as costar with Emilio Estevez in *Repo Man,* directed by Englishman Alex Cox. Four years before, French director Bertrand Tavernier gave him a significant, if not starring, role in *Death Watch.*

Harry Dean's Travis Henderson has "a strong appeal to us," said Swiss director Sophie Huber, who produced and directed the award-winning 2013 documentary *Harry Dean Stanton: Partly Fiction.* "These sort of characters don't exist in Europe. It is American characters."

Uncertain at first, Harry Dean eventually saw the role as a natural fit. "The whole film evolved on a very organic level. It almost had a documentary feel to it. It wasn't odd to be in the lead. I took the same approach as I would to any other part. I play myself as totally as I possibly can. My own Harry Dean Stanton act. . . . I don't know what happened to Travis. I'd say . . . it's me. Still searching for liberation, or enlightenment, for lack of a better way to put it, and realizing that it might happen, it might not."

The parallels aren't exact. Harry Dean never married, but he once confessed there's "one kid I'm pretty sure is mine." Travis Henderson bought the land on which his parents first made love: "I started out there." Harry Dean Stanton, the oldest of three sons born to Ersel and native North Carolinian Sheridan Stanton, said this about his own conception: "I don't think they had a good wedding night, and I was a product of that."

Sheridan Stanton was a tobacco farmer and barber who used to tell the oldest of his three sons, "Go straight ahead till you hit something." The oldest of nine children, Ersel Moberly married Sheridan to get away from the crowded home of her parents. Living with Sheridan in little West Irvine, Kentucky, she gave birth to her first son on July 14, 1926. They were strict parents, and mother and son were never close. "I think she resented me as a kid," Harry Dean once said. "She even told me once how she used to frighten me when I was in the cradle with a black sock."

Another memory from childhood was that of his first love. "I learned to sing when I was a child. I had a babysitter named Thelma. She was eighteen, I was six, and I was in love with her. I used to sing her an old Jimmie Rodgers song, 'T for Thelma.' 'T for Thelma, T for Tennessee, that girl made a wreck out of me.' I was singing the blues when I was six. Kind of sad, eh?"

Later in life, after seeing a psychiatrist and getting group therapy, Harry Dean confronted his mother. "I called her one night and told her I hated her. We made up shortly before she died. Got pretty close then, actually. That's how it goes sometimes." Acting became a vehicle for dealing with the anger from those early years. "You can do stuff onstage that you can't do offstage. You can be angry as hell and enraged and get away with it onstage, but not off. I had a lot of rage for a long time, but I let go of all that stuff a long time ago."

The strict fundamentalist faith practiced around him colored his views of religion. His parents weren't particularly religious, but his brothers, Arch and Ralph, both would become Bible-quoting "Jesus freaks," in the words of Harry Dean's niece Whitney Fishburn. Religion in Kentucky, as across all of the South, is as much the backbone of the culture as tobacco, cotton, or music.

His parents divorced when Harry Dean was in high school. "As a child," he recalled, "I felt rage against adults who didn't treat me as a person, adults that were brutalized themselves by having an angry, vindictive God watching them all the time. I come from a broken home, and I realize it's the rule rather than the exception."

He was a singer before he was an actor, singing in a barbershop quartet as a young man and later, with a twenty-four-piece choral group, performing in stores and on the streets of small towns across the country. During World War II, he was a ship's cook in the US Navy and saw action in the Battle of Okinawa in 1945. "I was lucky not to have been blown up or killed," he has said about the experience. "I was there when the Japanese suicide planes were coming in. Fortunately they missed our boat. Took me a while to readjust after I went back home and went to college in Lexington, Kentucky."

He studied journalism at the University of Kentucky, switching majors several times before eventually gravitating to a drama group that gave him his first experience on stage. "I acted in *Pygmalion* with a Cockney accent. I knew right then what I wanted to do, so I quit college and went to the Pasadena Playhouse in 1949."

Founded in 1916 by actor-director Gilmor Brown, the Pasadena Playhouse was one of the premiere acting schools and community theaters in the country. Productions there ranged from Roman comedies, Shakespeare, and George Bernard Shaw to the latest works of modern dramatists, such as Eugene O'Neill and Tennessee Williams. Students learned everything from Japanese Noh plays to how to build and design sets. The great dramatist and screenwriter Horton Foote enrolled in the school's two-year program in the 1930s. Lee J. Cobb and Victor Jory were among the long line of famous actors to study and perform there.

"I started out on the stage, doing Shakespeare, but I preferred movies," Harry Dean once admitted. "Money, travel, women. Every man wants to get laid. That's all you think about."

He went to New York City, struggled, and eventually made his way back to California, this time Hollywood, early on appearing in the New York City–filmed 1954 television series *Inner Sanctum* and later getting an uncredited appearance in Alfred Hitchcock's *The Wrong Man* (1956). Over the next couple of decades he made countless film and television appearances, including four episodes each of *Zane Grey Theater, The Lawless Years,* and *Rawhide.* Between 1958 and 1968 he was in *Gunsmoke* eight times.

The roles got juicier in the 1960s and 1970s. He roomed for a time with future star Jack Nicholson, appearing with him as the innocuously grinning stagecoach robber "Blind Dick" in Monte Hellman's *Ride in the Whirlwind* (1966). Nicholson not only starred in but also wrote the script for the film. It was one of several films directed by Hellman that included Harry Dean in the cast. Others were *Two-Lane Blacktop* (1971), in which he played an Oklahoma hitchhiker (credited as H. D. Stanton), and *Cockfighter* (1974), which starred his friend and fellow Kentuckian Warren Oates. He showed the world his vocal chops and guitar-playing skills as well as his acting ability in *Cool Hand Luke* (1967), playing Tramp and crooning "Just a Closer Walk with Thee" while Paul Newman as Lucas Jackson visits with his chain-smoking, soon-to-die mother Arletta, played by Jo Van Fleet. In that film, he also performed "Midnight Special," "Ain't No Grave Gonna Hold My Body Down," and "Cottonfields."

"Singing and acting are very similar things," Harry Dean once said. "Anyone can sing and anyone can be a film actor. All you have to do is learn."

Cool Hand Luke "was a film with great character actors," noted director Frank Darabont has said, "the great mix of faces and personalities from different walks of life" that you get in a prison film. Along with Harry Dean, the film's cast included fellow character actors George Kennedy, Strother Martin, Anthony Zerbe, and Morgan Woodward.

Six years later, he was in the cast with Bob Dylan and Kris Kristofferson—two of his close pals—in Sam Peckinpah's *Pat Garrett and Billy the Kid* (1973). Six more years, and he was the bogus blind preacher Asa Hawks in John Huston's film version of Flannery O'Connor's *Wise Blood* (1979).

Harry Dean was part of the "New Hollywood" movement of the 1960s and 1970s that challenged the old film establishment and brought new life into filmmaking. New directors and screenwriters, including Hellman, Martin Scorsese, Francis Coppola, Peter Bogdanovich, Alan Pakula, and William Friedkin, embraced the "auteur" theory of director as artist and set about making films that mattered and that dared to challenge the still lingering Hollywood formula of the old studio system. Actors like Nicholson, Robert De Niro, Al Pacino, Harvey Keitel, and Gene Hackman "banished the vanilla features of the Tabs and Troys, and instead brought to the screen a gritty new realism and ethnicity," wrote Peter Biskind in his landmark study of the era, *Easy Riders, Raging Bulls*. Similarly, Faye Dunaway, Ellen Burstyn, Diane Keaton, and Jane Fonda "were a far cry from the pert, snub-nosed Doris Days of the 1950s."

These directors, screenwriters, and actors "produced a body of risky, high-quality work . . . work that was character- rather than plot-driven, that defied traditional narrative conventions, that challenged the tyranny of technical correctness, that broke the taboos of language and behavior, that dared to end unhappily," Biskind wrote. As part of this new approach to filmmaking, Harry Dean played an FBI man in Coppola's *The Godfather: Part II* in 1974, and more than a decade later, in 1988, a cynical Apostle Paul in Martin Scorsese's *The Last Temptation of Christ.*

By the 1980s, however, the New Hollywood was already fading, just in time for the Hollywood arrival of directors like Wenders from the German New Wave and, later, Werner Herzog.

In *Paris, Texas,* Harry Dean told the *Guardian's* Sean O'Hagan in 2013, he finally got the role he'd wanted for decades. "It's my favorite film that I was in. Great directing by Wenders, great writing by Sam Shepard, great cinematography by Robby Müller, great music by Ry Cooder. That film means a lot to a lot of people. One guy I met said he and his brother had been estranged for years and it got them back together."

Should he have gotten better roles earlier in his career? "In the end, you end up accepting everything in your life—suffering, horror, love, loss, hate—all of it. It's all a movie anyway." Harry Dean turned to Shakespeare's *Macbeth* to explain further. "'A tale told by an idiot, full of sound and fury, signifying nothing.' Great line, eh? That's life right there."

In one scene in Sophie Huber's documentary, a friend of Harry Dean's declares him a "philosopher," and over the years the actor's philosophical musings became part of his legend. An amalgam of Beat poetry, the writings of Alan Watts, Jiddu Krishnamurti, and Arthur Schopenhauer, Buddhist and Zen wisdom, the I Ching, and existentialism, it's a philosophy that is both fatalistic and yet, as Nietzsche would say, "all too human." Harry Dean's image as hip, off-beat philosopher was stoked by some of his later-career performances—his role as Mormon prophet, polygamist, and sect leader Roman Grant in the HBO series *Big Love* (2006–2010) and even earlier, in David Lynch's *Twin Peaks: Fire Walk with Me* (1992), in which his Carl the trailer-park manager is an island of normalcy in a world of weirdness.

"There's a Buddhist saying, 'To think you're an individual with an individual soul is not only an illusion, it's insane.' It's frightening, terrifying, but joyous, too," Stanton told the crowd at the 2014 Harry Dean Stanton Fest in Lexington, an event organizer Lucy Jones then called the only annual film festival dedicated to a living actor in the country.

Prologue

A sixties-era sensibility hovered about the Stanton philosophy, honed in part during those years when he was in a Southern California circle that included not only Jack Nicholson but also rock stars David Crosby and Cass Elliot. Kris Kristofferson even composed a song inspired by Stanton that became the theme song for their 1971 film together, *Cisco Pike,* and also served as the inspiration for the title of Huber's documentary on Harry Dean.

Journalist O'Hagan once described the enigmatic actor, singer, musician, and philosopher as "a kind of lone drifter in Hollywood." Yet the loner became a cult figure to many in the Dream Factory, and everyone's friend, too, it seemed, a decades-long regular at Dan Tana's in West Hollywood, where he used to hang out with Warren Oates and buddies Dabney Coleman and Ed Begley Jr. Eventually he became a kind of patron saint to a younger generation of actors, including Sean Penn and Johnny Depp.

He was "perhaps the last of that generation of great American postwar character actors," O'Hagan says, using a term Harry Dean never much liked. He was not the last. As of the writing of this book, one-hundred-year-old Nehemiah Persoff was still around, and so were L. Q. Jones and Cloris Leachman, both in their nineties. O'Hagan is right, however, when he calls Harry Dean "certainly one of the most singular."

Moviegoers "see themselves in the relatable situations and realistic idiosyncrasies these actors present on screen," write Cynthia and Sara Brideson in their 2012 collection of essays on great character actors, *Also Starring. . . .* "Like the average member of a movie audience, supporting players worked hard, if not harder than leading stars. They voiced little complaint as to their salaries or the redundancy of their types of roles. . . . Their back-to-back assignments did not diminish their abilities to give memorable performances."

Harry Dean, however, did grow weary of the redundancy, and that's why those tequila shots with Sam Shepard in Santa Fe led to *Paris, Texas.*

Still, director William Friedkin has called such acting "a lost art," which he believes is a shame because "character actors . . . solidified themselves into the audience's memory bank."

It's a memory bank that often focuses on the character actor's face, and Harry Dean's was as recognizable on the screen as any since Wallace Beery mugged it up with young Jackie Cooper in *The Champ* (1931). He knew how crucial effective use of his physical presence was to his art.

Let's talk about that face.

With "his lean face and hungry eyes," film critic Roger Ebert once wrote, "Stanton has long inhabited the darker corners of American Noir. . . . He creates a sad poetry." *Harry Dean Stanton: Partly Fiction* is essentially a "portrait of his face," Huber says about her documentary.

Harry Dean's was a face where many saw guilelessness and vulnerability even when he was a bad guy, such as gangster Homer Van Meter in *Dillinger* (1973). Above all, it was the face of a quiet man. Again we turn to writer Sean O'Hagan: "Stanton has made silence and stillness his most powerful means of onscreen communication."

Like Travis Henderson, Harry Dean was a quiet man on a long journey, a man whose roots clung to him even as he journeyed on, searching for something that maybe he didn't find, or maybe he did.

"I've always felt like an outsider," he once said. "I've been rebellious . . . any iconoclastic thing. It's true about the industry but also about society as a whole. I don't blame anyone, but I think that society is negative in that people are terrified to be free. I was born on the edge of the mountains in Kentucky and now although I live in Hollywood I still feel more related to nature. It's an attitude. I have a pool, but it's to do laps in, not a status symbol."

1

"Something Went Wrong"

Filmmaker Sophie Huber had to tell a lie to get Harry Dean Stanton to agree to a documentary about his life and work. She had known him for twenty years, but he kept saying no. "It took a full year to do it," she said. "At the end, I told him, 'Let's not think of it as a documentary. I come to the house. We film a song and go and talk.' When I said it was not about him but the music he was willing to do it."

What was Harry Dean hiding that he didn't want a documentary made about him?

Huber believes she knows the answer. "He felt his whole childhood would be brought up, and he didn't want that." She and famed Los Angeles podcaster Marc Maron talked about this after Maron confessed his failure to get to the real Harry Dean Stanton in his own interview with him.

"Even though he lives in the present, there is a heartbreak, a struggle going on there," Maron said.

"You know something went wrong," Huber told Maron, "a pain" that motivated him "through all these films and the music."

Jiddu Krishnamurti, a spiritual teacher and writer Harry Dean greatly admired, famously advised audiences to free themselves "from the background in which you have been brought up, with its traditions and prejudices. . . . Before we can understand the richness and the beauty of fulfillment, mind must free itself from the background of tradition, habit, and prejudice."

Harry Dean's background, with its traditions and its memories, clung to him like a wet suit. It was there even in his rebellion against it, his rejection of organized religion, in his music, his aloneness, even his cigarettes.

Glenn Wilson, Harry Dean's cousin, put it this way: "You can't change your roots. You can't get out of your skin, the way you became. It is engrained . . . the who you are, the way you are raised."

Where the Bluegrass Kisses the Mountains

On a little winding street in tiny West Irvine, Kentucky, near the town ceme-
tery, sits a double-wide trailer on the spot where Harry Dean Stanton was
born July 14, 1926. The house where the Stantons lived was white clapboard
with a green-tiled roof, a red chimney, and a small front porch, the kind of
house lived in by midcentury Southerners of modest means from Kentucky
to Louisiana.

The house sat midway up a hill in the part of central Kentucky local
chambers of commerce describe as "where the bluegrass kisses the mountains." You don't see mountains along this edge of Appalachia as much as you
see what the locals call "knobs"—steep, cone-shaped hills of limestone, sand-
stone, and shale—and they're both east and west of the Kentucky River that
divides West Irvine from its mother city, Irvine.

Irvine today is smaller than it was when Harry Dean was born. Fewer
than 3,000 souls reside in this Estill County community, which was prime
hunting and fishing territory for the Shawnee and other Indian tribes before
Daniel Boone and a party of North Carolina hunters stumbled onto it back in
1769. It became part of Boone's "Wilderness Trail," which stretched as far
south as Kingsport, Tennessee. Many of the town's 2,400 citizens can trace
their roots back to those early white explorers and settlers. Estill County got
its name from Captain James Estill, who died fighting Indians in the Battle
of Little Round Mountain in 1782. That battle, waged after the scalping of a
young white girl, produced another local hero, William Irvine.

The flatboats that carried tobacco, hemp, logs, and other goods to markets
as far south as New Orleans helped create a viable economy in the area, and
eventually they were replaced by steamboats and tugs before traders looked
beyond the river to the new railroads connecting markets. With the discovery
of iron ore in the area, the economy grew strong enough by 1848 to support
the 120-room Estill Springs Hotel, which included riding stables, tennis
courts, bowling alleys, and the largest ballroom in all of Kentucky. The old
hotel burned down in 1924, two years before Harry Dean was born.

Although British journalist Alistair Cooke once called Kentucky the most
self-consciously Southern of states, rural Estill County supported the Union
during the Civil War. Many there, however, were on the side of the Confederacy.
Confederate troops under Colonel John S. Scott actually held Irvine captive
for a few hours during the Battle of Irvine in late July 1863, but Union colonel
W. P. Sanders eventually routed them.

During the second half of the nineteenth century, Irvine became a railroad town with the development of the Richmond, Nicholasville, Irvine, and Beattyville Railroad Company to haul coal from eastern Kentucky. Later, the Louisville and Atlantic Railroad Company and its successor, the Louisville and Nashville (L&N) Railroad Company, became major employers. The emergence of the automobile created a demand for crude oil and with it an oil boom in Estill County that lasted through World War II.

Tobacco has been a mainstay of the economy of central Kentucky since the late 1700s, when the Spanish lifted their embargo on New Orleans, opening up markets as far away as Europe. The burley tobacco grown in central Kentucky and adjacent states is harvested differently than the flue-cured tobacco farther south in the Carolinas. Whole stalks of burley tobacco are harvested at the same time, while only the ripened bottom leaves of flue-cured are picked at each harvesting.

The story of central Kentucky tobacco goes to the heart of the culture and history of the region.

"Burley tobacco, as I first knew it, was produced with an intensity of care and a refinement of skill that far exceeded that given to any food crop that I know of," the Kentucky-born philosopher, farmer, and author Wendell Berry has written. "It was a handmade crop; between plant bed and warehouse, every plant, every leaf, was looked at, touched, appraised, lifted, and carried many times. The experience of growing up in a community in which virtually everybody was passionately interested in the quality of a local product was, I now see, a rare privilege."

The growth of Big Tobacco, led by James B. Duke's powerful American Tobacco Company and the British-owned Imperial Tobacco Company, led to a late-nineteenth-century trust that essentially locked out smaller competition and put farmers at its mercy on the price they received for their crop. In those heady days of an unregulated capitalism that favored government-sanctioned monopolies like the Tobacco Trust, farmers rebelled in the same spirit that created the People's Party, or Populists, the Grange movement, and the Farmers Alliance in the rural South and Midwest, and the rise of labor movements in the cities. In Lexington, Kentucky, farmers created the Burley Tobacco Growers Association to protect their livelihood from the powerful forces back east. They met with some success initially, but when the trust began buying off individual farmers many turned to violence.

The so-called Night Riders, singing church hymns and waving their Bibles, began attacking and whipping farmers who'd sold out to the trust, raiding warehouses and factories. In what historians called the "tobacco wars," plant beds were destroyed, tobacco stored in trust-friendly warehouses ruined, lives threatened. The farmers ultimately failed to muster the financial wherewithal to withstand the trust. However, in 1907 Congress passed the Sherman Antitrust Act, and in 1911 the US Supreme Court weighed in to break up giant trusts like John D. Rockefeller's Standard Oil Company and the Tobacco Trust as well. Out of the American Tobacco Company came new companies like R. J. Reynolds, P. Lorillard, and Liggett and Myers.

As important as tobacco was to the economy of central Kentucky, the people, even the farmers, often found themselves conflicted by it. The Night Riders may have waved their Bibles in one hand and a sword in the other against the Tobacco Trust, but many evangelical preachers also waved their Bibles from the pulpit against the sin of tobacco.

From the revivals of the Great Awakening in the 1700s and the birth of the fundamentalist movement in the 1870s to the rise of Bible-thumping evangelical "old-time religion" preachers like Billy Sunday and Kentucky-born William B. Riley (it was Riley who gave "fundamentalism" its name) in the 1920s and even until today, religion has been at the core of the life and culture of people in Appalachia. To many hard-shell Baptists and their even more fundamentalist brethren like the Pentecostal Holiness, tobacco was an evil enjoyment on a level with demon rum. It's ironic that tobacco was an important part of the religious rituals of Native Americans when the first colonists arrived in the New World.

"There have always been people who disliked it," Wendell Berry wrote. "There has long been a vague religious antipathy to it, though in tobacco country, to date, churches have generally been glad enough to receive their tithes from it."

As a future tobacco farmer with an aversion to smoking, Sheridan Harry Stanton brought some of that internal conflict with him when in 1910, at the age of seventeen, he arrived in Berea, Kentucky, to attend school at Berea College. A native of White Rock, North Carolina, Sheridan later moved to Dayton, Ohio, for work and then to South Carolina for service in the Medical Corps during World War I before settling in Irvine. A barber and intermittently a tobacco farmer, he married Irvine native Lula Dozier in May 1920, and she gave him two daughters, Quincy Alice and Lillian, before dying of pneumonia just eight months after Lillian was born.

Ruddy complexioned with hazel eyes, Sheridan carried a mere 125 pounds on his five-foot-one-inch frame, the reason he was known simply as "Shorty" to most. He had an athlete's build, however, and was a sharp dresser, a dapper man who liked gold pocket watches and nice cars, even if he was a terrible driver. He was quiet and held his own counsel, but he knew how to tap dance and had an eye for the ladies. He caught their eyes as well, including seventeen-year-old Ersel Greene Moberly, fourteen years his junior, a free-spirited, fun-loving, sharp-witted and sometimes sharp-tongued native of the little nearby town of Waco who was anxious to get out of her crowded home and into a life of her own. The oldest of nine children, she was a pretty young girl with green eyes, dark hair, and an artistic bent. She played guitar, sang with a low voice, and loved to paint. Like Sheridan, she would also later prove to be terrible behind the steering wheel of an automobile. When she and Sheridan married in 1925, four years after Lula's death, her father, Archie Moberly, who worked with the L&N Railroad Company in Irvine's neighbor city of Ravenna, pulled Sheridan aside to give him the same warning he would give any prospective husband of his three daughters.

"If you ever lay a hand on my daughter, I'll kill you."

"And he meant it, too," his granddaughter Joy Spicer told me during an interview in Irvine in the summer of 2018.

Ersel "was an outgoing, fun-loving lady," her nephew Jim Huggins Sr. recalled. "I enjoyed being around her."

Sheridan operated a two-chair barbershop on Broadway in downtown Irvine. He had the first chair, and his colleague Albert Witt had the second. It was a full-service barbershop offering a bath as well as a shoeshine. Ersel worked as a beautician. She learned how to handle hair from Shorty. The year after their marriage, Harry Dean was born, followed by Ralph a year later and then Arch two years after Ralph.

After their mother's death, Sheridan's daughters by Lula went to live with their aunt Marie Dozier, who had never married, lived on Garrett Avenue near where Sheridan and Ersel would live, and worked at the Carhartt clothing factory in Irvine. Quincy Alice was four when Sheridan remarried, and Lillian was just one.

Some of Harry Dean's earliest and best memories were not of his parents, brothers, or half-sisters. They were of Thelma, his eighteen-year-old babysitter and his first love. He and his brothers would hide under the table or bed when she came in the house, but eventually they would come out. She inspired the musician in him, and he would sing to her.

"One day I just got up and started singing 'T for Texas, T for Tennessee, T for that girl who made a wreck out of me," he told Sean O'Hagan of the

Guardian. "I guess you could say that was the birth of my blues, but it's also when I went into show biz."

In Mississippi country crooner Jimmie Rodgers's 1927 classic song, "Thelma" runs off with another man, and the singer looks forward to the day he would "buy me a pistol just as long as I am tall" so he could "shoot poor Thelma just to see her jump and fall."

It's doubtful little six-year-old Harry Dean contemplated such revenge, but no doubt his own Thelma must have broken his infatuated heart. It wouldn't be the last time a woman did so. Harry Dean's Thelma, however, helped him discover his passion for music. By the time he was eight, he was using any opportunity he was alone to climb up on a kitchen stool and sing songs from his growing repertoire.

Nearly all of the Stantons and Moberlys were musical, but Harry Dean's repertoire grew in part due to Ersel, who would sing ballads to the boys. "When I was young, they were trying to teach me about music," he once told his close friend and fellow musician Jamie James. "They made me sit in this tub till I got it right. It was a horrible experience." Later, after his parents began to argue more and more, arguments that would ultimately contribute to their divorce, Harry Dean would escape into his room and listen to records to drown them out.

Music was always important in the Stanton household, and eventually Harry, Ralph, and Arch would join with a friend and form their own barbershop quartet, fitting given their father's occupation. "They'd sing, and then they'd argue," Harry Dean's nephew Ralph Stanton Jr. recalls. "All the Stantons were all meaner, tougher, and smarter than the other one." Ralph Sr. was the more serious brother, but he looked up to Harry Dean and tried to impress him whenever he got the chance. Arch was outgoing and loved a good time, but he also could be preachy, particularly to Harry Dean. Both Ralph and Arch would later develop an evangelical bent and ask people questions like "Do you accept Jesus Christ as your Lord and Savior?" Their father was a strict disciplinarian, but three rambunctious boys could still be a handful.

Harry Dean liked movies, too. He once told his longtime personal assistant in Los Angeles, Logan Sparks, that he first wanted to be an actor after going to the movie theater as a young boy. He'd walk out of the theater "thinking I was Humphrey Bogart."

On Sunday afternoons the Stantons would follow another old Southern tradition and take a ride. "I lived up in the hills, and we'd go visit the relatives on Sunday," he told filmmaker Tom Thurman in the 2011 documentary on the actor, *Crossing Mulholland*. "I remember traveling down this country dirt road, or gravel road. I was six or seven years old, maybe five, I don't know. I remember passing this house and saw this old couple sitting up on the porch in their chairs rocking and watching the traffic pass by. I remember thinking someday I'm going to get out of there."

Logan Sparks alluded to that notion in a comment he made in Sophie Huber's documentary about Harry Dean that folks in Kentucky still haven't forgotten or forgiven. Harry Dean "says 'Do nothing' all the time," Sparks said, talking about the actor's Zen-like philosophy of life, "which is bullshit. If he did nothing, he'd still be in a rocking chair in Kentucky."

Like Southerners everywhere in the region, Kentuckians get bristly when non-Southerners like Sparks put them down and invoke the old stereotypes of ignorance and backwardness. Estill County historian Jerry Eltzroth, a native of Ohio, said many people in Ohio, even if it's only the Ohio River that separates them, call Kentuckians "Briar," and it's not a complimentary term.

Harry Gets His Gun

When the boys were still very young, the family moved to the town where Sheridan was born, White Rock, North Carolina, and where he gave up barbering for tobacco farming. Managing a farm at the height of the Great Depression was no easy trick, and Sheridan, like all Southern farmers, had to turn to the federal government to help bring what writer Pete Daniel has called "supply and demand into harmony" so farmers could get a decent price for their crop and a livable income for their hard work. In North Carolina as in Kentucky, farmers had long resented the large tobacco warehousemen and manufacturers, and they found in Franklin D. Roosevelt's administration the kind of ally that they had not seen during the Republican administrations of the 1920s.

Located near the Tennessee border in the Blue Ridge Mountains north of Asheville, White Rock is in rural Madison County, former Cherokee territory and so isolated that its Scotch-Irish folk traditions remain strong even today. Named for President James Madison, the county was partly carved out of neighboring Buncombe County, home to one of North Carolina's most prominent politicians, Civil War–era governor and postwar US senator Zebulon V. Vance, a county that inspired the word "buncombe" and phrase "full of bunk" because of the meaningless verbosity of an early nineteenth-century Buncombe County congressman's stump speeches. Tobacco and timber have always been the area's economic mainstays.

The move to North Carolina may have been a coming home for Sheridan, but it was a disaster for Ersel, who found herself far from her roots and in charge of increasingly rowdy boys. James Huggins Sr., whose mother, Christine, was Ersel's sister, remembered the family stories about their stay in North Carolina. "My mom was not that much older than Harry, and she was very close to Harry. She went down to North Carolina to babysit for the three children. My mom said it was one the worst experiences in her life. They got into a fight. Harry got a .22 rifle and fired at them. They were completely out of control." Harry Dean often told the story of another childhood incident with a gun.

"I killed a mockingbird," he remembered. "It was singing. I had a BB gun that didn't shoot straight, and I didn't think I'd hit it. This mockingbird was singing, and I didn't think I would hit it, and the singing stopped."

He told this story a final time in his last film, *Lucky,* and his personal assistant and *Lucky* coscreenwriter Logan Sparks said the incident still rattled Harry Dean. "He said it was the saddest moment in his whole life," Sparks told the *Independent* in London. "Filming the mockingbird scene really affected him. I drove him to the set every morning and on the day the monologue was filmed, he said, 'I don't want to do that.' I told him it was an opportunity to get it off his chest and share that pain with the world. He rode in silence for a while and then said, 'Well, I'll give it a shot.' When he finished the scene, there wasn't a dry eye in the house."

In White Rock, the Stantons lived in a small house that likely reminded Ersel of her own crowded childhood home. "They weren't there too long, maybe a year or two" Huggins Sr. said. Ersel "didn't like it at all. That might have been a contributor to their divorce."

The family would eventually return to Kentucky, but to the larger city of Lexington, north of Irvine. This time Sheridan would both resume his work as a barber and continue his tobacco farming.

Farming Tobacco in the Athens of the West

When the Stantons arrived in Lexington, Kentucky, named after the town in Massachusetts where the Colonists first engaged in battle with the British Redcoats in the Revolutionary War, the city was much smaller than the thriving metropolis of 320,000—roughly a half-million in its metro area—it is today. Even with only 45,000 residents in the 1930s, however, Lexington was known as the "Athens of the West" and played an important role in Kentucky's culture, history, and economy.

Kentucky's most famous statesman, Henry Clay, settled in Lexington to practice law after leaving his native Virginia in 1797. Called the "Great Compromiser" for his successful deal-making on the bitter "nullification" issue that was an early test of Southern resistance to federal mandates, Clay served as speaker of the US House, US senator, and US secretary of state, but he never attained the presidency he tried three times to win. One of Clay's greatest admirers was Harry Dean Stanton.

"There is one part I really want to play, but it hasn't been written yet," he told journalist Steve Oney in 1986. "I want to play Henry Clay, the man who held the Union together for so long before the Civil War. I want to play him because he's credited with the line, 'I'd rather be right than be president.'"

Clay's home still stands in Lexington, as does Hopemont, the home of Confederate general John Hunt Morgan and Nobel Prize–winning geneticist Thomas Hunt Morgan. Abraham Lincoln lived in Lexington, and his wife, Mary Todd, grew up there. Confederate president Jefferson Davis lived there, too, and Colonel Harland Sanders lived in nearby Winchester and Nicholasville before becoming famous for his Kentucky Fried Chicken chain of restaurants.

The distance between Irvine and Lexington is less than fifty miles, but the two were, and are, worlds apart in many ways. Lexington is the self-proclaimed "Horse Capital of the World"—Ersel would become a devoted racetracker, both with the horses and dogs—and boasts horse farms, the prestigious Keeneland Race Track, bourbon distilleries in every direction, fine old homes surrounding its growing city skyline, and proud universities. Irvine is on the border to, and once was part of, Kentucky's fifth congressional district, one of the nation's poorest. The region around Irvine still consists of small farmers, rail workers, factory workers, and much poverty. Before and during the Civil War, those farmers were hostile to the "uppity pro-slavery Bluegrass region to the north." Indeed, Lexington then had the highest concentration of slaves in Kentucky. Still, in the second half of the nineteenth century and the early years of the twentieth, those same disgruntled farmers to the south would come to Lexington to organize their resistance to the Tobacco Trust, because Lexington was also a major tobacco market, with giant warehouses where the farmers' crops were bought and sold. In fact, the city seal of Lexington includes a tobacco leaf.

For the Stantons, Lexington was a natural move. It was the nearest larger city to Irvine. Relatives already lived there. It offered more work opportunities for Sheridan and better schools for the boys. Sheridan continued his tobacco farming but would eventually return full time to barbering for a living.

Unlike cotton farmers, tobacco farmers can make a decent living from their cash crop on a small farm. Like all tobacco farmers, Sheridan put his family to work on his new farm east of town, on Lexington's Liberty Road near Winchester Road. "We'd hang it in the barn, let it dry out," recalled Harry Dean about his family's crop in his interview with podcaster Marc Maron.

Burley tobacco farmers like Sheridan would harvest their crop from mid-August to September. Unlike most flue-cured farmers in the Carolinas and Georgia, who harvest, or "prime," over the course of six weeks, picking only the ripened yellow leaves at the bottom of the stalks each time, burley tobacco farmers harvest entire stalks at a time. It's hard work.

"Cutting tobacco is strenuous work that requires speed and coordination," wrote John van Willigen and Susan C. Eastwood in their landmark 1998 study, *Tobacco Culture*. "It can be dangerous to miss the target when cutting a stalk of tobacco or when spearing the plant onto a stick. Common injuries include impaling one's hand on the spear or cutting one's leg with the tobacco knife." Another risk is green tobacco sickness, which can cause vomiting and dizziness when nicotine from wet tobacco is absorbed into the skin. Tobacco cutters often smoked or chewed tobacco as a means to keep the sickness at bay.

Harry Dean and his brothers worked in the field as well as in the barn. Even later, as a young man, he cut tobacco to earn money so he could go to California. Harry Dean and his brother Ralph once even burned down a tobacco barn by mistake, nephew Ralph Stanton Jr. recalled.

Workers generally hung the tobacco in the barn the same day it was harvested. Hanging tobacco-laden sticks in the barn was "difficult and dangerous," wrote van Willigen and Eastwood in *Tobacco Culture*. "Each laborer must be able to keep his balance while straddling loose tier rails or poles and reaching down to pull up the heavy tobacco sticks. Occasionally a man 'falls out of the barn.' That is, he falls from the tier rails to the floor and can be severely injured or killed." Kentuckian Nell Collins told them, "It is a dangerous thing, standing up on those tier rails. . . . That's the most dangerous part about tobacco—hanging it in the barns."

The barns, each with three to five tiers connecting the slopes of its roof, are filled from top to bottom at harvest time. The curing begins after the barns are filled, with farmers burning coke or using gas heaters to dry the tobacco. This is when barns occasionally burn, and that's probably what happened to

Harry Dean and Ralph while they, as the two oldest boys, were fulfilling their chore of watching the barn one evening.

For those working in the field and at the barn, the best time of the day during a harvest was the noon meal, a time of "banter" and sometimes boasting by or about tobacco cutters who could "cut twelve hundred to sixteen hundred sticks a day," according to van Willigen and Eastwood.

This writer of this biography will never forget the noon meals on "priming" day while working in his cousins' tobacco fields in North Carolina as a young teenager in the early 1960s. Black and white workers—primers, hangers, stringers (who'd string the tobacco onto sticks), and handers (who'd hand the tobacco to the stringers)—would gather together around the barn to drink RC Colas and eat sandwiches, sometimes fried chicken from the farmhouse, or simply "nabs" (peanut butter crackers), while talking about the music and musicians playing on the transistor radio, baseball, school, the weather, the harvest that day, or sometimes just life itself.

The three Stanton boys played as well as worked, however, and their cousin Etta Clay Moberly Hamilton played with them. "We were just kids running and playing in the yard, hide-and-seek and other games," the ninety-one-year-old told me in July 2018. She remembered, too, that Harry Dean was always humming and singing.

The Stantons liked practical jokes, too, and Harry Dean's half-brother Stanley McKnight Jr. remembered that Ersel was the target of one in particular. "Sheridan and she would go on the road to carnivals. They liked to take photographs. They were on the road a lot. One time they were coming back from a trip, and Harry had stuffed a sheet with pillows and made it look like a person lying on the floor. He poured ketchup all over it, and Ersel came in and thought it was Ralph. He would do stuff like that to piss off his mother."

Harry Dean had a particular fondness for his Aunt Beulah, Ersel's sister, who also lived in Lexington for a time. "He loved my mother dearly," her daughter Joy told me. "Harry Dean once borrowed fifty cents from her to go swimming at Harrington Lake, and my mother said, 'Okay, but promise me you won't dive off the cliffs.'" Harry made the promise to his aunt, but when he came back he also made a confession to her. "He came back and told her, 'I dived off the cliffs!'"

Even after his stint in the US Navy during World War II, Harry Dean would return to Harrington Lake. "His brothers Archie and Ralph, they would go over to Harrington Lake and dive off the cliffs," recalled his nephew Jim

Huggins Sr. "They'd take me along. When the brothers would give me a hard time, Harry would intercede. He was an excellent swimmer."

Joy Spicer also remembered going to weddings and funerals with the Stanton boys, and how they would always make her laugh at the most inappropriate times. "His brothers were funny. Arch was especially funny. We'd find something to laugh at."

Although neither Sheridan nor Ersel was overtly religious, their children got plenty of exposure to the Baptist ethos that permeated the culture of Kentucky and the entire South. In his interview with Marc Maron, Harry Dean talked about the Southern Baptist world in which he lived. "It's all based on fear, all religions, fear of God, the father figure. It's all bullshit. These preachers would come through, the evangelists. Brother Gibson was one of them. We'd go down and shake hands with him after the ceremony. He moved me on. Shook hands with me and moved me on. Like something's wrong with this picture."

"She Just Ran Off"

Ersel was glad to be back in Kentucky. Her sister Beulah lived in Lexington, as did other members of her family. The marriage to Sheridan was on shaky ground, however, after the disaster of living in North Carolina. Maybe the troubles had begun before then, in Irvine. Although they had the three boys—she was closest to Arch, her youngest—she had lost a fourth child. Harry Dean mentioned that loss once in an interview. "I was there the night it happened," he told Mark Matousek of Andy Warhol's *Interview* magazine. "The radio was playing a song called 'Roll Along Kentucky Moon.' I think my father buried the baby out in the field. I remember yelling and screaming. Pain."

In addition, some time after the return to Kentucky, Ersel found herself again in the kind of crowded household she thought she'd escaped for good at age seventeen. Marie Dozier, like her sister, died a premature death after collapsing in her home in West Irvine, and Sheridan's two daughters who had been living with her needed a home, so they moved in with Sheridan's new family.

Maybe raising five children—her own three growing, headstrong boys plus two teenaged daughters whose mother was another woman—and coping with a taciturn husband who was preoccupied with his tobacco farm and eventually his new barbershop were too much for Ersel. In 1940, she was thirty-two and had never enjoyed the freedom that she had desperately desired since she was a young girl. As the oldest child, she had had to help care for her eight younger siblings. Pregnant with Harry Dean within months of her marriage to Sheridan, Ersel left one household full of responsibility only to begin another. As with her oldest son, hers was a free spirit with an artist's sensibility. She liked music. She liked good times. She liked fun, and she had had precious little of any of it.

She liked drinking, too, and often would disappear for days at a time.

Then one day she packed her bags in their little home on Liberty Road and left for good.

"She just ran off, left them [the children] with Sheridan," Ralph Stanton Jr. said. "He had to take care of the children. My sister told me they wound up in an orphanage for a time, but that may be just hearsay."

If Sheridan hadn't been able to take care of his daughters after their mother's death, how could he take care of five children? This time Sheridan wouldn't find another wife to help carry the load. He never remarried; and his daughters, particularly the younger daughter, Lillian, who turned sixteen in 1940 and was listed in the US Census that year as a "children's nurse," would take over the mother's role in the household. Nineteen-year-old Quincy was described in the 1940 Census as a "sales clerk" and probably helped her father in earning an income for the family.

"He had an older sister named Lillian, and she raised them like a mother," Harry Dean's ninety-four-year-old high school friend Paul Sturgill said in an August 2018 interview. "That was up during grade school and high school. . . . The mother was not in the picture. She didn't live in the house. Lillian, his half-sister, was a very fine lady, one or two years older than I was. She took care of those three boys."

Another high school friend, Richard "Dick" Derrickson, ninety-two when I interviewed him, recalled visiting the Stanton house in those days. "It didn't have anything but beds in there. His dad did the best he could. . . . he just tried to make ends meet. His dad would give him money to go eat on." Sixteen-year-old Lillian's cooking skills were limited. "I would bring him [Harry Dean] home with me. My mother was a good cook. He would really enjoy eating a home-cooked meal. My mom would fix steak and mashed potatoes and green beans. Stuffed peppers, pork chops."

"One of Those Guys Who Just Kind of Hung Around"

At Lafayette High School and later college, Harry Dean developed a reputation as a friendly guy who dated occasionally and liked to sing. "Harry was a likable guy," Dick Derrickson recalled. "One of those guys who just kind of hung around. He had a dry sense of humor, liked to sing. I remember his brothers. Archie was kind of a little comedian. Ralph was more serious."

Harry Dean "was a young boy like any other young boy," Paul Sturgill added.

He liked to play pickup basketball but never got good enough to make Lafayette High School's legendary—six state championships—basketball team. Still, he had a significant impact during at least one game. "Their arch-rival was Henry Clay [high school], and their sporting event was a major affair," Jim Huggins Sr. said. "One heated basketball game came down to the wire with one point difference. A Henry Clay guy was fouled and getting ready to throw a free throw. It was at the end of the game. Harry got into the light controls and turned out the lights. The gym and the pace erupted in a riot!"

Apparently, Harry Dean had help from his brothers. "Both his brothers admitted [it]. Harry tried to deny it later." This was classic Harry Dean, Huggins Sr. said. "Harry liked to have fun, joke around. He had a great sense of humor. If you'd be with him, he was always cracking jokes."

High school also provided Harry Dean with opportunities to develop his love of singing. "I've always been a singer," he once said. "I sang in high school, glee clubs. I was a soloist. I was singing when I was five years old. I had a lot of speech training and a lot of voice training and I was just blessed with a good voice and a good ear for music." Already picking a guitar and playing harmonica, Harry Dean also played drums in the school's marching band.

Sheridan and Ersel lived their separate lives by the time Harry Dean was in high school. A dispute with another landowner regarding timber sales may have contributed to Sheridan's turning his attention mostly to barbering again. "He got into a dispute about land someone sold him, that he was selling timber off of land that wasn't his," Ralph Stanton Jr. said about his grandfather. So Sheridan set up a barbershop on Liberty Road. "It was a three-seat walk-in, just like you'd see in the movies."

Eventually Sheridan had a "little shotgun" room built onto the barbershop that would become his permanent residence after the children left. Although Sheridan had three seats in his barbershop, he mostly barbered alone.

"He had his rules," Ralph Jr. recalled. "I would want to sit in his barber chair, and I would flip one of those metal bars [on the footrest], and the seat would swivel back and forth. It would irritate the crap out of him. You just didn't do that."

Even though Sheridan had made his living as a tobacco farmer, he despised smoking. His chain-smoking eldest son remembered how much his father hated it in his interview with Marc Maron. "People would smoke in his chair. He would take out a little syringe and dab it on the end of their cigarette and make it go out. They'd give up."

On her own without husband or children, Ersel (who, like her son, loved to smoke) made a living as best she could. "She always needed money," her niece Joy said. Ersel worked as a cook and beautician during the day, and she tended bar at night. She learned to drive and liked to get behind the wheel. "Ersel drove this old car and was a terrible driver, not looking where she was going," Joy said. "I remember someone saying to her, 'You need to be careful,' and she said, 'Oh, nobody's going to hit this old car with their new one.'"

Ersel and Sheridan officially divorced in 1941. She was thirty-four, Sheridan forty-eight. Their oldest son was fifteen. Ersel remained single for a few years, but after the war married Stanley Morris McKnight Sr. Eight years younger than his new wife—they shared the same January 10 birthday—McKnight was a Springfield, Missouri, native who had spent part of his childhood and youth in Kansas and then Colorado. He served four years in the US Navy during World War II, including a stint on an LST (Landing Ship, Tank) with a landing at Normandy Beach. He was just ten years older than fellow Navy veteran Harry Dean. Ersel and Stanley would have a son, Stanley Jr., in the late 1940s, but the age difference in the half-siblings was great, and relations were often less than ideal.

Even after the divorce, Ersel stayed in touch with Shorty, including working for him at his barbershop at one point.

Ralph Jr. said his father "treated him [Stanley] like a little brother," but he also considered Stanley Jr. pampered and spoiled and sometimes "wanted to step on him like a bug."

Ersel's drinking worsened after her marriage to Stanley McKnight, as did her health, with numerous visits to the hospital, once for a nervous breakdown. "She was a whiskey-loving woman," Stanley McKnight Jr. said during a 2018 interview. "There was a guy named Red Williams. Every Friday he would visit at Aunt Beulah's house [in Irvine], and she would have whiskey in a jar. That was something we looked forward to. The bootlegger's name was Clarence Williams. His son was [named] Red, who later became a pot dealer."

Ersel's disappearances worsened, too. "Ersel would leave her children [Harry Dean and his brothers] for days or weeks at a time," granddaughter

Whitney Fishburn told me. "With my dad [Stanley Jr.] it was months at a time. She'd always say, 'I'm going to go fishing.' Code for going out drinking."

Stanley Sr. was a salesman who had a window and awning business. "He was real jolly, could sell anything," Joy said. "He'd sell you something, and if it was defective and you brought it in, he'd sell you something else before you walked out."

Later in life, after living for a time in south Florida, Stanley McKnight developed a heart condition; he died of a heart attack in the summer of 1967. He was fifty-one years old. Ersel was less than a fully committed caregiver during those latter years.

As her second husband's heart condition worsened, Ersel complained to her sister Beulah, "Now I have to be nice to him all the time."

Harry Dean never liked to talk much about his mother or her abandonment of the family, but he made a confession during the filming of Sophie Huber's documentary *Partly Fiction* suggesting that Ersel's leaving set the stage for the Harry Dean Stanton he would become. "I was fourteen and I was terrified," he said, "thinking there was nothing out there. I was alone. Parents divorced."

Lots of therapy later in life helped Harry Dean overcome his deep-seated anger with Ersel, and when she was dying in 1974, he sent her a present. "I sent her a heart, a ceramic heart," he told Marc Maron, "and the nurse broke it and sent it back to me. I glued it back together." Harry Dean went to her funeral in Lexington that August, but he was stoned when he got there and didn't stay long.

"He came in from Hollywood," Stanley McKnight Jr. recalled. "We did a big old doobie right before her funeral. We went to the funeral high. We showed up late. Some old biddy said, 'Which of them is the movie star?'"

At the open-casket service, Ersel's good hand covered the one crippled by rheumatoid arthritis, a request she had made of Beulah. As Harry Dean rushed to leave right after the service, a relative asked, "What's the hurry?"

"I have to get back to play backup guitar for Bob Dylan."

2

"Riding a Stick of Dynamite"

In his last film, *Lucky,* Harry Dean Stanton, in the title role, tells a fellow World War II veteran, played by Tom Skerritt, that he got his nickname because he was a ship's cook, which was "supposed to be the easiest job" in the US Navy. He found out, however, that every sailor in the crew was on board "a long, slow target" that "was like riding a stick of dynamite."

He tells Skerritt's character that he faced that reality at one point when he looked up in the sky and saw that "a suicide plane was coming right toward our ship." A single Japanese kamikaze pilot could take out an entire ship, and many of them did in World War II. "A hundred yards away it went up in the air and then slid down into the water. Some of our small arms fire got it."

Harry Dean was "Lucky," and his story, like many in the film, was true.

Drafted after finishing high school in Lexington, Harry Dean spent part of 1944, all of 1945, and part of 1946 aboard the USS LST-970, a tank landing ship that carried up to 1,900 tons of military hardware, including tanks, weapons of all sorts, ammunition, artillery, both wheeled and tracked vehicles, and even pontoons to use as causeways once troops disembark and are on land. He would receive a commendation for coolness under fire, but "I was damn lucky I didn't get blown up or killed," he once recalled. An LST always ran the risk of going "up like a Roman candle."

And they often did. LSTs, a kind of ship used mainly in World War II and to a lesser extent in the Korean War, were a favorite target of Japanese bombers. Sometimes it didn't even take a Japanese bomber. Five ammunition-loaded LSTs blew up in a single day due to a chain of giant explosions in Pearl Harbor on May 21, 1944. When the Japanese military began adopting suicide missions as a battlefield policy toward the end of the war, its death-defying pilots—1,465 Japanese pilots and planes went down in kamikaze attacks during the battle of Okinawa alone—aimed their guns and torpedoes mainly at smaller ships, like LSTs and destroyers, to attain the greatest effect of their last act of war. At one point, kamikaze attacks were sinking at least one US ship every day.

Harry Dean was one of several actors and future actors to see action in the Pacific. A torpedo sank the destroyer that character actor and writer Jan Merlin was on in the south Pacific. Lee Van Cleef, Denver Pyle, and Lee Marvin also fought in the Pacific. Pyle and Marvin were both wounded, and Van Cleef earned medals for his service aboard a minesweeper. In his book *Improvising Out Loud,* actor and teacher Jeff Corey, who later gave acting lessons to both Harry Dean and his friend Jack Nicholson, remembered his own encounters with kamikaze pilots while aboard the USS *Yorktown*, a ship similar to Harry Dean's, during World War II. "I was originally assigned to what they called a Kaiser's coffin, which was a small ship used strictly for transporting airplanes and never would have seen combat," wrote Corey, whose duty was to photograph and film his ship's war effort. "I spent two years in the Pacific on the Yorktown and was in fourteen major combat engagements."

Corey, later a victim of the House for Un-American Activities Committee blacklist, would relive the kamikaze attacks against the *Yorktown* a full year after his release from the military. While living in Los Angeles, he would wake up in the middle of the night with the shakes, soaking in sweat and talking out of his head. In one dream, he recalled, his family was "at the top of the Griffith Park Observatory. We had a clear view of downtown Los Angeles. Suddenly, a huge airplane crashed into City Hall and exploded. I had another dream I was sitting in Greenblatt's Delicatessen on Sunset Boulevard, directly across from the Actors' Lab. Again I watched as a plane crashed into the building across from me."

Historians say that fighting in the Pacific, particularly in the war's last major battle at Okinawa, led to more mental issues and mental breakdowns among US soldiers and sailors than at any other time in the war.

Like other eighteen-year-olds in 1944, Harry Dean got his draft notice around the time he graduated from Lexington High School. "You were drafted when you were eighteen, and they put you where they wanted to put you," his high school friend Paul Sturgill told me.

During World War II, every young man had to register for the draft, and local draft boards decided who would dig foxholes and who would swab decks. They also decided who got to stay home. "The draft was lawful and rational, perhaps even right, but no power on earth could make it fair," wrote Jerry L. Rogers in his compelling book *So Long for Now* about his late brother Elden's experiences on board the USS *Franklin* during World War II. Married men, and especially married men with children, had a better chance to stay at home.

"The 'Dogfaces' of the Army and the 'Leathernecks' of the Marine Corps faced danger in personal and individual ways, slogged through and slept in dust and mud, and often ate packaged rations when and where they could," Rogers wrote. "Sailors faced danger as members of crews, unable to duck or dodge or jump into a foxhole, but they slept in clean and sheltered bunks and for most meals sat at tables to eat freshly cooked food."

Harry Dean was assigned to the US Navy and soon shipped off to boot camp. There, he got his shots and his Navy buzz cut, his likely ill-sized uniform, a hammock, a pillow, and two pillow covers. He got his orders to box his civvies and send them home. The Navy issued him a Bible and a Bluejacket's Manual, which contained instructional information on proper sailor conduct both on- and offshore. He got his seabag and stenciled his name on the side.

Six weeks of boot camp included middle-of-the-night commands from the chief petty officer: "Up and at 'em, drop 'em and grab 'em, fire drill, scrub down that deck, inspection, move it, Boot. Now, I ain't your mommy asking you. It's me. I'm telling you." These were orders that came after a ten-hour day of marching, rifle drills, calisthenics, and pulling oars in a boat. "Boots" like Harry Dean also had to "climb up a rope ladder on the side of a wall 18 feet high and jump off the other side and swing over a hole of water about three feet deep," wrote another World War II–era "boot," Elden Rogers, Jerry L. Rogers's brother, in a letter to his parents. Of course, duties also included swabbing the deck.

After boot camp, Harry Dean was assigned to the USS LST-970, which was launched on December 16, 1944, and commissioned January 13, 1945. Its commanding officer was Lt. William W. Rader, and it sailed with a company of 13 officers and 104 enlisted men. Harry Dean's uncle Earl Moberly was on the same ship, and the veteran helped get his nephew assigned as a cook, third class. "You didn't have to know a lot," Harry Dean later told podcaster Marc Maron.

Roughly four months after its commissioning and after a stay in California, the LST-970 left for Hawaii on April 16, 1945. From there it went to the Nansei Islands, arriving May 22. Also known as the Ryukyu Islands, the Nansei stretch as far south as Taiwan (Formosa) and include the Okinawa Gunto (group), the largest of several groups of islands.

Although Harry Dean may have been lucky to get cook duty, he was no natural-born man of the sea. "I don't like the ocean," he also told Maron. "That's for fish."

Harry Dean's future stepfather, Stanley Morris McKnight Sr., would also serve in the US Navy a full four years.

"Earl somehow got Harry Dean a job in the kitchen," cousin Jim Huggins Sr. said. "That was a cushy job, rather than being a gunner dodging the kamikazes." However, Huggins said, he and his son Jim Jr. learned after visits to Harry Dean's home in Los Angeles years later that the actor apparently learned few lasting culinary skills in the Navy. "If he was a good cook, he kept it hidden. Jim [Jr.] ate cold pizzas."

A Navy ship's mess hall usually was two decks down from the galley topside where the food is prepared. It was a noisy, crowded place where sailors stood in line cafeteria-style to get their meat, two vegetables, soup, dessert, and coffee or cold drink. "The chow line, perhaps because it was a break from serious work, seems to have been a place for conflict as well as for laughing, joking, and talking," Jerry L. Rogers wrote. Fights would break out when a sailor "grubbed the line—sailor slang for cutting in." Back in the galley, cooks like Harry Dean had to keep a constant and often unsuccessful vigil to make sure weevils stayed out of the flour, and sailors often found them baked into their bread. After months at sea, they "gradually learned to think of them as adding texture and protein" and generally "found the chow good," Rogers wrote.

A sailor's life, like a soldier's life, was always a mix of boredom, tedium, long hours of hard work, camaraderie, homesickness, and the occasional intensity of battle and all the emotions battle brings with it. Harry Dean likely watched a lot of movies as he was crossing the Pacific and making occasional "liberty" stops along the way, films like *Hitler's Madman* featuring John Carradine, Alan Curtis, and Patricia Morison. Sailors listened to music by makeshift or visiting bands playing Glenn Miller or Tommy Dorsey hits and songs like "Pistol Packin' Mama," the biggest hit in the USA in 1944. Maybe he got to see an occasional USO show, too, featuring movie stars and comedians.

Probably less entertaining were the evening "Zero Hour" broadcasts by Tokyo Rose on the radio, particularly as the LST-970 came closer to the Philippines and Japan. She could be grossly inaccurate. She was known sometimes to announce the sinking of a US ship as the sailors on that same ship calmly listened to her.

Enlisted men got a ration of only three cans of beer per week. These were 3.2 percent alcohol at that, and some sailors desperate for a real drink "knocked back a slug" of what author Jerry L. Rogers called "torpedo juice." Torpedo juice consisted of methanol—the fuel that propelled torpedoes—strained through bread, the kind of cocktail that could (and did) cause blindness or death.

Like all enlisted men, Harry Dean learned quickly the old military truism to "never volunteer for anything" because it produced few rewards, and he had plenty enough to do anyway. He likely developed the "wide-paced, swaying" kind of walk sailors learned, as Rogers described it, "to cope with the moving platforms beneath them." Every sailor got homesick, and so did Harry Dean, regardless of what the situation was at home.

The LST-970 arrived in Okinawa May 24, 1945, in the middle of a raging eighty-two-day battle that would prove to be one of the most significant in the entire war. The LST-970 would remain in Okinawa until the battle ended in late June.

Even before Harry Dean and the LST-970 reached the Far East, the Japanese were already seeing the handwriting on the wall. They were going to lose this war. As effective as their attack on Pearl Harbor had been on December 7, 1941, they essentially had planned "too much to fight the last war and too little to fight the technologically different war they had ignited," Rogers wrote. Yes, they destroyed eight US battleships with their big guns at Pearl Harbor, but they missed the US carrier fleet, which was away at sea and would prove crucial in the subsequent war effort. After losing the battle of Midway Island in June 1942 and Guadalcanal in late 1942 and early 1943, the Japanese fought with the kind of mad ferocity that only a dark sense of fatalism might produce. Suicidal "banzai" attacks by Japanese troops at the bloody battle of Tarawa in November 1943 cost many US Marines their lives, but ultimately proved futile in stemming defeat. The same was true in February and March 1945 at Iwo Jima, a place once described as "something out of *Frankenstein*," where all but 200 of 21,000 Japanese troops died in battle.

Tom Skerritt's character Fred in the film *Lucky* tells of this ferocity as he sits in a café with Harry Dean's Lucky. He talks about the Japanese convincing local civilians that they faced rape and death at the hands of the Americans, and how many committed suicide rather than meet that fate.

The kamikazes were a last act of desperation and frightening to their targets. The man of war who cares no more about life and fully expects to die will do anything to wreak as much as damage as he can.

Admiral Chester W. Nimitz, commander in chief of the Pacific Fleet, and Admiral William F. Halsey, commander of the Third Fleet, were prepared to avoid a long engagement in the Philippines by going directly to Formosa en route to Okinawa and ultimately the Japanese mainland. However, General Douglas MacArthur convinced them and President Roosevelt otherwise, and the Philippines campaign began in October 1944 with the invasion of the island of Leyte. Both Tom Skerritt's character, Fred, and Harry Dean's Lucky talk about fighting in the Philippines. After the Philippine islands were largely secured, the main thrust of the US military campaign in the Pacific shifted to Okinawa, which became the centerpiece of Operation Iceberg, the prelude to Operation Downfall, with its planned invasion of the Japanese mainland. The battle of Okinawa raged from early April to the end of June 1945 and caused the worst loss of ships in US Navy history. This also was the battle that included the worst unleashing of kamikaze attacks in the war. The US Navy lost 900 sailors in the battle of Okinawa, and it was this event and its ferocious demonstration of Japanese determination to go to the death fighting that led to the decision to drop atomic bombs on the cities of Hiroshima and Nagasaki.

Harry Dean and the LST-970 stayed in the Far East for a while after the war ended as part of the occupation. Both men and ship eventually returned home, Harry Dean to civilian life and the LST-970 to its decommissioning and sale to a private firm for merchant service in the Chesapeake Bay.

3

From the Lexington Stage to a New York Park Bench

Over the next several years, Harry Dean would live a peripatetic life, returning from his stint in the Navy and war experience in the Pacific to Lexington for several years of study on the GI Bill and getting his introduction to the stage at the University of Kentucky. Then he pursued those studies with greater intensity at the famed Pasadena Playhouse in Pasadena, California. From there, he traveled across the country with a male choral group before trying his luck in New York City and sleeping on park benches in the process.

Finding Home on the Stage of the Guignol Theatre

The great war cartoonist Bill Mauldin returned from World War II's European front to an America much different from the ticker-tape parades shown in the newsreels of RKO Pathé News. He found a world full of "pressure groups, black-marketers, used-car shysters, highjacking landlords, crooked congressmen, left-wing dilettantes, professional red-baiters, religious bigots," as described on the cover of his 1947 book *Back Home*. With the rising hysteria led by Communist witch-hunters Joe McCarthy and the House Un-American Activities Committee, Mauldin had one laid-up vet in a hospital ask his famous cartoon vets Willie and Joe, "How's things outside, boys? Am I still a war hero or a drain on th' taxpayer?"

Mauldin writes about how Pacific front veterans like Harry Dean arrived back home just after "several thousand young uniformed punks, who had fought the war within the continental limits of the USA, had torn up several West Coast cities in celebration of VJ Day," fueling already widespread suspicions that "returning soldiers are trained in killing and assault and are potential menaces to society." Despite a lot of bragging and brouhaha from railroads and airlines about their commitment to the nation's fighters, they "were doing a magnificent job of failing" those fighters in securing seats on their trains and planes so they could return home. "The result was that many thousands of soldiers, sailors, and marines spent their first postwar Christmas on American soil in barracks and tents in military encampments because they couldn't get home and couldn't even find a hotel room."

If Harry Dean ran into such troubles upon his return from the Pacific and departure from the Navy in May 1946, he never talked about it. "He never talked about his military experience," recalled Lois Pemble, who dated Harry Dean when he was a student at the University of Kentucky and active in the Guignol Theatre there. "He was moving on."

Soon after Harry Dean returned to Lexington, he took advantage of the GI Bill and enrolled at the University of Kentucky, where he would be a student for the next three years and get his first real chance to perform on stage. "I changed majors every year," he told Tom Thurman in his documentary *Crossing Mulholland*. "I took singing lessons although I learned singing from speech lessons, breathing, being articulate, breathing from your stomach and all that. I changed majors from music, I took journalism. I could be a writer, still could be, but too lazy. The muse never hit me. I did radio announcements, commercials. I couldn't handle commercials."

Eventually Harry Dean found his way to the university's Guignol Theatre, which was under the direction of Wallace Neal Briggs. Briggs, an Indiana native whose childhood experiences in a tiny town near Hattiesburg, Mississippi, are recounted in his book *Riverside Remembered*, saw Harry Dean's potential as an actor, as did others who performed and worked with him in those days.

"I saw him perform on stage, and he was marvelous," recalled veteran actor Ed Faulkner in a June 2017 interview. A Lexington native and fellow student in the Guignol Theatre program, Faulkner, eighty-five at the time I spoke with him, became famous for his supporting roles in many John Wayne films, including *Rio Lobo, Chisum, McLintock!, Hellfighters,* and *The Green Berets*. "I was in a scene with him. He knew what to do. I felt like he had a future."

Faulkner and Harry Dean appeared together in a production of Sidney Kingsley's *Detective Story,* which would be made into an Oscar-winning film starring Kirk Douglas and Eleanor Parker in 1951. "Harry Dean Stanton was the cat burglar," Faulkner recalled. "I was the detective. He was really an outstanding actor. I thought, 'This young fellow knows what he is doing.' Instinct told me that. He had a handle on that."

Lois Pemble, who was a high-school student when she first met the returned veteran and worked and performed with the Guignol Theatre herself both in high school and college, agreed that Harry Dean impressed everyone, including Wallace Briggs. "Harry could read *Hamlet* and make you weep. He could do absolutely anything. Hanging around a bunch of wannabes, we all wanted to go to New York and be famous."

Harry Dean was one of several veterans on the GI Bill who were studying drama at the University of Kentucky, she said. "They were a chunk older than most of the other students. They kind of hung together because of that, their shared experience in the military. Harry was mostly quiet, but he had a very wry sense of humor."

Coming back home also meant adjusting to a firmly divided family. Sheridan still operated his barbershop. Ersel worked as a beautician and sometimes as a bartender. Before she met and married World War II veteran Stanley McKnight, she lived in Lexington with her sister Beulah, Harry Dean's favorite aunt, and already had a reputation for her bad driving. Once she drove from Louisville to Lexington, a seventy-eight-mile distance, "in second gear the whole way," Beulah's daughter, Joy Spicer, said with a chuckle.

Ersel's nephew, Jim Huggins Sr., said his father was also a veteran, and he recruited Harry Dean to go with him on his beer truck to make deliveries. On occasion, they would take young Jim along, too. "One time they made their delivery and had a few beers themselves, and Harry said I told him, 'You 'mell bad,'" Huggins said with a laugh.

Harry Dean would get together with his brothers Ralph and Arch and go back out to one of their old favorite haunts, Harrington Lake, where they would dive off the cliffs. In addition to his studies at the University of Kentucky, Harry Dean would do stints on local radio, even playing Santa Claus one Christmas. "It was so funny," Joy Spicer said. "Jim Huggins and I listened to him."

More important, however, was the barbershop quartet that the Stanton brothers formed. At various points, their fourth member would include friends Homer Randall and Jock Sutherland, who would gain local fame as the sportscaster announcing the games for the Louisville Cardinals. They kept the quartet active off and on for several years. "Every time we would get together they would always start to sing," Ralph Stanton Jr. said. "They would start a tune and wind up in an argument halfway through it and never finish the tune."

The Stanton brothers were pranksters as well as singers, and Joy Spicer said she'd never forget one prank they played on her father, who worked for the railroads. "My father worked third shift, and he'd sleep in the back of the home with the window open since there was no air conditioning. One night Harry Dean and his barbershop quartet stood outside his window and played 'Goodbye, My Coney Island Baby.' Woke my father up. I'll never forget it." ("Goodbye, My Coney Island Baby," a tale of a young man's decision to leave his girlfriend "forever" to enjoy his bachelor days, has been a classic part of every barbershop quartet's repertoire since it was composed in 1924 by Les Applegate.)

Harry Dean would go out on dates, too, of course, and was a perfect gentleman, according to Lois Pemble, a native of Tennessee who moved to Kentucky when she was twelve and later lived much of her adult life in New York state. "He was sweet and funny, an interesting guy," she recalled. "We talked a lot about the theater, average, casual kinds of conversations, never deeply involved. He talked about his home in Irvine and the music that was part of their family. He had so many of these rural things."

The two went to see movies several evenings, but it was a night at a local club that signaled the end of their dating days. "We all went out after some rehearsal to a local bar, and I was very definitely underage for drinking rules at the time. I ordered a whiskey sour. They served me, and everyone was giggling. I spilled the drink, and Harry looked at me and said, 'Well, I'm not going to buy you another one.' And that was that, the end of my drinking career for that evening. When he found out I was still in high school, he didn't ask me out anymore. He didn't want to rob the cradle."

Pemble left high school her junior year and started college at the age of sixteen. She had already been active with the university's theater program, however. "You could do that then," she said. "I was the enfant terrible of the UK theater group. I built sets, painted things, did whatever I could. I would leave high school in the afternoon and spend my afternoons helping build sets. That was my thing, my last year in high school."

Roger Leasor, another alumnus of the Guignol Theatre who studied there much later, from 1969 to 1971, said that the drama program stressed the value of learning from mistakes. "I learned a lot of bad habits, acting wise, but they were so useful to you, and it wasn't hard to unlearn them. . . . Key is to get [actors] to learn how to communicate."

It was one of Harry Dean's performances—his first actual stage play— at the Guignol Theatre that would determine his future. He played the character Alfred Doolittle in George Bernard Shaw's *Pygmalion*. It's a role that requires a cockney accent. Alfred Doolittle is a "dustman" full of class consciousness and strong opinions about it and, in many ways, is key to Shaw's play. As Eliza's father, he's a working-class stiff who later enters the middle class, but retains a hearty skepticism about its values. He's a philosopher of class distinction. He also is important to the humor in the play, challenging stereotypes the audience might have about the working and middle classes. "I was pretty good," Harry Dean told *Venice Magazine* writer Alex Simon in 1997. "I had a good ear for dialects, so I guess it was a pretty good stage accent, but a real cockney probably would've turned over in his grave, or a Brit."

"Theater allows you to examine alternate possibilities for yourself," Leasor said. "It enables you to examine where you could go if you work hard enough, or where you might go if you're not careful. . . . On stage, you know what's going to happen there. It's life that's uncertain. The theater unlocks a treasure chest of possibilities."

Harry Dean said much the same about his Guignol Theatre experience in Tom Thurmon's documentary about him. "I was at home on the stage. I could be myself. Once I did the play [*Pygmalion*], I knew I could be myself on stage. You can't be off stage, not in this society." In another interview in 2011, he said this: "I had to decide if I wanted to be a singer or an actor. I was always singing. I thought if I could be an actor, I could do all of it."

So, in some fundamental way, Alfred Doolittle convinced Harry Dean Stanton he was an actor, and that would be his future.

Perhaps that's what Wallace Briggs also saw in Harry Dean as the young actor performed that important role on the stage. "You have the potential to be a great actor," Briggs told him, and he also told Harry Dean he'd learned all he could learn in Lexington. It was time to move on to Southern California, where he would continue learning his craft at the famous Pasadena Playhouse.

Harry Dean took Briggs's advice. "I made it a point not to graduate. I thought that was a positive, independent kind of statement. I never liked being ordered around—which, of course, was an overreaction. I eventually found out that I didn't mind being ordered around at all when it was by someone who knew what he was doing."

Maybe this attitude was a kind of holdover from his days in the Navy. Bill Mauldin had it, too. "In the Army [I] had my fill of pompous little men in positions of authority," he wrote.

So, after working a while in tobacco fields to help raise funds for the trip, Harry Dean got a ticket on a Greyhound Bus and took off for California.

Journey to a Temple in Another Athens

Harry Dean left one Athens of the West to go to another, this one given its name by the same George Bernard Shaw who wrote *Pygmalion*. Shaw compared the Pasadena Playhouse to the Great Dionysia theater festival that took place in ancient Athens in the sixth century BC. Honoring the Greek god of wine, Dionysus, the festival featured carousing and wine drinking, but more importantly stage productions of tragedy, comedy, and the "satyr" play, a burlesque treatment of an otherwise heroic figure.

The Pasadena Playhouse "has been rightly called a temple of the arts," wrote author Carl Rollyson in his biography of actor Dana Andrews, *Hollywood Enigma*. Andrews studied at the playhouse—"a cathedral built in mission style with a baroque fountain in a courtyard of Florentine proportions"—from 1936 to 1938.

A pipeline of actors and screenwriters to nearby Hollywood for much of its century-long history, the playhouse was founded by theater impresario Gilmor Brown in 1917. It became a key force in the "Little Theatre" movement that had spread across the country in the first decades of the twentieth century, a movement that championed community-supported and community-staged productions, including experimental works by new artists and those of the nineteenth- and early twentieth-century European theater, as well as the innovations of such artists as German director Max Reinhardt.

The movement came into being just as movies were making their mark as mass entertainment, and "little theaters" were established in cities such as Chicago, Boston, New York City, and Provincetown, Massachusetts, all of them "reflections of an arts movement organized around local communities," Rollyson wrote. "The movement was spearheaded by groups of amateurs and professionals who wanted to create and perform work that entertained but also edified, dealing with serious issues in a more realistic style than that of the melodramas of the nineteenth century."

Gilmor Brown was an energetic and talented fundraiser as well as director, and his efforts produced contributions from more than a thousand wealthy citizens in the local community, enough for him to purchase the land at 39 South Molino and build the Spanish Colonial Revival–style, nearly 700-seat capacity main theater in 1925 that still stands today. He organized the Pasadena Community Playhouse Association and secured city funds, enabling him eventually to add additional buildings to a growing campus, including a restaurant, an "Ivory Tower" where classes were held, and the Play

Box, which offered the nation's first theater-in-the-round productions, where the audience literally surrounded the stage.

"He knew how to raise money," Pasadena Playhouse archivist and alumnus Ross Clark said. "He knew how to keep twelve balls in the air at the same time. He looked at every opportunity as a way to finance the playhouse."

Brown became such a vocal champion of American theater that he was appointed Works Progress Administration chairman of the arts for the Western region during the Great Depression. "No greater changes are going on in the world today than in the theater," he told the Van Nuys (California) Woman's Club during a luncheon on October 25, 1934. The theater is a place where America's youth can "find themselves and stand on their own feet."

The playhouse would produce all thirty-seven of Shakespeare's plays, Roman comedies, and plays by Oscar Wilde, John Millington Synge, Henrik Ibsen, and George Bernard Shaw. It staged world premieres by playwrights Noel Coward, Eugene O'Neill, and Tennessee Williams and novelist F. Scott Fitzgerald. Playwright and screenwriter Horton Foote recalled seeing a powerful dramatization of Fyodor Dostoevsky's *The Brothers Karamazov* in the fall of 1934 that featured two actors from the company of German director Max Reinhardt. "They seemed to be doing really very little but with such concentration and quiet authority that you really watched no one else," Foote later wrote.

In 1937, the California Legislature designated the Pasadena Playhouse as the official state theater of California.

Even more than its productions, however, the playhouse's reputation centered on its school, established in 1927 as a two-year program. It produced some of the greatest actors in the nation's history. Its alumnae include not only Horton Foote and Dana Andrews but also Victor Jory, Robert Preston, Lee J. Cobb, Robert Young, and later luminaries such as Dustin Hoffman, Gene Hackman, Nick Nolte, and Sally Struthers. During his time at the playhouse in the 1930s, Victor Mature appeared in more than sixty plays. The faculty eventually grew to three dozen, serving a student body of three hundred.

The training was intense and demanding, a breeding ground of good acting and soon "a veritable talent funnel for the radio, television and film industry explosion that occurred in Los Angeles during the '30s, '40s, and '50s," according to the playhouse's official history. Dubbed the "Star Factory" during its golden era between 1920 and 1945, the playhouse, with its courses in voice and diction, was key in helping actors transition from silent films to "talkies" in the late 1920s and early 1930s. "Hollywood agents scouted theater productions like college coaches at high school games," wrote Judy O'Sullivan in her book *The Pasadena Playhouse: A Celebration of One of the Oldest Theatrical Producing Organizations in America*. Brown even placed a magazine ad in 1931 that said, "Want to be a movie star? Your best bet may be the Pasadena Playhouse." The playhouse would later be an innovator in training writers as well as actors to adapt to the new medium of television and established the West Coast's first television station.

A typical school day lasted from 8:00 AM until midnight. Students took classes all morning and until five in the evening, including courses in makeup, costume design, fencing, literature, and voice. "From early morn till late at night I run from one appointment to another—dramatics, voice, orthodontist, dance (for free body movement), speech, fencing, and besides all this I have to study for parts and go to rehearsals every day," Dana Andrews wrote his parents during his stay at the playhouse.

After their coursework during the day, students were expected to spend two hours at play rehearsal. Every week students listened to an inspirational speech from Gilmor Brown, whose core philosophy was "learn by doing." As many as four plays were produced every weekend on the playhouse's several stages. "We had three student [training] theaters, and they were going all the time," recalled playhouse archivist Ross Clark, who was in the school's last graduating class in 1969. "The student productions were typically one week. It was like summer stock all the time, one of the best training grounds."

Aspiring actors learned all aspects of their craft. "You were doing everything from set design on," Clark said. "That was not a choice. That was part of the curriculum. They would say, 'Okay, for the next six weeks . . . by the way, you are going to stage manage your show.' If you don't do every aspect of the theater, you were asked to leave."

To be allowed to continue their studies, students had to be invited back, both at midyear and at the end of the year.

Harry Dean's first days in California and at the Pasadena Playhouse remain something of a mystery. However, his arrival in Southern California likely differed from that of Horton Foote in the 1930s. Foote "was greeted by his Aunt Mag and Uncle Walt," Foote's biographer, Marion Castleberry wrote. "After the usual hugs and handshakes, the couple took Horton to eat, then drove him around the city to see the sights. They rode down the Miracle Mile of Wilshire Boulevard, past the original Brown Derby, and past the Coconut

Grove Ambassador Hotel with Aunt Mag ceaselessly quizzing Horton about their family in Texas."

With no family in California, a stranger in a strange land worlds away from Kentucky, Harry Dean more likely felt what Horton Foote felt after his aunt and uncle dropped him off at the YMCA in Pasadena. "Although he tried to remain positive, in truth he was scared and lonely, and memories of his hometown left him melancholy," Castleberry continued.

With a faculty at the playhouse that included such notables as actor-teacher Raymond Burr, later famous for his television role as attorney Perry Mason, Harry Dean early on made something of an impression, securing his first role as a guitarist in a Mainstage production of Charles Dickens's *Cricket on the Hearth* on December 21, 1949. "As a rule, first-year students did not appear on the Mainstage. That would be a very, very rare occurrence. By the time you did, you would have done eight or nine productions," archivist Ross Clark said. And although Harry Dean's role was small, the Mainstage was the largest and most prominent of the playhouse's four stages. (The other stages were the Play Box and the East and West Patio.)

Casting Harry Dean as the guitarist was no accident. In fact, he played a musician or a street singer in his first four productions at the playhouse. After *Cricket on the Hearth,* they included playing a musician in Anton Chekhov's *Three Sisters* on February 16, 1950 (West stage), a musician in Edmond Rostand's *The Romancers* on April 27, 1950 (West stage), and a street singer in Lillian Hellman's *Monserrat* on July 25, 1950 (Mainstage). The dates refer to opening nights, and student productions typically lasted a week. Even in Harry Dean's next role, as the rogue Autolycus in Shakespeare's *Winter's Tale,* he took advantage of his musical skills, as Autolycus sings and dances to perform his acts of trickery on others.

Gilmor Brown's faculty and staff were always quick to recognize specific talents in their young students and take advantage of them. "If there was a student who could do something, they figured out a way to use it," archivist Clark said.

As at the University of Kentucky's Guignol Theatre, student performers at the Pasadena Playhouse were encouraged to value and learn from the mistakes they made on the stage. "The philosophy here [at the Playhouse] was if you work enough different things, you are going to learn," Clark said. "You might be doing a comedy this week, a Shakespeare play after that. You needed the discipline to make that happen. There were plenty of people around to help you do that. They were not afraid here to let you fail. It seemed failure was your guide to your next success. I remember being told here that this is the best place to fail because next time you are not going to do that."

From its very origins, the Pasadena Playhouse preached a kind of practical wisdom in the theater arts that paid little attention to the emerging theories of the great Russian actors and directors Konstantin Stanislavski and Eugene Vakhtangov that would inspire the Group Theatre in New York City in the 1930s and the Actors Studio led by Elia Kazan and later Lee Strasberg in the 1940s. Those theories, embodied in the so-called Method school of acting, embraced a deep emotional commitment to a role that took into account psychological motivation, an understanding of a character's personal history prior to the setting and time of the play.

The great character actor Nehemiah Persoff, ninety-seven at the time of my interview with him at his home in Cambria, California, in the summer of 2016, studied the Method under Lee Strasberg at the Actors Studio. "He was the only person I worked with who really knew what he was talking about," Persoff recalled. "What he taught was the need to tap into yourself and get truthful behavior that is real, that really comes out of your guts. Truth behavior as compared with pretend behavior."

Persoff recalled encountering the greatest of Method actors, Harry Dean's later friend and neighbor, Marlon Brando, during an early training session at the Actors Studio. "When I was on leave from the Army in 1942 or '3, I went to visit my old teacher Stella Adler in her studio. When I opened the door, I saw a young actor doing a monologue from a European play, *Hannale's Way to Heaven*. This is a play many actors did in class, so I knew it. The young actor that was on stage was mesmerizing. My hair stood on end. This was a boy called Marlon Brando. I don't know if much of his ability came from his teacher Stella Adler. He was clearly a naturalistic actor who had access to his innermost feelings."

Stanislavski told his students that "it is the actor's function to reveal the human condition!" Here is how Vakhtangov put it: "You must be serious and not feign seriousness. You must come to believe that whatever arises within you under the circumstances which are given by the author to the character are yours and not those of the character, that they will make you remake yourself, that is, they will make you the character."

At the Pasadena Playhouse, "they really didn't follow the drumbeat following the Russian Method acting," Clark said. "It was more on your feet and work lots of different kinds of roles to get those emotions out. That was the philosophy of the Pasadena Playhouse."

Young Horton Foote was exposed to the teachings of writers like the famous New York drama critic Stark Young, who once wrote, "The greatness of a man's acting will depend on the extent to which the elements of life may be gathered up in him for the spring toward luminous revelation, toward more abundant life." Yet Foote grew frustrated with the determined preachings of teacher-directors at the playhouse like Tom Brown Henry for him to get rid of his Southern accent, and with learning the "antiquated" methods of playhouse-recommended tutors like Blanche Townsend, who required that he translate every word of Shakespearean monologues into phonetics. Foote's frustration eventually drove him to New York, where he discovered Russian teachers like Tamara Daykarhanova, who told him on their first encounter, "You will have to forget everything you learned at the Pasadena school."

Harry Dean would study two years at the Pasadena Playhouse and stay on for another two, performing in a wide range of productions. He was Ephraim in Eugene O'Neill's *Desire Under the Elms*, Vic Rousseau in Sinclair Lewis's *The Jayhawker*, Squeak in Herman Melville's *Billy Budd*, part of the ensemble in Robert E. Sherwood's *Abraham Lincoln in Illinois*, Bob in George M. Cohan's *Broadway Jones*, Joe Saul in John Steinbeck's *Burning Bright*, and both Fred Mayon and Richard Walters in John Wexley's *The Last Mile*. (He played Fred Mayon in a production of that play in 1951 and then Walters in 1953, his final year at the playhouse.)

During Harry Dean's time there, the Pasadena Playhouse was beginning to feel pressures that would escalate after Gilmor Brown's death in 1960 and later lead to a sixteen-year shutdown of the theater—pressures that included competition from other theaters and from the film schools at the University of Southern California and University of California at Los Angeles, rising production costs, and declining ticket sales. Like Horton Foote, Harry Dean would eventually find his way to New York and later broaden his acting training through teachers such as Nehemiah Persoff's fellow Actors Studio alumnus Martin Landau and actor-teacher Jeff Corey.

However, a newspaper advertisement would result in Harry Dean's taking a break between his acting experience at the Pasadena Playhouse and his foray into the highly competitive world of the New York theater.

Singing His Way across the USA

Harry Dean stayed at the Pasadena Playhouse a comparatively long four years—from 1949 through 1953. "I should've gone to New York, like everyone was telling me," he told Alex Simon. "That's when the Actors Studio was really hot, and the Neighborhood Playhouse. But I found a home in Pasadena and stayed there two more years [after his studies] doing plays, then I went back east." He returned to Lexington, doing a play while he was there, and then spotted an ad in the newspaper that read "Singers Wanted."

Answering the ad, he contacted the American Male Chorus, a twenty-four-piece choral group that toured the nation. The group was led by "this Baptist preacher who wanted to spread the word of God through song," he later recalled. They would go into a town, give concerts, and pass out leaflets to the crowd. "Twenty-four guys on a bus playing small towns," he described the gig to Sean O'Hagan of the *Guardian* in London. "When I quit, there were only twelve guys left. The rest deserted along the way. We sang on street corners, in department stores, and, at the end of the week, in a local venue."

Then with a dose of irony, he told O'Hagan, "It's called paying your dues."

Choral groups had become popular with the 1950 hit "Tzena, Tzena, Tzena," as recorded by Mitch Miller and his orchestra, a large-scale version of an old Israeli folk song that had also been a hit for the groundbreaking folk group The Weavers that same year. With his giant-sized choral group, Miller tapped into a changing postwar America and the changing tastes of the middle class, who were populating the growing suburbs around the nation's major cities. Miller was riding high at least until the summer of 1953, when Elvis Presley entered Sam Phillips's Sun Records Studio in Memphis, Tennessee, and paid receptionist Marion Kreisker $3.98 to record two ballads. Mitch Miller hated rock 'n' roll; as a Columbia Records executive he once had the chance to sign Elvis, but refused to pay Phillips the $18,000 he was asking for the artist.

Miller's brand of American music inadvertently helped open the door to the folk song craze of the 1950s and 1960s—something Harry Dean could appreciate—by turning Weavers and Pete Seeger songs into pop. With his all-male choruses and various Boy Scouts and Girls Scouts groups chiming in, Miller had America singing along to "The Yellow Rose of Texas" and whistling "The Colonel Bogey March" (from the movie *Bridge on the River Kwai*) through much of the 1950s.

During Harry Dean's time with the American Male Chorus, he drove the bus as well as sang, and he and his twenty-three compatriots likely sang more hymns than the kind of folk-turned-pop tunes Mitch Miller recorded. Much later, however, some of those tunes would find their way into Harry Dean's repertoire when he performed at The Mint and The Troubadour in Los Angeles—songs such as "Sunny Side of the Street" and "Stardust."

A Kentuckian Arrives in Bebop Land

Writer Norman Mailer, in his 1959 book *Advertisements for Myself,* boiled down the difference between the "hip" and the "square" in 1950s America, particularly his hometown New York City. In fact, he made a list.

Hip	Square
wild	practical
romantic	classic
instinct	logic
Negro	white
Catholic	Protestant

Deeper into the list, we get this:

Hip	Square
sex	religion
rebel	regulator
sin	salvation
doubt	faith

After his time with the American Male Chorus and another year in Lexington, Harry Dean cast his eyes toward New York City, where he figured he could best put to use the training he had received during his four years at the Pasadena Playhouse and three years at the University of Kentucky's Guignol Theatre. He was twenty-eight years old, a World War II veteran with a lot of training in theater, and jobless. He was ready for Gotham.

Although film production would shift toward Hollywood by the end of the decade, Gotham in the early and mid-1950s was still in many ways the epicenter for serious acting, home of the great acting schools—including the Actors Studio, founded in 1947, an outgrowth of the earlier Group Theatre—and teachers such as Lee Strasberg, Harold Clurman, and Stella Adler. The new medium of television, in what has since become known as its "Golden Age," was based in New York and offered compelling dramas by such writers as Paddy Chayefsky, Rod Serling, Reginald Rose, Horton Foote, and Stirling Silliphant, dramas that, in the words of producer Fred Coe, explored "the dark corners of the human heart." This was the time of groundbreaking live drama shows, including the *Philco-Goodyear Television Playhouse, Studio One,* and

45

the *Kraft Television Theatre*. "The best actors, writers, and directors are in New York," Chayefsky once wrote. "The only definite advantage Hollywood has is the steady sunshine required for any planned photography."

Method-trained actors like Nehemiah Persoff had to perform before live audiences as the television cameras rolled. "Live TV made demands on the actors that film did not make," Persoff told me in the summer of 2016. "The actors had to be able to sustain the show from beginning to end. There were no such things as retakes. What you did was out on the air. It was very demanding and frightening. It didn't frighten me, because I was a beginner and I had nothing to lose. There were a whole bunch of us beginners—Kim Stanley, Martin Balsam. I remember doing a show with [Hollywood actor] Tony Quinn, and he was sweating bullets."

Harry Dean was a beginner, too, and he came from a place worlds away from New York. He may not have fit Mailer's description of "hip"—he wasn't "Negro," "Catholic," and maybe not even "wild," but the rebellion that had been within him since childhood had blossomed. Kentucky would always be a part of him, but it would never be home again. Not only had he left Kentucky; he also had put behind him the rural, Baptist culture he was born into in West Irvine. In Norman Mailer's lexicon, "hip," with a few exceptions, was pretty much the diametric opposite of Protestantism, which he described as "not so much a religion as a technique in the ordering of communities." Unlike Catholicism, with its inherent inability to "separate the mind from the body," Mailer wrote, Protestantism was "the means by which the mind could nose out into a new understanding of the universe while the body remained in the restraints of monogamy, family and the state."

Harry Dean had fought a war, come under fire, seen the world, and sung his way across the nation. He had trained for the stage with the best and brought to life the words of George Bernard Shaw, Eugene O'Neill, Sinclair Lewis, and John Steinbeck. No more preachers would be moving him on down the line to get to the more important members of the congregation. Not even the remotest chance he'd be someday on a rocking chair on some porch in backwoods Kentucky watching the traffic go by.

He was a rebel all right. Wild? Maybe sometimes. Romantic? What person who pursues a career on stage isn't? Doubt? It sure wasn't religious faith that would be Harry Dean's guide as he continued to shape his world view. Although he may have had his first thoughts about Buddhism and Tao during his time in Asia, a chance discovery of a used book by the transcendentalist Ralph Waldo Emerson while he was at the Pasadena Playhouse got him to thinking more deeply about life and its meaning. He likely had some important conversations in New York City about those belief systems, which would increasingly color Harry "Zen" Stanton's future philosophy of life. His ideas would crystallize later, in the late 1950s Los Angeles, where he, Jack Nicholson, and other habitués of Jeff Corey's acting classes would gather at Chez Paulette's, Schwab's, the Raincheck Room, Pupi's, or the Unicorn and debate "existentialism, the collective unconscious, Zen Buddhism . . . Alan Watts, Nietzsche, Sartre, and Camus," according to Nicholson biographer Patrick McGilligan. "Zen" would become a word often associated with Harry Dean.

Despite the lingering media image of the 1950s as a decade of sleepy conformity under a grandfatherly president, the nation—and particularly New York City—seethed with cultural rebellion, even revolution, that even Joe McCarthy and the House Un-American Activities Committee couldn't contain. Poets, troubadours, and dreamers were everywhere, and they often put their lives on the line with their art and their search for some form of ecstasy in life. Harry Dean arrived in the city the year after Welsh poet Dylan Thomas drank himself into oblivion at the White Horse Tavern in Greenwich Village. The year after he arrived, bebop jazz's cofounder, saxophonist Charlie Parker, would die of a heart attack, aggravated by cirrhosis and a bleeding ulcer, in the Stanhope Hotel suite of Baroness Pannonica de Koenigswarter, a scion of the Rothschild family. Parker was only thirty-four, but the coroner thought he might be sixty. That same year, 1955, Norman Mailer cofounded what would become the nation's premier underground newspaper, the *Village Voice*. In New York and out West, particularly San Francisco, Jack Kerouac, Allen Ginsberg, and other Beat Movement leaders were redefining America and finding truths in Buddhism that Christianity didn't offer.

Kerouac, Ginsberg, and poet Gregory Corso made poetry as they listened to the frenetic, madcap riffs and rhythms of Charlie Parker on sax and Dizzy Gillespie on trumpet and to the sharp-edged "brilliant corners" of Thelonious Monk's piano filling the air at the Three Deuces and other jazz clubs along West Fifty-Second Street.

Just how much folksong-crooning Harry Dean absorbed of all this is another mystery in his life. His later musical repertoire didn't include any bebop jazz vocals. As Bob Dylan would write in his 2004 autobiography *Chronicles,* Beat writers and poets "listened exclusively to modern jazz, bebop." They "tolerated folk music, but they really didn't like it."

The House Un-American Activities Committee and Joe McCarthy–led communist witch-hunt after World War II had taken its toll on the strongly

Left-leaning folk scene. By the autumn of 1952, "the New York folk scene had shattered," Joe Klein wrote in his 1980 biography, *Woody Guthrie: A Life.* Folk-blues musician Huddie "Leadbelly" Ledbetter had died. Folklorist Alan Lomax had fled to England. Burl Ives had cooperated with the House Un-American Activities Committee, and Woody Guthrie was diagnosed with Huntington's chorea.

Yet a revolution of renewal would soon afterward take place in the kind of music Harry Dean had known since he was a child, a folk music boom that would last well into the 1960s.

Woody Guthrie and Pete Seeger helped get that revolution underway as early as the 1930s and 1940s with seminal tunes like Guthrie's "This Land Is Your Land" and labor anthems such as Florence Reece's "Which Side Are You On?" Seeger formed the Almanac Singers in the early 1940s and later, with Fred Hellerman, Lee Hays, and Ronnie Gilbert, the Weavers, which would score a major national hit with the old Leadbelly tune "Goodnight Irene" in 1950. An important and usually overlooked element in the folk revolution was the dramatic rise of seminal country music artists like Hank Williams, Web Pierce, and Hank Snow in the early 1950s, each inspired by earlier artists such as Mississippian Jimmie Rodgers and the Carter Family in the 1930s, and each lending a unique authenticity to his music.

From 1949 to 1952, folklorist Alan Lomax, who had discovered blues great Muddy Waters on a Mississippi Delta plantation in 1941, recorded songs and stories with Kentuckian Jean Ritchie, a classmate of Harry Dean's at the University of Kentucky, whose 1955 book *Singing Family of the Cumberlands* would become a classic account of Appalachian music and culture.

It was this kind of music that would have attracted Harry Dean, rebel that he was in his own right, and he probably found it in the coffeehouses, cafes, and taverns around Washington Square and along MacDougal Street and Bleecker Street in Greenwich Village.

His fellow Kentuckian, Warren Oates, two years younger than Harry Dean, also arrived in New York City in the mid-1950s hungry for an acting job, and gravitated directly to Greenwich Village. Oates "immediately loved Village life," wrote Susan Compo in her biography of Oates. "The Village upheld the tenets of his personal faith: opportunity for vibrant friendships, passels of women to romance, scads of alcohol to consume, and cigarettes to smoke, all with the backdrop of art and possibility of similar intoxicants." Another aspiring actor, Steve McQueen, became Oates's friend and shared his views about the Village. "The chicks were wilder and the pace was faster," McQueen said. "I dug that."

Oates made friends and found odd jobs to tide him over between acting gigs, such as washing dishes at Sherman Billingsley's famous Stork Club and checking in customers' hats and coats at the 21 Club, where he once spotted cowboy film hero William "Hopalong Cassidy" Boyd and saw the reverence and respect people give a true "star."

At least Oates had an apartment, a "coldwater flat at Tenth and Bleecker streets" that was "a fifth-floor walkup and the definition of arty austerity," Compo wrote. Harry Dean's times in New York were even more of a struggle.

"When Harry Dean went to New York, he was sleeping on a park bench, he was so poor," his cousin Joy Spicer told me in the summer of 2018. Another relative confirmed this. "When Harry decided to go into acting, he got on a bus and went to New York," Ersel's nephew and Harry's cousin Steve Moberly said. "He would sleep on a park bench and go wash up if he had an audition. He would go into a public restroom and shave and wash up. He got down on his times."

Harry Dean sometimes got so low he would go back home to Kentucky to regroup, Moberly said. "The way the story goes was Harry had met a guy in New York, and he was wanting to come back with Harry. He didn't have the money, so my dad wired Harry enough money to come back home to Kentucky to get their act together and go back. I think the friend just wanted to get out of New York."

Harry Dean signed up to study with Method teacher Stella Adler. However, he soon found himself "stuck doing another miserable road tour with a children's play that went all over the country," he told Alex Simon.

The Strawbridge Children's Theater was founded by internationally known concert dancer Edwin Strawbridge, who gave up dancing to lead his touring repertory theater for children across the country. They crisscrossed the nation eighteen times, traveling an estimated 450,000 miles, performing before some four million children. They performed plays such as *The Brave Little Tailor* by the Brothers Grimm. Harry Dean signed up with the children's theater and soon was back on the road, traveling from one local theater to another, including Louisville, Kentucky, near Harry Dean's home. (Coincidentally, the mother of Harry Dean's future good friend and neighbor, actor Jack Nicholson, performed with the Strawbridge Dancers during her one performance on Broadway, in a 1934 production of *Fools Rush In*.)

Harry Dean never got a nod from *Studio One* or the *Philco-Goodyear Playhouse*, but he did land a spot, his first television role, in a segment of NBC's half-hour mystery series *Inner Sanctum*. Filmed in New York City, the series was based on a radio show with the same name. Harry played a character named Andrew in a segment titled "Hour of Darkness," which aired July 24, 1954. It was the twenty-ninth episode of a series that would end its run at thirty-nine episodes, and it starred veteran Broadway and film actors James Gregory and Jo Van Fleet. Van Fleet would win a Tony Award that same year for her performance in Horton Foote's *The Trip to Bountiful* on Broadway. She and Harry Dean would later work together in *Cool Hand Luke*.

With his first television credit under his belt, Harry Dean was ready for the movies, and he saw that actor Burt Lancaster was casting for the first major film that would be feature him as director as well as lead actor, *The Kentuckian*. The film was being shot in Owensboro in western Kentucky and in the Cumberland Falls area of southern Kentucky. "Harry shows up unannounced at our house, wondering if he could say with us," Harry's cousin Jim Huggins Sr. recalled. "He was going to try out for a movie, *The Kentuckian*, with Burt Lancaster. I was fifteen or seventeen. I drove Harry out to the state park where they were filming the movie. I picked him up later, and he was upset. 'I didn't get the part,' he said. 'To hell with the movies.' Then he went to New York to try to get into a play."

By now Harry Dean had grown weary of the constant touring he had experienced with first the American Male Chorus and then the Strawbridge Children's Theater. By the late 1950s, actors were finding it harder to get jobs in New York, even though the city remained the grand citadel of American theater. "Acting jobs were fleeing to the West Coast," Compo wrote. "The city's spirit had shifted less perceptively, but in television, the change was pronounced. Going, going, gone were the variety shows and thought-prodding dramas. In their place were a slew of game shows like *The $64,000 Question* and *Jackpot Bowling*. . . . West Coast westerns abounded." Oates, McQueen, and other actors, including Robert Culp, packed their bags and headed west. Actor Nick Georgiade asked a question many asked: "If all the work is in California, why are we here knocking on doors in New York City?"

In the words of writer Jon Krampner, "Television's center of gravity was shifting from New York to Los Angeles."

So Harry Dean packed his bags, too. He had had enough of New York, and Kentucky would never again be more than a rest stop. He may have told Jim Huggins Sr. "to hell with the movies," but he was bound and determined to get in one. This time he was going to California, and he was going for good.

This time, "Harry estranged himself from everybody when he left for California," nephew Ralph Stanton Jr. told me. "He left, and he wasn't looking back."

4

Early Days in Hollywood

Lois Pemble, Harry Dean's old girlfriend back in his days at the University of Kentucky, and everyone else in the Guignol Theatre group were impressed with the future Hollywood actor's skills on the stage. Still, they also saw an obstacle that might lay in his path. "Everyone who knew Harry and watched him work said, 'Here is a leading man in a character actor's body.'"

Paul Sturgill, Harry Dean's buddy at Lafayette High School back in Lexington, was always proud to have a former friend make it in the movie business. However, he, too, saw limitations. "He usually played the villain. He was not the best-looking guy in Hollywood."

Harry Dean's own notions about his future in those early days weren't so modest. The great character actor L. Q. Jones, who worked with him in television and in Sam Peckinpah's *Pat Garrett and Billy the Kid* (1973), teased him mercilessly on the set of the television Western *Gunsmoke* during the 1960s. "Harry Dean and I were doing the heavies," the ninety-year-old Jones said during an interview in February 2018. "I was the chief one. I kicked dogs. It's okay if you rape women. Just don't kick dogs. They ran it on a Sunday, and I was driving my MG with the top down, inching along with the rest of the traffic two or three miles. I was booed. People threw food at me, rocks, they cursed me."

With this kind of fan reaction to the "heavies" on the screen, big or small, Jones recalled, "Harry Dean had decided he was going to be a major romantic star. I was on his case day and night. I didn't see it that way. He was a helluva actor, but I could get under his skin. A day didn't pass that I didn't give him a hard time. It was so far-fetched I wasn't about to let him get away with it." Years after filming that segment of *Gunsmoke,* Jones connected with Harry Dean again as they prepared to do *Pat Garrett and Billy the Kid.* "I hadn't seen him in a while, so I rode him again. He was a talented man to work with. We need people in the business like Harry."

Just how Harry Dean traveled to Hollywood is a bit of a mystery. Some folks back in Kentucky believe he hitchhiked. Whether by bus or by thumb, he must have done a lot of thinking about his past and future as he watched the passing landscape along Route 66. "To ride or drive across the continental United States [in the late 1950s] was to encounter a transforming world," Susan Compo has written eloquently. "New buildings were often starkly linear or leaning toward whimsy, and a hitherto unnoticed breed—the teenager—could be found usually in clumps lurking sullenly or spiritedly beneath the neon signs of drive-in restaurants. The world of Tom Joad was in evidence, too. In bas-relief, now shabby auto courts abutted the two-lane highway, sometimes with campsites right beside them."

Harry Dean arrived in Hollywood with a solid education and extensive work on stage as a student back at the University of Kentucky and then at the Pasadena Playhouse. However, he had failed at his first bid for a movie role, in Burt Lancaster's *The Kentuckian*, and struggled mightily in New York City. Yes, he had done more stage work in New York and had an appearance on the television show *Inner Sanctum* (then billing himself as Harry Stanton), but little else to show producers as he made the rounds of Hollywood. Nevertheless, he felt he had the chops to make it big in the business. "When Harry Dean arrived in Hollywood during the 1950s, he was convinced that within a couple of years he'd become a star," journalist Steve Oney wrote. "His optimism, however, was undercut by the insecurities and frustrations he'd carried with him since childhood."

His Pasadena Playhouse connections helped him land an early gig for a US Air Force documentary. In addition to its stage productions and training, the playhouse did groundbreaking work in early television and collaborated with the US military in producing documentaries. With both the US Army and Air Force, "those people were trained here," playhouse archivist Ross Clark told me.

Hollywood had been going through major changes since the end of World War II. Anthony R. Fellow in *American Media History* described three major challenges the film industry had faced. "First, the federal courts would press the film industry to divest themselves of theater chains. The second challenge would be a series of investigations of the film industry by the House Un-American Activities Committee (HUAC). The third would be the unexpected rapid growth of television."

In the 1948 US Supreme Court case *United States v. Paramount Pictures, Inc.*, the Court had ruled that studios' "block booking" of theaters across the land—in essence, forcing theaters to book only their studio owners' films—was in violation of antitrust laws. The ruling effectively "broke the vertical integration of the studios" and "their control [of] production, distribution and exhibition," director-author Alex Cox wrote in his *Introduction to Film: A Director's Perspective.* The ruling reversed the 1918 Webb-Pomerene Act, which had allowed studios "to operate as an export cartel, fixing prices and essentially running a monopoly in the distribution of American films."

It also shook the very foundation of the studio system that producer Thomas Ince had created in the early decades of the twentieth century and that had dominated Hollywood ever since. The first great Western film star, William S. Hart, a committed professional actor and director who had spent his childhood in the West and vigorously worked to maintain authenticity in his films, clashed deeply with the early studio system in the 1920s and suffered as a result. After getting a contract to do two films with United Artists, a studio created by Charlie Chaplin, Mary Pickford, and Douglas Fairbanks Jr. for the purpose of maintaining artistic integrity, Hart worked with director King Baggot to create his masterpiece in 1925, *Tumbleweeds,* an epic account of the Oklahoma Gold Rush. Fans loved the film but had few chances to see it, as the major studios punished Hart's independence by locking it out of their theaters. "The big theaters in the big cities, where one must play to get adequate returns for an expensive picture, did not book me," Hart wrote in his 1929 autobiography *My Life, East and West.* "They were mysteriously closed to me." At the end of his book, Hart acknowledged defeat. "I fought cleanly, without rancor or malevolence but as sturdily as I knew how—I was whipped—I salute the victors."

The breakdown of the studio system that began in the years after World War II affected everyone, from the bit players and character actors to the biggest stars. The working stiffs in the supporting cast had benefited from the mass production of films under a studio system that could force theater chains to book both their best features and their long list of B movies. For the big stars like Gary Cooper, Clark Gable, Barbara Stanwyck, and Errol Flynn, "the collapse of the studio system meant limited choices and mediocre screenplays" as "the best actors, writers, and directors were going out on their own" to do independent films, Glenn Frankel wrote in his book *High Noon: The Hollywood Blacklist and the Making of an American Classic.*

As Fellow noted, two other postwar realities were shaking Hollywood to the core: the relentless communist witch hunt against Hollywood writers, directors and actors led by the US House Un-American Activities Committee (HUAC) and the rise of television.

With the Republican takeover of Congress in the wake of Franklin Roosevelt's death came a determination to trim the power of labor unions and wage a relentless campaign to weed out alleged "communists" and communist sympathizers across the land. The Republican Congress pushed through the antiunion Taft-Hartley Act over President Harry Truman's veto in 1947. HUAC specifically targeted Hollywood, where many screenwriters, actors, and directors had joined leftist organizations during the 1930s as part of the nation's widespread disaffection with an unhinged capitalism that had allowed the Depression to ravage the land.

Harry Dean landed in a Hollywood still reeling from the ravages of HUAC's investigations, which had led to the imprisonment of the so-called Hollywood Ten—mostly screenwriters who had refused to cooperate with what they felt to be unconstitutional interrogations and a clear violation of free-speech rights. Their crime? Refusing to "name names" of fellow travelers in leftist politics and ultimately contempt of Congress, which noted screenwriter and Hollywood Ten member Dalton Trumbo readily admitted. The HUAC tribunals, supported by studio moguls such as Walt Disney, who wanted to rein in the power of labor unions like the Screen Writers Guild, and by conservative actors like John Wayne and Ward Bond and liberal-to-conservative-transitioning Ronald Reagan, brought ruination to many careers, including that of actor John Garfield and Harry Dean's future teacher Jeff Corey, who had to give up his acting career and turn to teaching because he was forced to languish through much of the 1950s on the so-called blacklist, which prevented anyone targeted by HUAC from getting work in Hollywood.

"As far as the industry's cooperation with HUAC is concerned, blacklisting was not about Communists or democracy," Hollywood screenwriter Garrick Dowhen has written. "It was about economics. It was an overt attempt by Hollywood studio executives to squash, or at least cripple, the industry's trade unions" such as the Screen Actors Guild, Writers' Guild, and Directors' Guild. "One must understand that studio heads ran their studios like dictators. Studio bosses such as Harry Cohn and Louis B. Mayer hated the unions. Additionally, Walt Disney was one of the greatest anti-union icons in the industry."

Ironically, the miasma created by fascistic Republicans in Congress, aided and abetted by a corporate world that included Hollywood studio chiefs and executives, helped create film noir as a reaction. Often directed by European émigrés such as Fritz Lang and Robert Siodmak, those black-and-white crime dramas of the late 1940s and 1950s inevitably sent a protagonist spiraling into a dark, amoral world where greed and corruption ruled. "Film noir, the style if not the term, came to Hollywood on the verge of the industry's grimmest phase," write Paul Buhle and Dave Wagner in their 2002 book *Radical Hollywood.* "Eastern and central European refugees had, of course, fled fascism to escape not only censorship and unemployment but a worse fate. The approaching blacklist in Hollywood was nevertheless familiar in many ways: the third such to fall on those who abandoned Germany in 1933 and France six years later." Harry Dean would himself later appear in Alfred Hitchcock's noir classic *The Wrong Man,* his first film, and in later neo-noirs like *Farewell, My Lovely* with the quintessential noir actor Robert Mitchum.

Jeff Corey recalled his blacklist experience in the autobiography he co-wrote with his daughter Emily Corey, *Improvising Out Loud: My Life Teaching Hollywood How to Act.* "The men who oversaw the blacklist—Joseph McCarthy, Roy Cohn, J. Edgar Hoover, the committee heads and their staff—used patriotic rhetoric to their advantage. They were, in fact, not patriots. They were mean-spirited and out only for themselves. In all the years they did their dirty work, there were no genuine plots revealed to overthrow the government or any person singled out in Hollywood who legitimately intended to cause America's moral or political downfall. The only thing they succeeded at was destroying people's lives. It was the worst of America."

Indeed, the HUAC hearings helped launch political careers. "The Hollywood Ten hearings of 1947 were one of those moments in American political history that helped set the direction for the country for more than a decade," wrote Frankel in his book *High Noon.* "They introduced a trio of aspiring young politicians to the national scene—future presidents Richard Nixon (a HUAC member) and Ronald Reagan, and future US senator George Murphy." Both Murphy and Reagan were leaders of the Screen Actors Guild, which became active in scourging itself of left-leaning members.

An even more fundamental challenge to Hollywood after World War II, however, was the rise of television—and this was a more important change to the relatively apolitical Harry Dean Stanton. After a series of false starts and stops dating back to the 1920s, and delays in its technological development due to World War II, by 1952 television had become a mainstay in American life, with more than one out of every three homes featuring a television set. At the same time, attendance at movie houses dropped as much as 40 percent in areas where television was available. By the end of the 1950s, 86 percent of American homes had a television. It was the medium's Golden Age. Television was often live, and along with shows that had gotten their start on radio came a wave of Westerns and detective shows to fill the air.

The game and quiz shows that gave Harry Dean tremendous watching pleasure later in life and that began replacing the quality dramas in the late 1950s also gave television its first major scandal when the shows *Twenty-One* and *Dotto* were exposed as frauds. The scandal led to congressional investigations, cancellations, and federal regulations. TV Westerns, however, abounded.

Harry Dean's later buddy Jack Nicholson and other young aspiring actors in the late 1950s and early 1960s generally looked down on television acting as a lesser art, but they also often saw it as a lifeline. "Television was one way of filling the gaps of both time and money, even though they all scorned television as puerile and inartistic," Patrick McGilligan wrote in his biography of Nicholson, *Jack's Life*. "The general credo held that there was more purity in the worst motion picture than in the best television."

Harry Dean would eventually become a television mainstay, but he first sought out motion picture roles after arriving in Hollywood. He got his first bit part in 1956 as a Department of Corrections employee in Hitchcock's *The Wrong Man*. The part was uncredited.

Unlike any other Hitchcock film, *The Wrong Man* is a film noir that uses a documentary style to tell the true story of a man caught in the web of an American justice system all too ready to convict rather than abide by the principle that one is innocent before being proved guilty. The film starred Henry Fonda and Vera Miles. Alain Silver and Elizabeth Ward, in their book *Film Noir: An Encyclopedic Reference to the American Style*, call *The Wrong Man* "one of the bleakest films in the history of the cinema."

Veteran character actor Nehemiah Persoff, who played the brother-in-law of falsely accused holdup man Manny Balestrero (played by Fonda), vividly recalled the filming of *The Wrong Man* in an interview with the author in June 2016. "Alfred Hitchcock was an asshole," the ninety-seven-year-old Persoff told me at his home in Cambria, California. "He had one or two favorites, Vera Miles and Henry Fonda, and the rest were cattle. He said actors were cattle!" Persoff would go on to perform in Hitchcock's television drama *Alfred Hitchcock Presents* in 1957 and 1960. "He didn't give me calls on time, he made me wait, and he had a complete disregard for me. I just hated it."

Harry Dean's role in *The Wrong Man* was minimal, but he did go on to appear on *Alfred Hitchcock Presents* in a 1960 segment titled "Escape to Sonoita" and came away from the experience with a positive impression of the director. Hitchcock "trusted the actors," he told Tom Thurman in the documentary *Crossing Mulholland*. "He told us to work it out, and we did work it out. We did the whole scene on our own."

After his appearance in *The Wrong Man,* Harry Dean, billing himself now as Dean Stanton to avoid confusion with another actor named Harry Stanton, won small roles in two other feature films, both Westerns directed by veteran Western filmmaker Lesley Selander in 1957. *Tomahawk Trail,* starring future television stars Chuck Connors and John Smith and German American actress Susan Cummings, told the story of a veteran cavalry sergeant, played by Connors, who has to take command of his outfit after an Indian attack drives his commanding officer insane. Harry Dean played Private Miller, the orderly to George N. Neise's Lieutenant Jonathan Davenport.

Critic Derek Winner called *Tomahawk Trail* "tepidly routine . . . mundane and minor in every way." It was a B-movie effort that, if nothing else, helped launch the television Western careers of Connors and Smith, and it contributed to Harry Dean's résumé.

Harry Dean got an uncredited role as Rinty in *Revolt at Fort Laramie,* starring John Dehner, Greg Palmer, and Don Gordon. Eddie Little Sky, who also starred in *Tomahawk Trail,* played Red Cloud. The plot deals with dissension between Northern and Southern troops as they face a common enemy, the Sioux Indians, just prior to the Civil War. Critic Andy Webb wrote that the plot to *Revolt at Fort Laramie* offered great potential, but ultimately the film "ends up one of those Westerns from the mid-1950s which feels like it is part of a Western movie factory line."

Harry Dean also appeared in several television series, including *Suspicion, Panic!,* and *The Court of Last Resort.* His title role as "Country Boy" in a 1957 segment of *The Walter Winchell File* landed him a spot in another feature Western, *The Proud Rebel,* a major production starring Alan Ladd and Olivia de Havilland and directed by Oscar-winning director Michael Curtiz, whose list of credits included *Casablanca* (1942), *Mildred Pierce* (1945), *White Christmas* (1954), and other classics. Harry Dean played Jeb Burleigh, one of the evil sons of Dean Jagger's Harry Burleigh, who desperately wants the farm owned by Olivia de Havilland's Linnett Moore. Jeb burns down the barn that Alan Ladd's John Chandler helped build for Linnett. The $1.6 million film also deals with Northern-Southern division, but this one takes place in the years after the Civil War.

Financed personally by Samuel Goldwyn Jr. after United Artists told him it would only back a $1.2 million film, *The Proud Rebel* is in some ways a follow-up to George Stevens's 1953 classic, *Shane,* which also starred Alan Ladd and paired him with a young, blond-haired boy, played by Brandon deWilde, who idolized Ladd's Shane. In *The Proud Rebel,* Ladd plays a father desperately trying to find medical help for his blond-haired son, played by Ladd's real-life son David Ladd, for his inability to speak after witnessing his mother's death in a fire.

Shane was one of several key postwar films that reflected a new kind of Western, a darker kind of film with complex heroes and villains, films in which a lone hero may receive little or no support from the local citizenry for getting rid of the town's bad guys, or where the main protagonist is in some ways as flawed as the villains. Linked to earlier classics such as William S. Hart's silent Westerns and John Ford's *Stagecoach* (1939), these newer, darker Westerns included Howard Hawks's *Red River* in 1948, Samuel Fuller's *I Shot Jesse James* in 1949, Fred Zinnemann's *High Noon* in 1952, Nicholas Ray's *Johnny Guitar* in 1954, John Ford's *The Searchers* in 1956, and *3:10 to Yuma,* a 1957 film based on a short story by Elmore Leonard. In the case of *High Noon,* the West became a metaphor and not-so-subtle critique of Hollywood itself during the dark days of HUAC and its tribunals.

The Proud Rebel, with its caring father, loving son, and faithful dog, is cut from a more traditional, family-oriented cloth than these other films, but it includes some noteworthy exchanges, including one that takes place between Harry Dean's Jeb Burleigh and Alan Ladd's John Chandler.

"I'd like a little respect," Jeb says. "I told you before I don't like people I'm talking to to walk away from me. Look at me! You look at me when I talk to you."

Chandler looks at him but then says, "I'm lookin', but I don't see anything."

Did Harry Dean feel this way at times over the course of his long career?

Harry Dean went on to spend the rest of the 1950s and early 1960s in television Westerns and war and detective shows. He appeared four times on *The Lawless Years,* an NBC crime show set during the Roaring '20s that was overshadowed by ABC's phenomenally popular series *The Untouchables.* Ever versatile, he also appeared on *The Untouchables* three times, first as a newspaper hawker, then as characters Picolo and Moxie. He was on *Dick Powell's Zane Grey Theater* four times, appearing first in a 1958 episode titled "To Sit in Judgment" starring Robert Ryan. Harry Dean played Rob MacPherson, a young gunman who has vowed to kill Ryan's Sheriff Amos Parney for hanging his father. Rob dies by a bullet at the end, telling the sheriff with his last breath, "I don't like that badge you're wearing. I never did."

Harry Dean made single appearances in shows like *The Adventures of Rin Tin Tin, Gunslinger, Johnny Ringo, U.S. Marshal,* Oscar-winning screenwriter

Stirling Silliphant's *The Man from Blackhawk,* and *The Rifleman.* In a 1959 episode titled "Tension" in *The Rifleman,* Harry Dean played Clemmie Martin, a young bounty hunter with a crippled leg who gets mortally wounded in a shootout with Roy Coleman, the man he's hunting.

"You think a kid like you can ride me four miles to Texas," Coleman tells him just before the shootout.

"You think because I got a bad leg I can't shoot straight," Clemmie says. "Everybody thinks because I'm a kid and got a bad leg I ain't good for nothing!"

Both of them perish in the shootout, but just before he dies, Coleman says, "He was just a punk kid, a nobody."

Clemmie's father, Ezra, played by Robert H. Harris, and older brother Gavin, played by Jack Elam, both veteran character actors, believe Chuck Connors's Luke is actually Roy Coleman and vow revenge as they still seek the bounty on his head. Harry Dean appears only in the first few minutes of the episode, but his appearance is striking and sets the tone for the rest of the story.

In 1958 and 1959, he made two appearances in *The Texan,* starring Rory Calhoun as real-life fast-shooting cowboy legend Bill Longley. Critics complained that the series made a hero out of a notorious gunslinger and racist former Confederate who was hanged before he reached the age of twenty-seven. Harry Dean also made two appearances in *Have Gun—Will Travel,* four in *Laramie,* four in *Rawhide,* and five in *Gunsmoke.*

Along with his television appearances, Harry Dean got small, often-uncredited feature film roles, including in Melvin Frank's *The Jayhawkers!* and *Pork Chop Hill,* both in 1959.

In the long history of Westerns, these were important years. Television offered 119 network Western series between 1948 and 1978. Harry Dean joined Strother Martin, Elijah Cook Jr., Royal Dano, Jack Elam, Dub Taylor, Patricia Blair, James Best, Roberta Shore, Noah Beery Jr., Ben Johnson, Harry Carey Jr., Albert Salmi, Jeanette Nolan, Claude Akins, and Neville Brand in the long line of character actors who became familiar faces on the big and small screens, but faces with no name. Some, including Lee Van Cleef, James Coburn, Charles Bronson, and to an extent Warren Oates would become stars. Most didn't, although some, like Neville Brand, struggled hard to break out from the confines of the supporting cast. "Always on the lookout for the role that would lift him out of the thug stereotype (which Brand first played in the noir classic *D.O.A.* in 1949) and transform him into a Wallace Beery–type lovable tough guy, he more often found work as a nasty Viking (*Prince Valiant*, 1954) or Indian (*Mohawk*, 1956)," wrote Douglas Brode in *Shooting Stars of the Small Screen*.

Just as *High Noon* and *Shane* had introduced a new kind of Western to the big screen, adult Westerns like *Have Gun—Will Travel, Wanted: Dead or Alive, Gunsmoke,* and *Rawhide* did the same for the small screen. Actors such as Richard Boone and Steve McQueen, both trained at Lee Strasberg's Actors Studio, took their craft seriously and played protagonists much more complex than the cowboy heroes Tom Mix, Hoot Gibson, Gene Autry, and Roy Rogers portrayed. For a time, *Gunsmoke, Have Gun—Will Travel,* and *Wanted: Dead or Alive* "became part of a Western block that 'owned' Saturday night," Douglas Brode wrote. In some ways, these new cowboy heroes were closest to the first Western film star, William S. Hart. Hart "always played the outsider: the noble outlaw, or the cowhand who got framed and took justice into his own hands, or the sheriff under attack by narrow-minded citizens for doing his job without fear nor favor," Frankel wrote in *High Noon.* "Hart's characters lived by a personal code: they treated women with respect, were kind to animals and small children, always kept their word, and fought their enemies honorably—they never drew first."

Hart spent part of his childhood in the West of the late nineteenth century, once witnessed a gunfight outside a Sioux City saloon, spoke the Sioux language, and personally knew real-life Western legends, including Bat Masterson. A veteran and well-known stage actor by his forties, he got into the film business because he was shocked at the misrepresentations in early Western films and wanted to bring authenticity and realism to Western film protagonists.

The television Western *The Life and Legend of Wyatt Earp,* which ABC broadcast from 1955 to 1961 and which starred Hugh O'Brian, was a serious effort to keep the Hart vision alive in its commitment to authenticity. "We were the first adult Western," the eighty-seven-year-old O'Brian told this writer in a June 2012 interview. "The Westerns being done were Gene Autry and Roy Rogers. Look at the wardrobe—*Wyatt Earp, Rawhide,* and *Gunsmoke.* The first thing you wanted was to be authentic. What Wyatt wore was what a marshal wore. The reality of it. If you're going to try to do an adult script, then the dialogue, you did it so that it was the logical way."

Douglas Brode, in his history of television Westerns, noted that *The Life and Legend of Wyatt Earp* came closer to reflecting true Western history than even other lauded shows like *Gunsmoke.* The show offered "an alternative definition of what an 'adult' Western could be by offering accurate details of the day-to-day workings of a lawman with a highly political mayor, a self-serving town council, an often corrupt local judge, and other peace officers who may or may not have proved cooperative."

Harry Dean looked for opportunities to portray complexities in his early characters, but still he usually was the bad guy who ultimately had to pay the price for his bad deeds. His Rob MacPherson in *Dick Powell's Zane Grey Theater* may have been poor and an outsider, but he was also a young thug on the way to becoming a first-class murderer before Robert Ryan's deputy shot him down. His Clemmie Martin in *The Rifleman* was bitter and resentful about his crippled leg, and his anger made him vengeful and murderous. He would die angry.

In the early years of its long, twenty-year run (1955–1975), *Gunsmoke,* with writers like Sam Peckinpah and its opening shootout sequence (filmed on the same street where Gary Cooper had faced four gunmen in *High Noon*), resembled a cowboy noir with its dark, lonely streets, black skies, shadowy figures stepping out of alleys, a black landscape lit only by the garish lights of the Long Branch Saloon. The cinematography of largely forgotten Fleet Southcott at times evoked that of Karl Freund in F. W. Murnau's *The Last Laugh* (1924) and John Huston's *Key Largo* (1948), as well as other great noir cinematographers like Nicolas Musuraca, John Alton, and John F. Seltz. In Amanda Blake's Miss Kitty, proprietor of the Long Branch saloon, *Gunsmoke* also offered audiences "a proto-feminist progression as the original two-dimensional 'whore with a heart of gold' became the most three-dimensional female on TV," Brode wrote.

Director Sam Peckinpah got his start in television Westerns, writing scripts and directing episodes of *Gunsmoke* and *The Rifleman,* a series he created out of an episode of *Dick Powell's Zane Grey Theater.* As he would do in his later feature films, Peckinpah showed a certain predilection for the villain. "Peckinpah was fascinated by the perverse vitality of such characters," Peckinpah biographer David Weddle wrote, "and lavished on them much more attention and humanity than he ever did to the steel-girder figure of Lucas McCain. He had begun to break down the stereotypes of TV westerns by introducing villains who were more complex, interesting, even sympathetic than the clench-jawed heroes who gunned them down."

Peckinpah would later direct Harry Dean in *Pat Garrett and Billy the Kid* (1973). In that film, the outlaw Billy the Kid, flawed as he is, emerges as a much more sympathetic character than the intrepid, relentless lawman Pat

Garrett, played by erstwhile character actor James Coburn. Harry Dean plays one of Billy the Kid's gang members. By the mid-1960s, Peckinpah, Coburn, and Harry Dean would all emerge from the fertile soil of television, and particularly the television Western, to put their stamp on the big screen. Peckinpah and Coburn would become household names. For Harry Dean, the road was longer and harder.

5

Zelig in La La Land

Whitney Fishburn, the daughter of Harry Dean's half-brother Stanley McKnight Jr., grew up thinking of the actor as "this weird uncle of mine" who "is in every movie ever. You can't watch a movie and he isn't in it. I love Westerns. I'll be watching a Western, and there is Harry."

"He is like Zelig," she told me in a November 2018 interview, referring to the 1983 Woody Allen film about a 1920s character named Leonard Zelig, who seems to be everywhere and becomes a celebrity because of his constant appearances in newsreels.

Harry Dean's career was in full gear in the 1960s, with continued appearances on a wide variety of television Westerns, dramas, and even comedies, including a role as duck-and-chicken poacher Ringo in a 1969 episode of *Petticoat Junction.* Caught with a duck feather stuck in his motorcycle, the leather-jacket-wearing, mustachioed Ringo tells the suspicious game warden Orrin that he and his fellow poaching biker friend are "just saving up to stuff a pillow." Ironically, this episode, titled "One of Our Chickens Is Missing," also included fellow actor Harry Stanton as the voice of the disgruntled sheriff. It was because of this Stanton that Harry Dean billed himself as Dean Stanton in those days.

As he had done in the late 1950s, Harry Dean made the rounds, appearing in *Daniel Boone, Adam-12, Mannix, The Virginian, The Andy Griffith Show, Cimarron Strip, The Wild Wild West, The Fugitive, The Guns of Will Sonnett, Bonanza, The Big Valley,* and a host of other television series. However, his appearances on the big screen became more frequent, too. He played a beatnik in *The Man from the Diners' Club* in 1963, his role uncredited. It was famed comedian Danny Kaye's last film, and one that the *New York Times* panned.

By the middle of the decade, Harry Dean was in Monte Hellman's iconic Western *Ride in the Whirlwind*—an important role for him—with his buddy and soon-to-be housemate Jack Nicholson. In 1968 he appeared in *Day of the Evil Gun,* a Western starring Glenn Ford, and *A Time for Killing,* a Civil War film also starring Glenn Ford along with George Hamilton. Hamilton, embodying the Hollywood star image, was chauffeured to the Kanab, Utah, set in his Rolls Royce by his "butler-chauffeur [who was] on the set with him most of the time, a gentleman's gentleman who hopped around lighting his cigars and dusting the red Utah earth off his wardrobe," according to the Columbia Pictures pressbook for the film. No doubt Harry Dean and the rest of the supporting cast lit their own cigars and cigarettes and dusted off their clothes themselves.

Also in 1968 Harry Dean played Spook in *The Mini-Skirt Mob*, putting the lie to the claim by noted film critic Roger Ebert that "no movie featuring either Harry Dean Stanton or M. Emmet Walsh in a supporting role can be altogether bad." The film was patently awful, a late-sixties psychedelic teen exploitation film that featured Harry Dean again in a leather jacket, a gang member who proclaims at one point, "I may be a damn drunk redneck, but I ain't no killer." At the dawn of the next decade, audiences saw him as a harmonica-playing GI in *Kelly's Heroes,* a comic spoof of the hugely popular film *The Dirty Dozen.*

It was the 1960s, however, that finally put Harry Dean Stanton's face into what director William Friedkin called the "audience's memory bank" of character actors whose faces are instantly recognizable even if their names aren't, and the main reason was his appearance as Tramp, the singing, guitar-strumming convict, in *Cool Hand Luke.*

Hanging Out at Schwab's

Harry Dean was one of many young journeyman actors going from job to job, mostly in television, occasionally in films, and spending a lot of time between jobs in places like Schwab's Pharmacy on Sunset Boulevard, Chez Paulette just opposite 77 Sunset Strip, the Raincheck, and Pupi's, the latter named after the eccentric Madame Pupi, who grumbled that actors spent too much time lingering over a single cup of coffee and dessert, taking up space, talking movies and Zen Buddhism with only a rare ring of the cash register. Sally Kellerman worked as a waitress at Chez Paulette, where Harry Dean's fellow Kentuckian and aspiring star Warren Oates liked to play chess. Actors Will Hutchins and Jack Nicholson also were regulars.

Schwab's had been a legendary hangout in Hollywood for decades, reputedly the spot where Lana Turner was discovered. Many of its legends were just that, legends and not facts, but Humphrey Bogart, Marilyn Monroe, the Marx Brothers, and Orson Welles had all spent plenty of time at Schwab's. Billy Wilder had a replica of the place built on the set of *Sunset Boulevard* for the scene where struggling screenwriter Joe Gillis, played by William Holden, laments that Schwab's was "a combination office, coffee klatch, and waiting room. Waiting, waiting, waiting for the gravy train."

Harry Dean's close friend Jamie James remembered a tale about Schwab's that Harry Dean loved to tell. It involved fellow actor Clegg Hoyt, a heavyset veteran of television shows like *Cheyenne, Sugarfoot, Death Valley Days, Wanted: Dead or Alive,* and *Wagon Train.* "He had some guys that back in the '60s they used to hang out there. Clegg Hoyt, a character actor who was in a lot of Westerns. Harry Dean did a lot of Westerns, too. Clegg had this glass eye that he liked to take out and scare women with it. Well, Warren Oates, who hung out there, too, went out and bought a two-piece corduroy suit. Harry had a little money, and he admired that suit. So now he bought a two-piece suit. Well, one day, Harry walked in with the same kind of suit that Warren Oates had. Clegg said, 'Look there. Harry Dean Stanton, a study in corduroy. Like a stand-in.' That was kind of humbling for Harry."

Like his friend Jack Nicholson, Harry Dean was also continuing to study his craft in acting classes taught by Jeff Corey and later Martin Landau. Both Corey and Landau were strongly influenced by the Method theories of Stanislavski and the Actors Studio in New York City, where Marlon Brando had studied. Method actors reached deep into themselves for a kind of "sense memory" that would allow them to utilize their own experiences and emotions in connecting with the characters they were playing and thus to inform their performances.

Corey's stage career dated back to the 1930s, and his film credits included Robert Siodmak's classic noir *The Killers* in 1946 and Mark Robson's *Home of the Brave* in 1949. He fell victim to the Communist witch-hunts of the House Un-American Activities Committee despite his commendable war record with the US Navy, having served in fourteen major battles in the Pacific. Refusing to "name names" before HUAC, Corey was blacklisted in 1951 and spent the next decade as an unemployable actor who turned to teaching to earn a living. His classes became legendary in Hollywood and included top stars like Kirk Douglas as well as relative unknowns like Jack Nicholson and Harry Dean. Over the decade of the 1950s and into the 1960s, Corey also taught James Dean, Dean Stockwell, Richard Chamberlain, Carole Eastman, Louise Fletcher, and Robert Blake.

Of the young Nicholson sitting in his class in 1957, Corey wrote in his notebook, "Have to select more carefully what it is you are playing. There is a kind of undisciplined wandering. Too vague, not fixed enough. Make yourself a surer target. You move and filibuster as though to keep from committing yourself."

In his teaching, Corey wrote in his autobiography, *Improvising Out Loud,* "my purpose was to help them find some essential aspect of the scene that everyone in the audience would relate to in his or her own life's experiences. I often invoked Stanislavski's imprecation, 'It is the actor's function to reveal the human condition!'" Corey refused to teach "technique," calling it a kind of dogma and a "word not to be trusted." Rather, he pushed his students to look within themselves "to discover one's own voice."

Theater critic and novelist Stark Young wrote about such discovery back in 1923 in his book *The Flower in Drama: A Book of Papers on the Theatre:* "The greatness of a man's acting will depend on the extent to which the elements of life may be gathered up in him for the spring toward luminous revelation, toward more abundant life."

At his backyard studio behind his home at the intersection of Cheremoya Avenue and Chula Vista Way in Hollywood, Corey offered students what he called "études," in which they would do things like go to a blackboard and, with a piece of chalk, rid themselves of all their thoughts, then select a character they'd played or would like to play and begin writing down word associations about that character. Another étude would be to pick a character out of a fictional story and portray that character "within the framework of a conflict implicit in the story." He charged his students $25 a month for a biweekly, three-hour class.

Corey wanted his students to engage their emotions organically. "An organic connection to anger does not mean playing the anger with feeling," he wrote. "It means identifying the anger and then doing what people do every day—progress with the emotion. In reality, emotion is like a series of concentric circles. While anger may be at the center, from there comes an intricate array of feelings: fear, injury, rage, a sense of injustice, a desire to be alone, anxiety about being left alone, as well as a desire to transcend the anger."

Harry Dean paid attention to Corey's teachings, and that's perhaps one reason why director David Lynch later praised him as one of Hollywood's most organic actors, with a combination of "innocence and naturalness that's really rare."

Eventually Harry Dean and Jack Nicholson left Jeff Corey's classes to study under Martin Landau, a veteran actor whom Monte Hellman had encouraged to teach and whose classes were held at the corner of Western and Fernwood. Landau had been a student of Brando's teacher, Lee Strasberg, at the Actors Studio. Other Landau students included Nicholson's future wife Sandra Knight, actor Bruce Dern, and Monte Hellman himself. As Patrick McGilligan described in his biography of Nicholson, Landau wanted his students to "physicalize" their inner emotions and tensions. He forced them to improvise scenes from bare-bones ideas or do exercises such as sing "Happy Birthday" or "Three Blind Mice" in such a slow, painstaking way that each syllable was emphasized.

The friendship between Harry Dean and Jack Nicholson would become lifelong. Their lives connected on many fronts. After quitting high school in 1934, Jack's mother, June, performed on Broadway with Imogene Coca and the Edwin Strawbridge dancing troupe. (It was Strawbridge's traveling Children's Theater that Harry Dean had joined in New York City.) Nicholson would later cowrite the script to the 1968 film *Head,* which featured the manufactured rock band The Monkees, whose leader, Michael Nesmith, would later produce Harry Dean's 1984 film *Repo Man.* In 1962, Harry Dean was best man at Nicholson's marriage to Sandra Knight. Five years later, when the couple separated, Nicholson moved in with Harry Dean at his home on Utica Drive in Laurel Canyon, where McGilligan said Jack made do with "a bed, a desk, and a record player."

Nicholson and Harry Dean shared a complicated family background. Harry Dean had a tortured relationship with his mother. Nicholson grew up believing that his grandmother, Ethel May, was his mother and his actual mother, June, was his sister. A fledgling dancer who dropped out of school at sixteen to pursue a career in entertainment, June had left home after becoming pregnant. (The father was believed to be dancer-singer Don Furcillo-Rose, who was already married to someone else.) Ethel May told the world she was the mother of June's young baby boy. Nicholson wouldn't learn the truth of his parentage until 1974, when he was thirty-seven years old and awaiting the release of *Chinatown.*

For a time, both actors also shared the frustration of struggling careers at a time when "all those good-looking guys had the jobs," as Warren Oates once complained. Fred Roos, veteran casting director and producer, agreed. "It was the era of the pretty guys." So did B-film specialist Roger Corman. "When he [Nicholson] started, it was the tail end of the Rock Hudson–Tab Hunter school, with the straight, clean-cut, all-American actor playing the lead."

Harry Dean was getting plenty of roles, and so was Oates, but they were all in the supporting cast. The best Nicholson could score were roles in Corman's Edgar Allan Poe movies and horror flicks like *The Terror.* The A-list leading jobs went to serious actors like Paul Newman and Warren Beatty, beach-boy surfer types like Troy Donahue and Frankie Avalon, or attractive TV Western heroes like Robert Fuller, James Drury, or Ty Hardin. Like Harry Dean, Nicholson settled for bit roles in television shows and appeared in military training films to help secure membership in the Screen Actors Guild.

Long afternoons at Schwab's and Pupi's ate up their spare time and also led to lots of intellectual investigations, with discussions of Zen Buddhism, Alan Watts, and existentialism. Patrick McGilligan, in his biography of Jack Nicholson, wrote how the young actors could hear Allen Ginsberg and Lawrence Ferlinghetti recite their beat poetry at coffeehouses on Venice Beach and listen to Billie Holiday tunes in area jazz clubs while reading Ginsberg's *Howl,* Jack Kerouac's *On the Road* and Albert Camus's *The Myth of Sisyphus.* Nicholson, maybe because he never went to college, was a notorious name-dropper of writers and books he'd read or wanted to discuss. He came from the "In-Between Generation, coming of age at the end of the Beat Generation and the start of the Love Generation," McGilligan wrote. Harry Dean, a decade older than his pal, was of the Beat generation, and both absorbed the Zen Buddhist notions that Kerouac described in *The Dharma Bums* and *Desolation Angels.* Zen philosophy, with its emphasis on what British writer Alan Watts called "the immediate now," which frees one from anxieties and concerns about the past and future, was a good fit for actors who were constantly worried about winning their next part. Harry Dean and Nicholson smoked a lot of marijuana and hashish and would eventually become friends with LSD guru Timothy Leary. By 1963 Nicholson was taking LSD at the recommendation of his therapist. "I never did it for fun," Nicholson would later say in the 2011 documentary on director Roger Corman, *Corman's World: Exploits of a Hollywood Rebel.* "It was too strong. You want to confront God for fun?"

Although Harry Dean would later eschew drugs harder than his beloved marijuana, Whitney Fishburn, his half-brother's daughter, believes he had to be tripping along with Nicholson back in the early 1960s. "Harry hung out with Timothy Leary. He must have done LSD. He talked like someone who did." In fact, Warren Oates's sidekick Warren Miller told writer Susan Compo about a road trip to San Antonio in 1975 with Oates, Stanton, and L. Dean Jones when all of them, high on LSD near the Mexican border, watched in utter fascination as lightning flashed across the sky before "falling back into a pile of what turned out to be a dung heap."

When Nicholson moved in with Harry Dean in 1967, their Laurel Canyon pad became wild party central, with lots of drugs, booze, and women, a hedonism that Alan Watts believed ran counter to the Zen experience of the old masters. "As *The Dharma Bums* made plain, it [what Watts called "beat Zen"] combines a voluntary and rather joyous poverty with a rich love-life, and for Western, and much Eastern, religiosity this is the touchstone of deviltry." Yet rock musicians like David Crosby and Cass Elliott had a blast at the Stanton-Nicholson household, and so did a lot of the "burgeoning Laurel Canyon rock aristocracy of the time," Sean O'Hagan of the *Guardian* wrote.

Enter Monte Hellman

Roger Corman gave Nicholson his first break in a feature-film leading role in 1958. The film was *The Cry Baby Killer*, "one of the cycle of misunderstood teenager flicks, imitative of *Blackboard Jungle* and *Rebel without a Cause*," McGilligan wrote. Corman, sometimes dismissed as a schlockmeister whose repertoire was a Hollywood version of the Grand Guignol, was a pivotal figure in the New Hollywood era that would emerge out of the late 1960s, an old hand at moviemaking who got his start as a messenger boy and then a reader and script doctor with 20th Century Fox. He began making his own films with *Monster from the Ocean Floor* in 1954. As a producer, he churned out hundreds of films, most of them B films—monster, biker, and terror flicks, with a special predilection for Edgar Allan Poe stories. They were cheaply and quickly made but, in the process, created what actor Bruce Dern called the "University of Corman," where future giants like Nicholson and directors Martin Scorsese and Francis Ford Coppola could develop their craft as they helped make movies.

With Roger Corman, "the whole world is so different from the Academy Awards world," actor David Carradine said in the documentary *Corman's World*. "This is full-on guerilla-style filmmaking."

Like his mentor Corman, Nicholson had toiled long and hard in the ranks, starting out as an eighteen-year-old gofer, his official title mail clerk, with MGM in Culver City at $30 a week. Working with Corman on his teenager and horror films "was humiliating, but it was good for me," Nicholson said in the Corman documentary. "Roger was the only one who'd hire me for ten years. He was my lifeblood to what I wanted to be."

Although they both were students in Martin Landau's acting classes, Nicholson really got to know Monte Hellman through Corman and their work together in films such as *The Wild Ride* in 1960 and *The Terror* in 1964. In *The Wild Ride*, Corman used Hellman as a production adviser as well as for help with sound and camera work, and it was during the filming of that movie in Contra Costa County that helped "cement the bond between Nicholson and Monte Hellman," McGilligan wrote.

Nicholson would later say this about Hellman: "Monte got me over the line of being exclusively an actor. He got me into writing and producing, and just thinking about films in general." At the same time, "Monte was the first person who was really interested in me as an actor. I mean really interested in me, not just to see me, but he felt a real rapport with whatever he felt my abilities were, and we worked very well together."

A native New Yorker educated at Stanford University and the University of California at Los Angeles, Hellman began his career in theater, once staging a production in Los Angeles of Samuel Beckett's absurdist drama *Waiting for Godot* that Roger Corman helped finance. He was drawn to the minimalism and absurdist elements in Beckett and Eugene Ionesco as well as the earlier existential dilemmas in the plays of Eugene O'Neill and Jean Anouilh.

Beckett's influence can be seen in the two Westerns Hellman collaborated with Nicholson on, *The Shooting* and *Ride in the Whirlwind.* Both released in 1966 with work on each beginning in early 1965 and filming done in a six-to-eight-week span, the two films constitute a Western tribute to Beckett, much like Hellman's production of *Waiting for Godot* in the late 1950s. "Without populations, lawmen, commerce or railroads," critic Michael Atkinson said about the two. "Only nature, survival, a little greed."

Nicholson starred in both films and wrote the script for *Ride in the Whirlwind,* which also featured Harry Dean as the one-eyed stagecoach robber Blind Dick. The germ of both films was born at a lunch date Nicholson and Hellman had at the Vine Street Brown Derby. As McGilligan tells it in his Nicholson biography, it was the day before Christmas, 1964, and the two decided they wanted to make "a B Western with some A nuances." Knowing the popularity of Westerns, Corman agreed to back the project, even suggesting they make two films rather than one, though he would later regret his decision and complain of the films, "There's no Indians. Where are the Indians?" No American theater showed either film until 1971, five years after their release, and their lack of commerciality was what primarily fueled the regret of their investor, who would title his autobiography *How I Made a Hundred Movies in Hollywood and Never Lost a Dime.*

One film did become two films, and both were shot back to back, *The Shooting* first, then *Ride in the Whirlwind,* near Zion National Park in Kanab, Utah. Joining the cast of *The Shooting* was another Harry Dean buddy, Warren Oates, and fellow Jeff Corey alumnus Will Hutchins, already well known for the lead role in the television series *Sugarfoot*. Cameron Mitchell, an established marquee name, starred in *Ride in the Whirlwind*, and Millie Perkins starred in both films.

Writing the script for *The Shooting*, loosely based on a Jack London story, was another Jeff Corey student, Carole Eastman. McGilligan wrote that "the young people who gathered in Corey's class in 1957 and 1958 would become . . . part of Roger Corman's stock company . . . and, to some extent, the vanguard of an entire generation destined to take over a doddering and out-of-touch Hollywood."

With Nicholson handling the script, *Ride in the Whirlwind* also features Beckett-like elements but within a more traditional, if more complex, plot and involving a larger cast. Nicholson, Mitchell, and actor Tom Filer play three wandering cowpokes who, welcomed by Harry Dean's Blind Dick with an innocuous smile that is one of his masterful moments on screen, end up spending the night in a bandits' nest. When the sheriff and his deputies show up to arrest the bandits for robbing a stagecoach, they believe the three cowpokes are part of the gang. The fight is on, with Blind Dick winding up dangling from a rope tied to a tree and Nicholson and Mitchell on the run for their lives. A heavy fatalism hangs over the story, with hints from Camus's *The Myth of Sisyphus,* one of Nicholson's favorite books.

As Nicholson's character, Wes, and Mitchell's, Vern, try to escape the sheriff's posse, they end up at the farmhouse of Evan, played by George Mitchell, who spends a lot of his time purposelessly chopping away at a huge stump in the yard. "How long has he been going at that stump?" Vern asks Evan's wife, Catherine, played by Katherine Squire. "Since yesterday morning," she answers. Jack Nicholson's Wes weighs in at one point, "I'd like to take a whack at that stump myself."

In the commentary that accompanies the Criterion Edition DVD for the two films, Hellman talks about how they tried to keep within a tight budget, using the same horses and as well as some of the same cast members in both films. Gregory Sandor was cinematographer in both films. Upon their release, the films quickly slipped into oblivion in the United States and then into television syndication in 1968. French director Bertrand Tavernier (who would later direct Harry Dean in *Death Watch*) and Parisian press agent Pierre Rissient did promote the films in France, arranging a public screening in Paris that alas was attended by fewer than thirty film lovers. The films were later shown at the Cannes Film Festival, but gained only limited attention. They have, however, both since gained cult status.

Just as *High Noon* and *Shane* signaled a new kind of Western in their day, Hellman's two Westerns opened doors to new possibilities for the tired genre. "Here we enter the altar space of American totemology through the side gate, when no one's looking, after grandeur and money and heroic individualism have wafted away with the night smoke and left only questions," film critic Michael Atkinson has written. "Monte Hellman's mitotic microwesterns *The Shooting* and *Ride in the Whirlwind* don't define their era—which barely saw them—so much as manifest a broader existential modernity rivaled only by Antonioni's in the same decade."

Ride in the Whirlwind taught Harry Dean important lessons about his craft. "Early on the whole point of acting was mostly getting a job and then the experience of doing it," he once said in an interview. "But when I did *Ride in the Whirlwind* with Jack Nicholson I discovered there was more to it. It was a key film for me because of that. Jack told me not to do anything, just let the wardrobe do the acting. It was a great revelation that became an acting principle—to be, rather than to do. You have to behave on screen as much as you do in real life. You don't kill anyone in life, but you understand the anger that may bring it about."

"Just a Closer Walk with Thee"

On the heels of his work with Jack Nicholson and Monte Hellman, Harry Dean scored a role in one of the most successful films of his entire career, *Cool Hand Luke.* He was still billed as Dean Stanton and only one of a long list of veteran character actors in the supporting cast, but this was the movie that would etch the singular face—if not the name—of Harry Dean Stanton in filmgoers' minds. In that face was not necessarily the "lean and hungry look" of Julius Caesar's assassin Cassius in Shakespeare's play, but lean and hungry nonetheless, with a dash of the hard-gained wisdom and weariness that was in Harry Dean's face even as a young man.

None of the long list of Harry Dean's earlier films and television appearances came close to the smash success and classic status of *Cool Hand Luke*—not *The Wrong Man* or *The Proud Rebel,* and certainly not the Monte Hellman films. Filmed largely on the San Joaquin River Delta between October and mid-December 1966 with a set that was built in Stockton, California, *Cool Hand Luke* cost roughly $3.2 million—a typical budget for a major feature at the time—to make. A huge box office hit, it earned four times that much, $16.2 million, garnering an Oscar for George Kennedy as Best Supporting

Actor plus nominations for Paul Newman as Best Actor and Argentinian jazz composer Lalo Shifrin for Best Original Score. Donn Pearce, the former prison inmate who wrote the book on which the film was based, and Frank R. Pierson also received a nomination for Best Adapted Screenplay. Many grumbled that it didn't get a Best Picture nomination and that Stuart Rosenberg's direction was overlooked, too.

Set in a south Florida prison in the early 1960s, *Cool Hand Luke* is the tale of Luke Jackson, a demoted but Silver Star–winning former soldier, born rule-breaker, and convicted parking meter decapitator who keeps escaping from his chain-gang existence and winning the respect and esteem of his fellow prisoners along the way. Newman's Luke Jackson brings "to the end of its logical development" the troublemaking "malcontent" and "loner" he portrayed to one degree or the other in his previous so-called "H" movies—*The Hustler* (1961), *Hud* (1963), *Harper* (1966), and *Hombre* (1967, the same year as *Cool Hand Luke*), in the words of film critic Roger Ebert. "Used to be the anti-hero was a bad guy we secretly liked. Then, with Brando, we got a bad guy we didn't like. And now, in *Cool Hand Luke*, we get a good guy who becomes a bad guy because he doesn't like us."

The film was director Stuart Rosenberg's first completed big-screen feature—an actors' strike had interrupted an earlier film, *Murder, Inc.*, in 1960—after a decade in television working on episodes of series including *Decoy, Alfred Hitchcock Presents, Naked City, The Untouchables, The Defenders,* and *Twilight Zone.* He would later go on to make noteworthy films such as *WUSA* (1970, also with Paul Newman), *The Pope of Greenwich Village* (1984), *Voyage of the Damned* (1976), *The Amityville Horror* (1979), and another prison film, *Brubaker* (1980). For *Cool Hand Luke,* he helped assemble a cast that included some of the finest character actors in all of Hollywood: George Kennedy, of course, in the role of his career as Dragline; Strother Martin as Captain, who runs the prison and utters one of the most famous lines in filmdom, "What we've got here is failure to communicate"; Jo Van Fleet, as Luke's mother, Arletta; Morgan Woodward as Godfrey, the sharp-shooting "man with no eyes"; Dennis Hopper as Babalugats; Clifton James as Carr, the floorwalker; and, of course, Harry Dean as Tramp, a ne'er-do-well whose bunk is next to fellow newcomer Luke's, who gets sick the first day in the field, and who is the prison camp's guitar-picking balladeer.

Jack Lemmon and Telly Savalas were originally considered for the part of Luke, and Bette Davis was in line to be Arletta, in some ways a more reasonable choice than Jo Van Fleet, who was only ten years older than Newman.

For Newman, who had trained at Lee Strasberg's Actors Studio, the role solidified his status as a major star.

Cool Hand Luke was one of a long line of prison films in Hollywood history and was the most searing indictment of the Southern prison system since Mervyn LeRoy's *I Am a Fugitive from a Chain Gang* in 1932, which starred Paul Muni in an Oscar-nominated role as fugitive James Allen. Even though *Cool Hand Luke* was largely filmed in California, Rosenberg wanted authenticity in his film. In one scene, where the prisoners are laying down a mile of asphalt to build a road, he ordered his actors to do the actual back-breaking work. He wanted real sweat and real exhaustion. He had tons of Spanish moss brought in from Louisiana to give his set a real Deep South feel, and he refused to allow women—including Newman's wife, Joanne Woodward—on the set. He even kept the cast's most prominent female, the voluptuous, car-washing Joy Harmon, separate from the male cast during filming.

Harry Dean holds his own in a strong cast, performing "Just a Closer Walk with Thee" during the pivotal scene when Luke is visited by his dying mother, and singing three other songs during the film: "Midnight Special" while Luke digs dirt out of the boss's ditch, "Ain't No Grave Gonna Hold My Body Down" during another digging scene, and finally "Cottonfields."

Harry Dean's singing of those songs was another key element in the realism director Rosenberg wanted in this film. Harry Dean sang with the authenticity that his Kentucky upbringing had instilled in him. These were songs he had heard all his life, and when he sang them during the filming of *Cool Hand Luke,* they likely made him think back, and it gave his singing a special sincerity that in turn made them seem that much more real to the audience.

Since he was cast as a singing, guitar-playing prisoner, Harry Dean at one point decided to take advantage of an opportunity. His musician friend Jamie James tells the story. "The guitar they brought him was some rinky-dink Sears. He pulled a fast one, one of the few times he pulled a fast one. He said, 'No, I need a specific guitar.' They got him a Martin." Harry Dean later gave the Martin, known for its quality and much more expensive than a Sears guitar, to James as a gift.

A "Lot of Poison in the Family" Back Home

Some of Harry Dean's relatives and friends believe he never really looked back once he got established in Hollywood. He didn't travel back to Kentucky much, but he stayed in touch with the family by telephone. In the late 1950s and early 1960s Harry Dean's half-brother, Stanley McKnight Jr., used to dread those early morning phone calls from Los Angeles to their mother Ersel.

"Our mother, she was a little bit crazy," Stanley recalled in an interview. "Today you would probably call it bipolar. When she added alcohol to the mix, it got worse. There was conflict between her and Harry Dean. When he would call, when the phone would ring, it would be two in the morning, only eleven in California. It would wake everybody in the house. I would later see her, my mother, in a manic episode and I knew I was in for a hell of a day. Don't know what the phone calls were, but I knew she was angry. When he would call her, I would get the shit beat out of me. She would remind me that the only reason to have me was to give my father a child."

After Harry Dean left and his brothers moved into their own homes, Shorty Stanton found himself living alone in the room he'd built in the back of his Lexington barbershop. He dated women, but he never married again. Ersel lived in Lexington and even worked for her former husband for a time. After all, Shorty had taught her hair care and enabled her to become a beautician. Ersel's second husband, Stanley McKnight Sr., had also been married before. His wife deserted him during the war, taking their baby daughter with her; he never saw his daughter again. According to Stanley Jr., Ersel told Stanley, "I'll give you a child as a present," and she did. But she never let that child forget what a favor she had done for his father.

Stanley Sr. and Ersel lived in Sarasota, Florida, for several years before moving back to Lexington, where Stanley Jr. enrolled at the University of Kentucky. In June 1967, Stanley Sr. had a heart attack and died. He was only fifty-one, an early death that stress brought on by Ersel's behavior may have aggravated—her disappearances sometimes for weeks at a time, her gambling at the racetrack on dogs and horses, her drinking and angry outbursts. "There's a lot of poison in this family," Stanley Jr.'s daughter Whitney Fishburn told me.

Stanley Jr. loved his dad, even if he's less than sure how much his mother did. He recalled how Stanley Sr. worked with his half-brother Ralph helping impoverished coal miners in the east Kentucky mountains during the Kennedy and Johnson "War on Poverty" years, installing aluminum siding, painting, and doing other home improvements.

Ersel moved back to Florida after her second husband's death. "My mother was drinking a lot," Stanley Jr. said. "She was drinking and living with other men."

Nearly exactly two years after Stanley Sr. died, Shorty did, too.

In his last years, Harry Dean's father had developed a reputation as a well-dressed, even dapper, eccentric, a loner but with an eye for the ladies, still a man of strict rules, just as he had been to his boys when they were young. He didn't smoke and he wasn't a drinker. "He cut every kid's hair in Lexington," his nephew Ralph Stanton Jr. recalled, but "he was sole to himself, very much a private person. He would come by at least once or twice a week for dinner to our house. He would always slip a dollar underneath his plate— for my mom. We always thought we could keep it if we found it. Never happened. He would bring a box of fudge bars."

At the barbershop, Shorty kept a strict eye on children like Ralph Jr., scolding them if they squirmed in their chairs or kept playing with the footrests, but he also showed a sense of fun at times. "I remember him doing a little dance, a tap dance. He would start and stop in the middle of whatever and dance, then go back to cutting hair. When the Beatles were coming out, I wanted bangs like the Beatles, and I would say, 'Give me bangs like the Beatles.' He'd give me a buzz cut."

Shorty was only five-foot-one, but he made quite an impression. "He was a real sharp dresser," Ralph Jr. said. "He drove a great big 1960 Grand Prix, a city block long. He rode with one foot on the brake and one foot on the gas. He would wear out the brakes. You couldn't tell him anything."

Ralph Jr. continued, "He had a gold pocket watch, always had a suit on. He was a dapper man with a gold chain, and he'd pull [the watch] out. You'd ask him what time it is, and he would not give you the time of day. He'd say, 'Half-past.' He would get out of his car, take his hat off the seat, put it on, lock his door, ask you directions. That's what he did. If he got out of his car, he would lock it, put [the hat] back on."

Shorty was seventy-six when he died in June 1969, but he was physically strong till the end. "The week he died, he and I were cutting down an oak tree with an axe," Ralph Jr. remembered. "He was a little guy, but he had muscles in his legs. He was just an athlete, and he took a shine to me. I was the only one who played football. He had played football and baseball. We just got along together."

Shorty and Harry Dean had a lot more in common than either probably realized. Harry Dean "was a kind of a guy to himself," Ralph Jr. said. "I believe he was happy enough being by himself. Never got married. He was like his father a bit. He wouldn't like to hear that."

6

Harry Dean and the New Hollywood

Monte Hellman looked younger than his eighty-five years, his hair longish but thinning, his eyes focused. Still, he was frail in his warm-ups and not feeling particularly well on the day we talked. He insisted on no photographs. I sat across from him at the bar in his Laurel Canyon home. It was March 2018, and I wanted to talk to him about Harry Dean Stanton and the three films of Harry Dean's that he directed: *Ride in the Whirlwind* (1966), *Two-Lane Blacktop* (1971), and *Cockfighter* (1974). The legendary director was a key figure in what has become known as the "New Hollywood" of the 1970s, but he was never impressed with such labels. "When I look back at my movies," Hellman said, "I basically made movies unconsciously. I am an intellectual in other areas, but not in making movies."

I looked around his home—lots of books everywhere, a workout machine, a pool outside, on the walls two photographs of the Obama family and an eclectic collection of art, much of it Asian. Prominent among the wall decorations was a framed photograph of a young Jack Nicholson, whose early career owed much to Hellman, with early starring roles in films such as *Back Door to Hell* (1964), *Flight to Fury* (1964), *The Shooting* (1966), and *Ride in the Whirlwind* (1966).

"You've been praised for the feminism in your films," I told him.

"It wasn't something I thought about. I have a lot of female protagonists."

"You saw film as an art form."

"We didn't think of it as art. We didn't think of it as anything. The problem was getting through each day, getting your pages shot."

"But the New Hollywood?"

"It didn't exist at the time. Eras are defined years after the fact, so what is this era now? Again, it is not something we thought about, or talked about."

I mentioned British film writer Brad Stevens's 2003 book *Monte Hellman: His Life and Films* and its high praise for Hellman's work.

"I've actually never read it," Hellman said. "It was fun working with him on that. We exchanged a thousand emails. I am sure a lot of the information imparted in those emails is in the book."

Hmmm. In his acknowledgments, Stevens gives special thanks to Hellman for his "thorough proof-reading/fact-checking of the manuscript."

Educated at Stanford University and the University of California at Los Angeles, a devotee of the work of Samuel Beckett and Jean Anouilh, Hellman was what Patrick McGilligan called "the perennial outsider in Hollywood," a filmmaker who may have come out of Roger Corman's low-budget, fast-on-the-draw, learn-on-the-job film "university" but who was always the intellectual among the vast population of high school and college dropouts in the film world.

With what film critic Michael Atkinson called their "existential modernity," Hellman's films both anticipated and became part of the New Hollywood era that defined the best films of the 1970s, a time that Hellman may deny as an "era" but one when indeed a new Hollywood shook the foundations of the Old Hollywood of Adolph Zukor, Jack Warner, Darryl Zanuck, and the creaky studio system they represented. Along with Hellman were young, emerging directors including Francis Ford Coppola, Martin Scorsese, Peter Bogdanovich, William Friedkin; writers William Goldman, Robert Towne, and Thomas McGuane; and new stars including Jack Nicholson, Faye Dunaway, Robert De Niro, Al Pacino, Jill Clayburgh, Gene Hackman, Dustin Hoffman, Ellen Burstyn, Diane Keaton—and, yes, smaller stars like Harry Dean Stanton.

Peter Biskind, author of arguably the foremost book on the New Hollywood, *Easy Riders, Raging Bulls: How the Sex-Drugs-and-Rock 'n' Roll Generation Saved Hollywood* (1998), has this to say about the era: "It was the last time Hollywood produced a body of risky, high-quality work—as opposed to the errant masterpiece—work that was character-, rather than plot-driven, that defied traditional narrative conventions, that challenged the tyranny of technical correctness, that broke the taboos of language and behavior, that dared to end unhappily. These were often films without heroes, without romance, without . . . anyone to 'root for.'"

The aims of the New Hollywood vanguard were revolutionary, Biskind argues. "At its most ambitious, the New Hollywood was a movement intended to cut film free of its evil twin, commerce, enabling it to fly high through the thin air of art. The filmmakers of the '70s hoped to overthrow the studio system, or least render it irrelevant, by democratizing filmmaking, putting it into the hands of anyone with talent and determination."

The New Hollywood was the film world's response to the late 1960s and the scandals of Richard Nixon, Watergate, and Vietnam of the 1970s, the idealism of those times, the radicalism of the youth, their vision of creating a new "society within the shell of the old," as stated in the preamble to the constitution of the Industrial Workers of the World, the Wobblies, at the dawn of the century.

Although Harry Dean's career stretched from the Old Hollywood days of studio moguls and McCarthy-era witch-hunts into the modern era of superhero–Stan Lee comic-book-hero movies, he hit his stride during the New Hollywood era. "It wasn't until he was in his fifties, when his age finally caught up with his looks, that Hollywood discovered his gentleness and range," writer Ian Nathan once said. "His best work comes in a middle-aged reel of hip movies."

"He fit perfectly alongside the individualists and weirdos of New Hollywood," writer Zach Vasquez said about Harry Dean, "and his unique screen presence captured the weathered, hungover aura of the films of the '70s better than perhaps anyone other than his close friend and frequent costar Warren Oates."

Indeed, many of Harry Dean's most memorable film roles came in the 1970s and first years of the 1980s, a time when he worked with many of the best directors in the business and appeared in only one television show, *Mary Hartman, Mary Hartman* (five episodes of it, however). He was in Monte Hellman's *Two-Lane Blacktop* (1971) and *Cockfighter* (1974), Francis Ford Coppola's *The Godfather Part II* (1974) and *One from the Heart* (1981), Sam Peckinpah's *Pat Garrett and Billy the Kid* (1973), John Milius's *Dillinger* (1973), Arthur Penn's *The Missouri Breaks* (1976), John Huston's *Wise Blood* (1979), Ridley Scott's *Alien* (1979), and John Carpenter's *Escape from New York* (1981) and later *Christine* (1983).

Other 1970s and early 1980s films with Harry Dean in the cast included *Kelly's Heroes* (1970), *Farewell, My Lovely* (1975), *Straight Time* (1978), *The Rose* (1979), *Death Watch* (1980), *Private Benjamin* (1980), and writer-director Thomas McGuane's *92 in the Shade* (1975) and *Rancho Deluxe* (1975, written by McGuane and directed by Frank Perry). McGuane was also the original writer on *The Missouri Breaks*.

Still, before his comparatively meatier roles in Huston's *Wise Blood*, Belgian director Ulu Grosbard's *Straight Time*, and French director Bertrand

Tavernier's *Death Watch,* Harry Dean remained mostly in the supporting cast, often playing a sidekick, such as his role as Moe in Coppola's *One from the Heart.* That film, starring Frederic Forrest and Terri Garr, proved a disaster, costing $27 million to make and earning only $2.5 million at the box office, a huge, misguided musical flop that would bankrupt Coppola's American Zoetrope studio and help bring an end to the New Hollywood era. The veteran Forrest would star the next year in the Coppola-produced, Wim Wenders–directed *Hammett*—a film replete with classic character actors including Royal Dano, Elisha Cook Jr., R. G. Armstrong, and Hank Worden—and then see his own short-lived time as leading man come to an end. After that film, he returned to the supporting cast that Harry Dean had never left.

Forrest once lamented the contrast between lead and supporting roles in a film. "It's a continual problem when you don't have the lead. There's always the possibility you'll get cut. You have no control. If there's a scene with a character who isn't the lead and it threatens the main story or detracts from it in any way, it doesn't make a difference how good it is. It goes."

Writer McGuane, who worked both with Harry Dean and Warren Oates on several films, told me in March 2019 that the label "character actor" is demeaning at best. "I think for people like Harry Dean and more especially Warren [Oates] it is a kind of kiss of death. Like 'writer's writer,' which means your books don't sell. You don't want to be called that within a working culture. It is a ceiling."

At least Frederic Forrest had been a lead. Harry Dean was usually either a sidekick or comic relief. If Forrest could complain to a journalist in 1980, "Next time, I'd like to get the girl instead of the horse," Harry Dean could say he had never gotten the girl and wasn't even first in line for the horse. In Peckinpah's *Pat Garrett and Billy the Kid,* he plays Luke, one of Billy's gang who welcomes Billy (Kris Kristofferson) back to the gang's bunkhouse after a long absence. "Sure is pleasurable seeing you back again, Kid," Luke tells him. Billy eyes the señorita in bed with Luke. "You had to take up with that low-down piece of old hide?" he asks her. Harry Dean's Luke meekly crawls out of the bed and lies down by himself as Kristofferson's Billy takes his place in the bed.

In Monte Hellman's *Two-Lane Blacktop,* Harry Dean has only a single scene, but it is a memorable one. His real-life buddy and fellow Kentuckian Warren Oates landed the lead in that road movie as hard-driving GTO, who picks up a hitchhiking Harry Dean in Oklahoma. Harry Dean plays a homosexual man wearing a straw cowboy hat and flaming red shirt who makes a pass at GTO; for this he is rejected and eventually ejected from GTO's yellow GTO in the rain. "Get your ass outta here," GTO tells him. "How was I supposed to know?" Harry Dean's clearly upset hitchhiker asks as he fights back the tears. "We can still be friendly, can't we?"

Hellman told me Harry Dean wasn't too happy when he learned about his role in *Two-Lane Blacktop*. "He was really kind of upset when he finally read the script. He didn't read the script until he came on location." What Hellman failed to mention, however, was that he refused to let any of the cast, with the exception of Warren Oates, read the script in advance. "He was really upset that I had cast him as what he called a homosexual, but he was great. That is one of the best performances ever, the one that he gives in that one scene."

Harry Dean puts in another great performance as Curt, the clumsy cowhand, in Frank Perry's *Rancho Deluxe*, a bumbler who's too shy to dance with Elizabeth Ashley's Cora Brown. He gets to show off the disarming smile he had in *Ride in the Whirlwind* when he beats Jeff Bridges's Jack McKee in a game of Pong in a bar (with Jimmy Buffett performing in the background) and casually informs him that he knows Jack is rustling cattle owned by Curt's boss, John Brown, played by Clifton James. In *Rancho Deluxe*, Harry Dean still doesn't get the girl, although he falls hard for one, Charlene Davis's hard-drinking, conniving Laura Beige, telling her, "You're so sweet and innocent," and telling his friend, "She's almost like Bambi."

In Dick Richards's 1975 remake of *Farewell, My Lovely*, based on Raymond Chandler's classic hard-boiled novel, Harry Dean plays junior detective Billy Rolfe, a racist, corrupt cop who despises Robert Mitchum's Philip Marlowe. "You're not a detective, Marlowe," Billy Rolfe tells him. "You're a slot machine. You'll do anything for six bits." Marlowe tells Billy's boss, Detective Lieutenant Nulty, played by John Ireland, to get Billy out of the room. "I feel like I got to slip him a fin," Marlowe says.

The 1975 film is considered by many a modern noir classic, the definitive film version of Chandler's novel and the one closest to the book. Roger Ebert called it "the most evocative of the private detective movies we have had in the last few years." Mitchum won kudos for his performance, as did Jules Styne's score. Harry Dean's malevolent Billy Rolfe is right on target, too. Hard-boiled writer Jim Thompson even had a cameo role in the film, as Judge Baxter Wilson Grayle.

Harry Dean's films in the 1970s helped define the New Hollywood era. He worked with its best directors at a time when the "auteur" theory had come into full flower in the United States, after this theory had provided the philosophical undergirding of the *nouvelle vague*, or New Wave, film movement led by François Truffaut and Jean-Luc Godard in 1950s France. First articulated by the writers in the French publication *Cahiers du cinéma* and in the United States by film critic Andrew Sarris, auteurism promoted the idea of film as a work of art largely guided by the vision of a single artist, the director.

Although he was becoming an increasingly familiar face on the screen, Harry Dean still chafed at the limitations that being a character actor in the supporting cast placed on him. Monte Hellman said he cast Warren Oates as lead in *Two-Lane Blacktop, Cockfighter,* and *China 9, Liberty 37* (1978) because "I saw Warren [Oates] as a leading man even though he was a character actor. I didn't see Harry as a leading man. This got to Harry. He wanted to know why Warren was getting all the other parts, and he was getting the second roles. I said I have to cast each movie the way they fall."

Supporting cast members may be in a film with a famous director, but how much do they actually interact with that director? "When I worked with Hitchcock and Kazan I was just playing little parts, and they didn't have any time to work with me," actor Bruce Dern told writers Robert Crane and Christopher Fryer. "You know, unless you have a big part, and go through the everyday give and take of an actor-director relationship, it's not the same thing."

Harry Dean was like Dennis Weaver, who played US Marshal Matt Dillon's limping, whining sidekick Chester Goode for nine successful years on television's *Gunsmoke* before he had enough of it. "Dennis left the show because he wanted to prove his versatility on the stage and in movies," James Arness, who played Matt Dillon, wrote in his autobiography. "I was particularly sorry to see Dennis leave us, since he'd become such an integral part of our seamless theatrical family. . . . I clearly understood his desire to move on, though."

As Hellman's comments indicated, what bothered Harry Dean was the fact that some of the actor friends who had struggled with him in those early years, taking Jeff Corey and Martin Landau's acting lessons and searching for parts, were now getting lead roles. He and Warren Oates were both chain-smoking, Buddha-admiring Kentuckians who had traveled the same dusty trail from New York City to Los Angeles through countless cowpoke parts on television. Now Harry Dean was second fiddle to Oates's GTO in *Two-Lane Blacktop* and Frank Mansfield in *Cockfighter.* He'd be third fiddle to Oates's Nichol Dance and Peter Fonda's Tom Skelton in Thomas McGuane's *92 in the Shade* in 1975.

Perhaps no actor more defined the New Hollywood era, however, than Harry Dean's decade-younger friend Jack Nicholson. After working for more than a dozen years in relative obscurity as an actor and screenwriter and paying his dues on television and in Roger Corman's horror flicks and Monte Hellman's existential Westerns and remote-location dramas, Nicholson had finally—and fully—ascended to stardom. He had reached what he liked to call the "Big Wombassa."

After his career-making success as the alcoholic Southern lawyer George Hanson in *Easy Rider* (1969), Nicholson had scored again and again in films such as *Five Easy Pieces* (1970), *Carnal Knowledge* (1971), *The Last Detail* (1973), *Chinatown* (1974), and *One Flew over the Cuckoo's Nest* (1975). Nicholson had earned Oscar nominations for *Easy Rider, Five Easy Pieces, The Last Detail, Chinatown,* and *One Flew over the Cuckoo's Nest,* the film that brought him the Oscar for Best Actor and an estimated $15 million in percentages in addition to his salary. "The careers of the surrogate family" of Jack's circle of friends, including Harry Dean, "with few exceptions, had gone in quieter directions," Patrick McGilligan wrote in his biography of Nicholson.

"They knew he was changing, moving away from them into another, more rarefied sphere," McGilligan wrote. "In most situations now, Nicholson had the upper hand, whereas before, especially with the men, the badinage had always been among equals. Competition, the glue holding together their relationships, was no longer there." Nicholson was on top, a star now. He had arrived. His buddies were in a different place, still hoping to arrive, no longer competition or even fellow travelers like they had been before.

The same held true for directors like Monte Hellman and Henry Jaglom, who had directed Nicholson in *A Safe Place* (1971). They could no longer afford Nicholson. His days of acting in "shoestring, independent films for scale and as a favor to friends" were gone, as McGilligan described it.

Harry Dean wasn't a star, but at least two of the films he was in, both feature films that fully embodied the New Hollywood's spirit of rebellion and challenge to the system, helped set the stage for larger roles later in his career, some years after the New Hollywood era. They were Sam Peckinpah's *Pat Garrett and Billy the Kid* and Arthur Penn's *The Missouri Breaks.*

Just One of Billy's Gang

Kris Kristofferson stood before the crowd of four hundred at downtown Lexington's ninety-five-year-old Kentucky Theatre and smiled his famous smile. "I'm wearing the same boots I wore in the film," he told them. The film was *Pat Garrett and Billy the Kid,* the 1973 Western directed by Sam Peckinpah and which starred Kristofferson as Billy the Kid, James Coburn as Pat Garrett, and what Kristofferson once called "the greatest collection of character actors assembled in one film." They included Chill Wills, Katy Jurado, Richard Jaeckel, Slim Pickens, R. G. Armstrong, Luke Askew, Matt Clark, Jack Elam, Jack Dodson, L. Q. Jones, John Davis Chandler, Gene Evans, Donnie Fritts, and Harry Dean Stanton. Another familiar face in the cast, if new to film, was Bob Dylan, who played a character named Alias, a newcomer to Billy's gang. Five years before the film, Dylan had recorded the story of another famous gunman of the Old West, John Wesley Harding.

Kristofferson was in Harry Dean's old hometown to introduce a screening of the film as a May 2017 preview event for the Harry Dean Stanton Festival, which would take place later that year. He and Harry Dean had been old friends. It was Harry Dean who'd helped launch the legendary singer and songwriter's film career, planting the seed during a gig at the Troubadour, a music hall just down the street from Harry Dean's favorite bar, Dan Tana's. From that seed grew a movie career for Kristofferson that included roles in films such as *Cisco Pike* (1972), *Bring Me the Head of Alfredo Garcia* (1974, another Peckinpah film), *Alice Doesn't Live Here Anymore* (1974), and *A Star Is Born* (1976).

"Working with Sam Peckinpah was a wild ride," Kristofferson told the crowd. "Working on this film was a dream come true. We got to ride horses, shoot guns."

A wild ride indeed.

Peckinpah was forty-eight years old and between two of his three marriages to Mexican actress Begoña Palacios, roller-coasting his way through his one-year marriage to Joey Gould. His up-and-down career, which had begun in the 1950s with directing and writing scripts for television Westerns like *Gunsmoke* and *The Rifleman,* included triumphs like *Ride the High Country* (1962) and the controversial, violence-drenched "masterpiece" (at least in the eyes of critic Roger Ebert) *The Wild Bunch* (1969). However, his filmography also included box-office and/or critically panned "failures" like *Major Dundee* (1965), *The Ballad of Cable Hogue* (1970), and *Straw Dogs* (1971), which critic Pauline Kael declared "the first American film that is a fascist work of art." *Pat Garrett and Billy the Kid* would be his last real Western, the genre for which he is most noted today.

Based in part on a book by Charles Neider, *The Authentic Death of Hendry Jones,* the film tells a different history from the gunslinging myth of William

Bonney. It tells of Billy the Kid being an obstacle to the land-grabbing Santa Fe Ring of crooked bankers and financiers—akin to some of today's venture capitalists—who were in cahoots with New Mexico cattle baron John Chisum in a push to expand their empire. Chisum hires Billy's old compadre, Sheriff Pat Garrett, to rid the area of the gunman's presence. When Billy refuses, Garrett kills him. (How different is the 1970 John Wayne vehicle, *Chisum,* which depicts the old emperor as joining up with Billy the Kid and Pat Garrett to fight the bad guys.)

"A rather ugly stench of ruthless business ethics, exploitation, corruption, opportunistic law and order mentality and political wheeling and dealing rises from the historical page containing the drama of Billy the Kid," film writer Jan Aghed said about the history that inspired the film, "and most likely Billy, despite the eventual notches on his gun butt, was one of its least antipathetic figures."

Peckinpah described the history this way to Aghed: "The inevitability of Billy and Garrett's final conflict fascinates me. . . . The same people who had hired Garrett to kill Billy years later had him assassinated because as a police officer he was getting too close to their operation." (Santa Fe Ring leader Albert Fall later became US secretary of state.)

Also influencing Peckinpah's story was the later history of the Teapot Dome Scandal of 1920, in which officials in the Warren G. Harding administration colluded with wealthy oilmen to help them grab lucrative oil leases in the West that had earlier been under the control of the federal government.

Pat Garrett and Billy the Kid grew out of a previous film, *One-Eyed Jacks* (1961), which starred and was directed by Marlon Brando—his only directing credit. Peckinpah wrote an early draft for the script of that film, but left the project as Brando shifted from writer to writer. The writer for *Pat Garrett and Billy the Kid* was Rudolph Wurlitzer, who had originally intended his screenplay for director Monte Hellman, but turned to Peckinpah after Hellman's *Two-Lane Blacktop* (which Wurlitzer also wrote) failed to score at the box office.

By the time Peckinpah began filming *Pat Garrett and Billy the Kid,* he was a battle-scarred veteran in an industry known for chewing up and spitting out opinionated, independent-minded rebels like himself who didn't consistently deliver on the bottom line. His long and usually losing battles with studio executives had created in Peckinpah a hatred of entrenched, money-obsessed power that would be reflected strongly in the story of *Pat Garrett and Billy the Kid,* a film that ultimately is a stinging indictment of blind, capitalistic greed and its destructive influence on people and the land. "You talking about a left-of-center movie. It really was," said actor-writer-director Billy Bob Thornton, who holds *Pat Garrett and Billy the Kid* in higher esteem than *The Wild Bunch.* "Nothing like it had been made before." Peckinpah's war with the studios would intensify with *Pat Garrett and Billy the Kid.* MGM would later cut sixteen crucial minutes—from the beginning and the end of the film—helping prompt a lawsuit from Peckinpah.

Peckinpah's battles with the studios had taken their toll. He was snorting lines of cocaine and drinking up to four bottles of whiskey or vodka a day, nursing a growing paranoia that led to sometimes explosive behavior both on and off the set. He already had a reputation for such behavior. He made the normally even-tempered Charlton Heston so angry on the set of *Major Dundee* that Heston lunged at him with a saber. Yet when Columbia Pictures fired Peckinpah from the film, it was Heston who came to his rescue and argued successfully for his reinstatement by offering to work free.

One night, after a day of filming on the set of *Pat Garrett and Billy the Kid,* Harry Dean and fellow musician and cast member Donnie Fritts paid a visit to Peckinpah in his bedroom and got a rude awakening themselves. "Harry and I went to his bedroom, and he had a .38 pointed right in our face," Fritts recalled. "Harry was smart and ran out of the room. I'm sitting there trying to reason with him. It wasn't the first time anyone pulled a .38 on me, but you don't get used to it."

Harry Dean didn't do much to endear himself to Peckinpah on another occasion during filming. As the ever-volatile director stared into the camera to make important decisions about the mise-en-scène for a particular shot, he spotted two joggers in the distance making their way across the Mexican landscape. Peckinpah recognized them immediately. They were Harry Dean and Bob Dylan. "You ruined the scene!" Peckinpah screamed at them. Peckinpah "had waited all day just to get this one shot right in which James Coburn rides off into the early morning light after killing me," Kris Kristofferson remembered. "Peckinpah was furious. He yelled at Harry, 'You just cost me $25,000.' Then he picked up a Bowie knife and threw it at him. It was a pretty close call."

"The man was crazy, and you got to be crazy to work for him," said veteran actor L. Q. Jones, ninety years old at the time he spoke with me in February 2018. Jones played Black Harris in the film, one of fourteen film projects he did with Peckinpah. "I think it was the worst picture Sam made. He was ill. He wasn't functioning properly. He was just a shell of himself. If you look at *Pat,* it depends on which cut you'll see. There'll be a spate of two minutes, five minutes, in which it is brilliant. Then it will dissolve into pure crap, then swing back."

With his multicolored bandana wrapped around his forehead and his eyes shielded by dark or reflecting glasses, Peckinpah had a way of creating a mood that affected the entire cast, Jones said. "You have to understand Sam, and I knew him fairly well, as well as anybody did. The way he operated it the first day. By the end of the third day, every actor hated every other actor. That was the way it was for about two days. Then Sam would put us back together, making a family of us. When we got to *Pat Garrett,* he took everything apart, but he didn't have the strength to put it back together. Sam shot himself in the foot. He was ill. He drank far too much. He was dependent on it." Peckinpah wouldn't even appear on the set until two or three hours after cast and crew had gathered for filming. Then, after "the prop man would put down a comfortable chair for him," he "would go to the chair and sit down with those reflective glasses that he wore. People said he was creating. Creating, my ass. He was trying to get his heart started."

Kristofferson agreed with Jones's assessment of Peckinpah's condition. "There were days when he couldn't raise himself from his chair."

Writer Thomas McGuane, who got to know Peckinpah during their days together in Montana with mutual friends like Warren Oates, has few fond memories of the director. "He was basically an asshole," McGuane told me in March 2019. "He made some great movies. No question about his capacity as an artist. He was just impossible to be around. Always coked up, the kind of guy who would chase his son around the apartment shooting up the walls. He was always dialed up to thirteen. He didn't have a normal range. A kind of sicko in many ways. Some of those long, elaborate stunt scenes were so he could do drugs and bring in hookers from Las Vegas. He was such a vivid character. He was kind of treacherous, kind of an angry person, hard to be around. That takes nothing from his achievement."

Actors like Oates and Harry Dean "had to defer to him," McGuane said. "It was a kind of sadistic relationship."

Still, McGuane said he understood Peckinpah's battles with the studios and executives. "The machinations of the producer class, they are vitiating. You want to take a shower after dealing with those people."

Critics who admire parts of *Pat Garrett and Billy the Kid* but acknowledge its failures as well point to issues like the miscasting of the legendary actor and director Emilio "El Indio" Fernández as a Mexican peasant and his subsequent death scene, where Kristofferson's Billy kills his murderers but then abandons the peasant's family in the desert to return to the ranch where his gang is holed up.

Despite all the problems, Harry Dean looked back at the experience with appreciation. Peckinpah "was a passionate, mad artist and poet," he told filmmaker Tom Thurman in Thurman's documentary *Sam Peckinpah's West: Legacy of a Hollywood Renegade* (2004), "and I loved him, really." In Thurman's documentary about Harry Dean's own career, *Crossing Mulholland,* Harry Dean talked again about Peckinpah. "All the directors I've worked with—Scorsese, Sam—all of them said something to me that had an impact."

Even with its flaws and initial panning by respected critics like Roger Ebert, who dismissed the film as "boring" and existing "almost entirely on one note—a low, melancholy one," *Pat Garrett and Billy the Kid* has become something of a classic. "This film is so rich, sensual, and lyrical that we could never simply call it hopeless," film scholar Gabrielle Murray has written. "There is a tension in *Pat Garrett and Billy the Kid* that exists between the mournful narrative and this film's aesthetic expressiveness."

Harry Dean's role in *Pat Garrett and Billy the Kid* is relatively small. Acting newcomer Bob Dylan, whom Kristofferson convinced Peckinpah to hire, gets more lines. However, the film was a memorable moment in Harry Dean's career. As an actor, he got to work with Peckinpah on a project that in many ways symbolized the rebellion that lay at the heart of the New Hollywood. In the film, he was the gang member who slept with Billy's señorita in Billy's absence and gave her back to him when he returned. He was there when Emilio Fernández's peasant led his family off into the wilderness and sure destruction. He was there with a bottle of whiskey in his hand as the reality hit home that Pat Garrett had indeed shot and killed Billy the Kid. Just a few scenes, but it was a marked presence that called attention to itself, the kind of understated, but undeniable, presence that became his trademark.

The film also gave Harry Dean an opportunity to solidify friendships with Kris Kristofferson and Bob Dylan, musicians like him who connected with him in important, lifelong ways. "The thing I remember most about that shoot is becoming friends with Bob Dylan," he told *Venice Magazine* writer Alex Simon in 1997. "We hung out quite a bit during the shoot. Drove together all the way from Guadalajara, Mexico, to Kansas City. We jammed together quite a bit. He liked my Mexican songs."

Three Mulholland Drive Neighbors in Montana

Marlon Brando is slumped into his chair at his Mulholland Drive compound. Across from him is his friend, writer Thomas McGuane, who has been staying at his house. They're talking books, movies, life, philosophy, all of it the very stuff of Brando's life, and Brando is so engaged he's oblivious to the two producers standing behind him, motioning feverishly at McGuane. They want the writer to say something to the actor to convince him to commit to their picture, *The Missouri Breaks*. It's McGuane's story, for heaven's sake. Get the man to commit.

"They are doing hand signals, wearing their double-breasted suits, waving their arms," McGuane told me with a chuckle in March 2019.

Brando is still highly bankable, despite the three-year hiatus since the success of *The Godfather* and *Last Tango in Paris* in 1972. Three years. Brando could use the money. One of the producers, Elliott Kastner, decides to arrange for a plumber to come to Brando's house and tell the actor that his house needs a major overhaul. "If you don't fix the plumbing, you can't flush any of the toilets in the house," the plumber tells Brando.

Brando is already in a financial bind due to a sea-farming project on his South Pacific island near Tahiti. He also needs financing for a film devoted to his current cause, Native Americans. Still, he remains uncommitted. He likes McGuane, but he doesn't believe this is a story that can become a movie. Kastner pulls another rabbit out of his hat. He goes to the director he wants, Arthur Penn, and then to two stars he wants, Brando and Jack Nicholson, and asks each, one by one, whether he'll do the film if the others sign on. Sure, Brando says; and so do the others.

In fact, if it had been up to McGuane, he himself would have directed the 1976 film and Warren Oates would have been cast in the role Brando eventually accepted, that of the sharpshooting regulator Robert E. Lee Clayton, whom cattle boss David Braxton has hired to capture the thieves stealing his stock. Instead of Jack Nicholson, McGuane would have cast Harry Dean in the other lead, as horse and cattle thief Tom Logan. Harry Dean would have gotten his first lead role in a major feature film eight years before *Repo Man* and *Paris, Texas*.

McGuane, who wrote the original script for *The Missouri Breaks* after extensive study of nineteenth-century cattle stealing in Montana, had gotten to know Harry Dean from his work in the film *Rancho Deluxe* (1975), a comic modern-day Western that McGuane wrote and that also dealt with cattle rustling in Montana. Their relationship further solidified with *92 in the Shade* (1975), written and directed by McGuane, a tale of rival fishing guides in Key West, Florida, that starred Harry Dean's old friend Warren Oates.

Harry Dean "had a kind of unique authenticity that even he couldn't do much about," McGuane told me. "He was just pure D Harry Dean Stanton. . . . Harry Dean was an actor who was more suited for a more intimate filmmaking.

He was one of those people whom the camera loved, what they used to say about Steve McQueen."

"I foresaw *The Missouri Breaks* as a kind of modest, moderate-budget movie," McGuane would say in another interview. "It was very kind of hard-edge, thoroughly gritty, and hopefully authentic Western. When it got inflated with all the *Paint Your Wagon* elements, and got kind of baroque, it was distinctly going in a different direction than the one I had in mind."

Important to a writer like McGuane was the film's story and the essential struggle of Montanans at moments in history when the cattle barons and industrialists were taking over. The story in *Rancho Deluxe* is similar: the cattle rustlers are much more sympathetic than the landowning cattlemen. "That's kind of the way I see the world," McGuane told me.

In his attempt to get Brando, Nicholson, and Penn on board, producer Kastner first went to Penn, a Hollywood rebel, veteran of the theater as well as film, a student of groundbreaking Black Mountain College in North Carolina, and proponent of and teacher at the Actors Studio. Penn had experienced great successes in Hollywood with *The Miracle Worker* (1962), *Bonnie and Clyde* (1967), and *Little Big Man* (1970), but also critical and box office failures such as *The Left-Handed Gun* (1958, another tale of Billy the Kid, this time starring Paul Newman), *Mickey One* (1965), and, most recently prior to *The Missouri Breaks*, *Night Moves* (1975). Burt Lancaster had even once fired him as director of *The Train* (1963) and replaced him with John Frankenheimer.

"It's something that could only happen in Hollywood," Penn told interviewer Claire Clouzot in *Ecran* in 1976 about Kastner's recruiting of Penn, Brando, and Nicholson by asking each if he'd sign on if the others did. Kastner, Penn said, "sent me Thomas McGuane's script, which I really liked, but at the time I wasn't really in the mood to make another film."

Then Kastner mentioned Brando's name. "I said yes." Kastner then went to Nicholson. "A deal was struck that said each of us would do the film only if the other two were on board," Penn said. "And everyone agreed. We weren't actually interested in the film so much as working with each other."

McGuane's vision of a "modest, moderate-budget movie" evaporated with the arrival of Brando and Nicholson. Although many pounds away from his romantic lead days, Brando was still Hollywood's biggest star, and his fee to do the film was $1 million for five weeks of shooting along with 10 percent of gross receipts above $10 million. As detailed in Patrick McGilligan's biography of him, Nicholson, a major star himself now, if not quite yet shining as brightly in the Hollywood stellar system as his neighbor Brando, commanded his largest salary ever, with $1.25 million for ten weeks of work on the set along with 10 percent of gross receipts above $12.5 million. (He would later sell Kastner 5 percent of his royalties for $1 million. Nicholson would file a lawsuit alleging Kastner failed to pay within the agreed-upon time.)

"Nobody disputes that, instantly, the star casting threw a modest script out of balance," McGilligan wrote in *Jack's Life*.

Harry Dean would be the only member in McGuane's originally envisioned cast to survive the changes after Penn and the superstars came on board. He would be cast as Calvin, Tom Logan's top partner and best friend in their joint theft ring, and not as Tom Logan himself. As with the other supporting-cast members, including Randy Quaid, Frederic Forrest, and John McLiam, Harry Dean's salary would be much closer to newcomer Kathleen Lloyd's $20,000 (it was her first feature film) than to Brando's and Nicholson's earnings.

Still, Harry Dean's role was at the top of the supporting cast. As Tom Logan's closest confidante, he led part of the gang on a venture to Canada to steal horses from Canada's famous Mounted Police while Nicholson's character reluctantly held house and home together in Montana. Harry Dean even got to sing a verse from "When the Roll Is Called Up Yonder" during the caper. The Canadian adventure is essential to the plot, as it sets the stage for the killing of Randy Quaid's Little Tod, other gang members, and eventually Harry Dean's Calvin, too, in a particularly wrenching scene. He is burned black in a fire set by the regulator, Clayton, and then tomahawked in the head. It is these deaths—particularly Calvin's—that put Nicholson's Tom Logan on a path of revenge against his buddies' murderer.

Critics would later say that one of the film's most effective scenes was the one where Nicholson and Harry Dean wrap up a long day by smoking and commiserating about life on a hillside above the farmhouse.

Despite a slew of badly received pictures in the mid- to late 1960s, Brando had seen his career rise again with an Oscar-winning performance in *The Godfather* and Oscar-nominated performance in *The Last Tango in Paris*. Thus he was a sought-after star by the mid-1970s. He had long been, and remained, a hero to both Nicholson and Harry Dean, just as he was a hero to a whole generation of actors after his landmark work on stage and in films such as *A Streetcar Named Desire* (1951), *Viva Zapata!* (1952), and *On the Waterfront* (1954). He was the quintessential Method actor, a student of Stella Adler's teachings on Stanislavski at the Group Theatre in New York.

"After *Streetcar Named Desire*, there was no actor who was not inspired by Brando, and many young actors began to imitate him," Actors Studio alumnus Nehemiah Persoff told me in 2016. "Suddenly it was acceptable to show behavior and emotion on stage."

In addition to his stature as an actor, Brando also had the additional appeal to Nicholson and Harry Dean of being a neighbor on Mulholland Drive in the very heart of Los Angeles. Film producer Bert Schneider had first suggested to Nicholson the Mulholland compound that adjoined and shared a common entrance with Brando's villa after the phenomenal success of *Easy Rider* in 1969. Nicholson bought the two-story, 3,303-square-foot home, and many years later after Brando's death he would buy Brando's home as well for a cool $6.1 million. In 1972 Harry Dean established himself on Mulholland Drive, purchasing a much more modest cabin up and on the other side of the road from Nicholson's and Brando's homes. It offered a pleasant view overlooking the San Fernando Valley, though perhaps not as pleasant as Nicholson and Brando's view overlooking Coldwater and Franklin canyons and the chaparral grassy meadows and sycamore and redwood trees below. Harry Dean got help from producer Fred Roos in finding his house, and he bought it without even seeing it first.

Neighbor and acting hero though he was, Brando brought with him a level of uncertainty. He was notorious for his behavior on and off the set and now was imbued with a deep sense of social consciousness regarding American Indians, so much so that he rejected his 1973 Oscar for *The Godfather* to protest Hollywood's treatment of them. He arrived on the set of *The Missouri Breaks* weighing more than 250 pounds. Even before getting there, he had already made demands for changes in the script that included converting Jack Nicholson's character into an Indian.

Temperatures were already on edge, not the least because temperatures in the Billings area that June were ranging as high as 112 degrees Fahrenheit. As befitting a superstar like Brando, the word "EXECUTIVE" was emblazoned on his air-conditioned trailer, which was larger than Nicholson's trailer. The rest of the cast and crew stayed in hotel rooms or other locations a half-hour's drive or more from the set.

Even though Nicholson and Brando were next-door neighbors, they really didn't know each other that well. Brando spent much of his time at his home in Tahiti. Plus, Nicholson's rising popularity sparked a competitive edge in Brando. He would later tell reporters that Nicholson had less talent than Robert De Niro, and that "I don't think he's that bright."

Brando could be contradictory. Writer McGuane, who stayed at Brando's home at times and got to know him well, told me the actor had little real respect for both Nicholson and Penn, despite the fact that their participation in the film sealed his own. "Brando had a very low opinion of Nicholson's acting abilities," McGuane told me in 2019. "He said at one point that watching him act was watching a man with one finger playing a piano in one key." Brando, often disconcerting to his admiring fellow actors for his seemingly cavalier attitude toward his craft, "really didn't want to be an actor," McGuane said. "He never saw the movie *The Godfather*."

When Brando wasn't "mooning" his fellow cast and crew—a long-favored but more substantial prank now with his weight gain—he was constantly thinking up ways to make Robert E. Lee Clayton more interesting. "Brando was right in thinking of Clayton as a man without a center of gravity, something that's quite obvious due to the fact that he keeps on changing his persona," Penn later said. "He spends his time looking for extravagant outfits that give him an unusual outward appearance."

Indeed, Brando's Clayton switches from an Irish brogue to a hillbilly Southern accent in different scenes, and his costumes change from buckskins to preacher's wear. A key scene occurs near the end of the film, when he kills Harry Dean's Calvin. As he and director Penn discussed various outfits for the scene, Brando was struck by what he considered a brilliant idea. "How about I play it as a woman?" he told Penn. Penn never forgot that moment. "He couldn't wait to get into this great calico dress and hat and came down and played it as old granny."

This was too much for Harry Dean. "Before filming the scene, Stanton jumped Brando, wrestled him to the ground, and ripped off the dress America's foremost actor had been wearing," Patrick McGilligan wrote. Later, Harry Dean told a reporter, "I just couldn't stand the idea of getting killed by a man in a dress."

More likely, Harry Dean's reason was that Brando was driving him and the rest of the crew crazy. Nicholson couldn't get over Brando's habit of using cue cards in lieu of simply memorizing his lines. "Why does the greatest actor in the world need cue cards?" Nicholson asked. At one point, Brando even asked actor John McLiam to stick cards to his forehead so Brando could read them when he and McLiam were in a scene face to face. McLiam complained, and the cards were instead placed strategically on a wall behind him.

"To be fair to Nicholson, Brando had turned his character into vaudeville and sleight-of-hand," McGilligan wrote. "He was out to prove he could out-shtick Jack."

Penn diplomatically praised Brando's performance after the film's release, and he insisted that he did not let the famously demanding actor run away with the $8 million project, noting "the lack of time and preparation" for it and the fact that United Artists shortened the agreed-upon deadline for completion by three months. The film "was made by three people who were really working very seriously, at the top of our form," he said. "We were trying, desperately, to take what was really a vestigial script and turn it into a movie under the enormous pressures of having to start and stop at a certain date.... I worked as hard as I've ever worked on a film and so did Marlon and Jack.... We had a terrific time making the film, even though we were like three drowning men. How were we going to keep our heads above water and get a movie made?"

While McGuane's own postrelease assessment included some praise for Brando, he insisted another actor would have done a better job. "There were lots of exciting things about the flamboyant stuff that Brando brought to it," he said, "but I think the movie would have been better if Warren had been cast in the role. I wanted the audience to feel close up to what it was like to be in that world. Warren would have been a great help in that sense because he always had an authenticity that reminded me of what harder-bitten types on the actual frontier might have been like."

Penn's own assessment of the film as a whole is telling. Calling *The Missouri Breaks* an "anti-Western," he said the film dealt with a "period when they were carving up Montana with as few owners as possible. They succeeded in doing so. There were enormous ranches owned by people who didn't hesitate to bring in armed gunmen to enforce their law." The film challenged "a sacred and untouchable" genre and told the story of a West "where the colonists and the wealthy set about establishing a system of rules and laws to protect their property." The film "held "a mirror up to the American people." Finally, he concluded, "it certainly isn't your average Western," and audiences weren't ready for it.

The film disappeared from movie theaters after only a month. Critic Andrew Sarris said Penn simply didn't understand the Western genre. Even in the heady days of the New Hollywood, the message its films conveyed sometimes could simply be too much for people.

The message may still be too much.

"Time has been kind to *The Missouri Breaks*," film critic Lee Pfeiffer wrote in a 2015 review for *Cinema Retro*. "The film's literate script and direction are a reminder of an era in which such projects would be green-lit by major studios who appealed to the intellect of movie audiences. Today, the project would never have seen fruition no matter who starred in it."

For Harry Dean, *The Missouri Breaks* became a stepping-stone, a passing through to a post–New Hollywood era that was already beginning to light the morning sky in the distance. The New Hollywood directors he had worked with—Arthur Penn, Francis Ford Coppola, Monte Hellman—would slip into decline. His old buddy Warren Oates would die with the era, and so would Sam Peckinpah.

Hollywood itself would see a resurgence of the big studios and, with it, an infatuation with high-tech, high-action, high-profit blockbusters from whiz kids like Steven Spielberg and George Lucas. The embodiment of the post–New Hollywood star was Tom Cruise, who would steal Harry Dean's girl and a few years later ascend as the quintessential Action Hero with *Top Gun* in 1986 and his more than a half-dozen *Mission: Impossible* films in the 1990s and beyond. Continuing the rebellion of the New Hollywood's character-driven, taboo-breaking, commerce-challenging directors would be European filmmakers, and it would be they who gave Harry Dean the best roles of his career.

7

The Passing and the Passing Through

Harry Dean and his half-brother, Stanley, are on the way to their mother's funeral, and they're late.

"Did they let her keep smoking weed?" Harry Dean asks, pulling out of his pocket a huge rolled doobie.

"Ralph's the one put her in the nursing home. He's evangelical Baptist. I doubt it very seriously."

"Yeah, he's still trying to convert me. Been doing it ever since I got here."

"Sometimes he'll call me up, out of the blue, and say, 'This is Ralph. I have just one question. Do you accept Jesus Christ as your Lord and Savior?'"

Harry Dean's eyes light up as he fires up the doobie. "What do you tell him?" He drags deeply and passes it to Stanley.

Stanley stares at it a moment. "I tell him, 'Ralph, we've been over this many times. This is why we don't have a relationship. Why do you keep asking me?' He says, 'I want to know if I will see you when I am in heaven.'"

Harry Dean shakes his head. "Good lord."

The two brothers don't resemble each other much. Harry Dean is twenty-two years older. He's lean while Stanley is more heavyset, but they share an impatience with religion, an artistic sensibility, and bruised memories of their mother.

They pass the doobie back and forth. "The weed was helping her with the arthritis," Harry Dean muses. "I knew it would. It's why I got her started on it."

"Why'd you get me started on it?"

Harry Dean turns to the passing landscape. It's mid-August in Kentucky and nearly ninety degrees, warmer than what he's gotten used to in LA. "Why'd she die? She was only sixty-seven."

Stanley ponders answers. She drank like a fish, smoked, and suffered from arthritic flare-ups, joint replacements on her feet, bad kidneys, and the shots the doctors made her take. "I don't know why she died."

"You think the weed had something to do with it?"

Stanley shrugs. "When I visited her in the nursing home a couple weeks ago, she was out of it."

"You know Arch took out a life insurance policy on her not that long ago. Even Ralph's mad about it."

"Archiegate."

"He says he didn't, but he's lying. He was always her favorite."

"Who cares? Arch sells life insurance. It's his business. He was entitled if he did. She lived with him in Florida. If he did, he was just getting paid back. You didn't put any shit into this."

They share the doobie in silence, smoking it down. Soon they're high and forget all about Archiegate. The heat's no longer bothering Harry. It never did bother Stanley. The funeral home comes into view, and there's a crowd.

The minute they walk in, people start talking.

"Which one of them is the movie star?" an elderly woman asks her friend above the buzz in the crowd.

"I know it's not the fat one," her friend quips.

Stanley hears it, pursing his lips in annoyance. Harry turns to him with a shit-eating grin, and they chuckle. Soon they're laughing, maybe more than they should, given the occasion.

Ersel

Harry Dean didn't hang around once the funeral was over that August day in 1974. After all, he had to get back for his gig with Bob Dylan.

The relationship between Ersel and her oldest had never been easy. She had a cruel streak. She liked to tell Harry Dean that when he was an infant she waved objects over his cradle just to scare him. She was just seventeen herself, having married mainly to get out of her parents' crowded house. Not long after Harry Dean came into the world arrived Ralph and then Arch, joined later by Shorty's daughters from his first marriage. She abandoned the family when Harry Dean was a teenager. It wasn't Shorty as much as it was everything else. Shorty had taught her hair care, given her a profession. He even gave her a job after she left him.

Mothering just wasn't Ersel's thing. She liked music and could play a mean guitar. She got that from her mother, Zouie, pudgy, four-foot-eleven Zouie, who was a champion dancer and could pick a five-string banjo like ringing a bell. Ersel was a rebel. She liked to have fun. She liked parties. Like her oldest, she liked to smoke. She liked to drink, too, and the Kentucky hills had plenty to offer, whether store-bought or from some local moonshiner's personal stock. She developed a lifelong taste for whiskey that likely aggravated what Stanley Jr. to this day believes to be her untreated bipolar condition and the "nervous breakdowns" that would put her in a hospital again and again later in life. "When she would go into a manic state, they would put her in the hospital and call it a nervous breakdown," Stanley Jr. told me.

Ersel also liked to gamble. Growing up in the heart of thoroughbred country instilled in her a love for the track, whether at Keeneland in Lexington or Hialeah in Florida. She'd spend hours at the track. It made no difference whether it was a horse or a greyhound, she'd place her bets on what she figured to be a winner. She bowled, she played cards, she disappeared sometimes for days, even weeks, at a time. She loved to fish and caught game fish that her son Archie helped her get taxidermied. Still, the family knew that Ersel's parting words "I'm going to go fishing" often meant she was going to go drinking, and who knew when she'd return.

As fun-loving as Ersel might have been, she had a temper that exposed as foul a mouth as Harry Dean and Stanley Sr. had ever heard in their Navy days. "Get that fuckin' piece of shit out of my driveway," she once told a friend of Stanley Sr. from Oregon. She didn't particularly like him or the fact that he'd driven his yellow convertible up onto their driveway after she had earlier thrown him out. When her husband's friend didn't respond fast enough, she grabbed a fistful of mud and threw it on the car.

One night when she and her granddaughter Whitney were sleeping in the same bed, the four-year-old discovered her grandmother's dentures under the pillow and screamed at the top of her lungs. "Dammit!" Ersel barked at the traumatized girl. "What the hell is your problem?"

A Better Grandmother than a Mother

Harry Dean's troubles with Ersel paled in comparison to Stanley Jr.'s. Other family members question some of Stanley's memories, but they're his and he stands by them. Every late night or early morning phone call from Harry Dean, probably drinking, to his mother would lead to Ersel's downing a few shooters of whiskey herself in the kitchen—and a beating for Stanley Jr. "I was six to ten years old when Harry would call. Ersel would get mad at me. I don't know what she and Harry would talk about. I would hear the phone ring, and I would notice it was two in the morning. Alcohol abuse causes phone-itis. Maybe it was just to start shit."

Both of Ersel's husbands were long dead by the time she passed away. In 1967 Stanley Sr., eight years her junior, suffered a fatal heart attack at age fifty-one that their son believed may have been caused by his wife's drinking, gambling, and disappearances. Shorty died two years after Stanley Jr., but he had reached the riper age of seventy-six. He died of a heart attack, too, but he had remained strong enough to chop down an oak tree a week before he died. He was a loner but a snappy dresser, and he liked the ladies, even if he'd never marry one again after Ersel.

For all of her issues, Ersel was a better grandmother than she was a mother, both her granddaughter Whitney Fishburn and Whitney's mother and Stanley Jr.'s former wife, Patty Wallace, agreed. "I do miss Mama Ersel," said Whitney, now a journalist in Washington, DC. "I was close to Ersel. She was sweet to me. She was my wonderful Mama Ersel. She brought me gifts. She was good to my mom. When she died I was devastated."

Patty Wallace said she saw a loving side to Ersel that Harry Dean and Stanley Jr. perhaps rarely saw. "She was very kind to me when Whitney was born. She just loved her to death. She actually used to tease me that if Whitney didn't have dimples she'd get sent back. Good thing she had them." Ersel had grown up in the foothills of Kentucky mountain country, where "when you're naughty, you get switched," where people are tough and self-sufficient, Patty said. "When you are young, you have your dreams, and you don't get to think about them very long. You're having children, and you get frustrated."

Riding the Wave

The death of Harry Dean's mother came just as he was riding the New Hollywood wave, even if he was still in the supporting cast. A fan base that included many of his fellow actors as well as fellow travelers in the New Hollywood rebellion had begun to grow after the Hellman and McGuane films, and it considered him important, even crucial, to other 1970s films, including *Straight Time* (1978), *Wise Blood* (1979), *Alien* (1979), *The Rose* (1979), and, in the same year his mother died, Francis Ford Coppola's *The Godfather: Part II*. In that film Harry Dean played an FBI agent, and to prepare for that role he went to his first cousin Jim Huggins Sr., a veteran FBI agent, for advice.

"I am playing an FBI agent, and I am with these witnesses," Harry Dean told him. "I need to know what kind of mannerisms I should have."

"I only guarded one Mafia witness, and that guy was a pain in the neck," Huggins Sr. told him.

Huggins Sr. went on to explain how he interacted with the witness. "I could tell [Harry Dean] was very serious, made sure he had it all down pat, how you dress as an agent, the training," Huggins Sr. told me in my interview with him in January 2018. "He was very serious about it. That's the way he always did in his roles. He called me often when he played a law enforcement agent."

As with his professional life, Harry Dean's personal life was showing signs of promise. He traded in his bachelor life with Jack Nicholson for a live-in relationship with actor Maggie Blye in a home in the Hollywood Hills–Beechwood Canyon area. Blonde, beautiful, thirteen years younger than Harry Dean, she was a Texas native who was in a number of television shows in the 1960s, including *Perry Mason, Ben Casey, Gunsmoke,* and *Hazel,* before gaining wider attention with her appearance in the 1967 film *Hombre* with Paul Newman and, two years later, *The Italian Job* with Michael Caine. By the late 1970s, however, her career was already in a downturn.

Blye always had "the glamour beat smile," Harry Dean's nephew Chad McKnight, who heads a casting company in Hollywood, told me. "I loved her, but she felt, like an actress, this desperation, and it never took off for her. It is sad at a certain age that stress started to eat away at her. A little lonely, never married. Hanging around Harry, she would dote on him. He was friendly. He wasn't affectionate. He was having his eye on the younger women."

If life was sweeter for Harry Dean, maybe laying to rest his mother and, along with her, his anger at her helped. "I sure wish I'd matured earlier," he would say during an interview a decade later. "There was such a long period in my life in which I was struggling to bloom, and as a result I did a lot of stupid things. I'd say that I'm now a lot more stable. I was just a very late bloomer."

His studies in Eastern mysticism—Alan Watts's writing on Zen Buddhism, the ancient Chinese poet Lao Tzu, and Indian philosopher Jiddu Krishnamurti —got a lot of the credit. Krishnamurti once wrote, "To investigate the fact of your own anger you must pass no judgment on it. . . . To live completely, fully, in the moment is to live with *what is,* the actual, without any sense of condemnation or justification—then you understand it so totally that you are finished with it. When you see clearly the problem is solved."

Getting rid of anger was a good career move. "I've only started getting good parts because I've changed, because I'm no longer so angry," Harry Dean said. "I'm much more confident now, and it comes through."

Not that every part was particularly good.

Like his late-1960s venture as Spook in *The Mini-Skirt Mob,* Harry Dean made some questionable decisions in the 1970s. One of them was likely a favor to his fellow musician and *Pat Garrett and Billy the Kid* jogging partner Bob Dylan. Harry Dean plays a character named Lafkezio in Dylan's nearly five-hour-long epic to himself, *Renaldo and Clara,* which is part concert performance and part Dylan's attempt at cinema verité. Critics roundly blasted the 1978 film, and audiences failed to show in such numbers that Dylan cut nearly half the film. What was left for rescreenings was mostly the footage from his Rolling Thunder Revue concerts in 1975 and 1976. Dylan and Sam Shepard received credit as writers, although *New Yorker* critic Pauline Kael lambasted the film as essentially having no writer and no director. "The participants seem to be saying whatever comes into their heads." Dylan apparently did do some editing, Kael wrote. "He has given himself more tight closeups than any actor can have had in the whole history of movies." Music legends including Ramblin' Jack Elliott, Joan Baez, and Ronnie Hawkins (playing Bob Dylan, with Dylan himself playing Renaldo) are in the film, and so is Beat poet Allen Ginsberg. Still, many viewers likely agreed with critic Phil Hall that the film may be "the very, very worst thing ever made."

Flatbed Annie and Sweetiepie: Lady Truckers was another questionable decision. Harry Dean played repossessor C. W. Douglas in the 1979 television truck-chase movie, which the *Hollywood Reporter's* Gail Williams decried as a failed attempt to bring back a "CB and trucker craze [that] is past its prime." Stars Kim Darby and Annie Potts "make assiduous efforts" and Harry Dean plays Douglas with "subtle humor," but the movie fails due to Robie Robinson's "flimsy" story, with its "numerous gaps in the plot," and Robert Greenwald's insufficient direction.

After a long ride through multiple television shows in the 1960s, Harry Dean focused mainly on feature films in the 1970s, with the exception of five appearances as Jake Walters during the two-season run of the television series *Mary Hartman, Mary Hartman.* Produced by Norman Lear, the half-hour, Emmy Award–winning series starred Louise Lasser as a blue-collar, toothy, and somewhat goofy Fernwood, Ohio, housewife with braided pigtails, little-girl dresses, and a husband who battles impotence. Once described by the *New York Times* as "postmodern before postmodern had a name," the show broke old taboos with its frank discussions of sexual issues like impotence, exhibitionism, adultery, venereal disease, and masturbation. Future close friends of Harry Dean, including Dabney Coleman and Ed Begley Jr., also appeared in the show.

"I met him at *Mary Hartman*," Coleman recalled in a 2018 interview. "We didn't hit it off immediately. It took a while. He got to know my children, three of whom are great singers. He was a musician. His passion was in music. He trusted my children before he trusted me."

Meet the Europeans

The year after *Mary Hartman, Mary Hartman* Harry Dean played ex-con Jerry Schue in Belgium-born filmmaker Ulu Grosbard's *Straight Time,* the story of the release from prison of another convict, Max Dembo, played by Dustin Hoffman, and his struggle with going straight under the sadistic eye of his parole officer, Earl Frank, played by M. Emmet Walsh. Film critic Roger Ebert once famously said that "no movie featuring either Harry Dean Stanton or M. Emmet Walsh in a supporting role can be altogether bad." Indeed, the film "is beautifully acted," *New York Times* reviewer Vincent Canby said at the time, not only by Harry Dean and Walsh but also by Hoffman and Gary Busey, who plays Hoffman's drug addict buddy Willy Darin. Initially directed by Hoffman before he fired himself and asked Grosbard to take over, *Straight Time* is a "leanly constructed, vividly staged film" done with "precision and control," Canby wrote.

Harry Dean's Jerry Schue went straight after his own stint behind bars, but now is bored beyond belief with his settled, middle-class life, with grilling burgers on his barbecue pit, with his swimming pool. He's so bored he joins with Hoffman and Busey for a couple of robberies. He's a thief of strict standards and complains at one point when things go awry, "It's very . . . unfuckin' professional." He's quickly put off by Busey's loosey-goosey character, whose ineptness ultimately will lead to Jerry Schue's death.

Hoffman later praised Harry Dean's acting in the film. "He has a personality that's very much like what you see. A very bright man filled with irony."

Based on a novel by real-life former convict Edward Bunker, *Straight Time* is a neo-noir that marks an important moment in Harry Dean's career: it is the first of several major forays with European directors, and one that got the attention of French director Bertrand Tavernier, who two years later would direct Harry Dean in another major film, *Death Watch,* with Harvey Keitel and Romy Schneider. "I had seen him in some Westerns and always liked him," Tavernier told me in an interview in August 2018. "Then I saw him in the film *Straight Time*. I remember when I saw the film with my cowriter, and we both loved what Harry Dean Stanton was doing in that film. It was so surprising, never was it something that you expected in the way he was playing it. I decided to contact him. I thought he would go very well with Harvey Keitel."

A Con Artist Preacher and the Church Without Christ

Director John Huston's genius lay in part in his skill in casting, which he once said was "ninety percent of a director's job." Indeed, the cast of Huston's 1979 film *Wise Blood* seems to have come directly out of the pages of Flannery O'Connor's strange, Christ-haunted first novel. Huston's star, Brad Dourif, is "the embodiment of Hazel Motes," the war veteran turned street preacher of the "Church Without Christ," wrote critic and Huston biographer Stuart Klawans. With eyes that "don't so much take in the world as beam emotions out to it," Dourif, as Haze, combines "frailty and menace in one package."

Harry Dean as the street-preaching con artist Asa Hawks, who pretends to have blinded himself in a religious fury, and Ned Beatty as the guitar-picking religious huckster Onnie Jay Holy "might as well not be actors at all, but found objects collaged into the frame," Klawans wrote.

That the film exists at all is another testament to Huston's genius. Perhaps Hollywood's greatest adapter of literary masterworks to the screen—from his film version of Dashiell Hammett's *The Maltese Falcon* in 1941 and B. Traven's *The Treasure of the Sierra Madre* in 1948 to Herman Melville's *Moby Dick* in 1956, Tennessee Williams's *The Night of the Iguana* in 1964 and Carson McCullers's *Reflections in a Golden Eye* in 1967—Huston faced a particular challenge in creating a visual account of O'Connor's book, with its insular look at a man battling with his soul.

Young producer Michael Fitzgerald, whose family had been close to and shared the deeply Catholic faith of O'Connor, traveled to Huston's remote home—accessible only by boat—on Las Caletas beach near Puerto Vallarta, Mexico, to propose filming O'Connor's book. Huston knew that the story of a street preacher's wrestling match with God in the fundamentalist Deep South wasn't particularly commercial and challenged Fitzgerald with raising the funds needed to make the film. He did, but Huston was right. The $1.6 million film won nearly universal praise from critics but couldn't find a major distributor to show it.

Inspired in part by T. S. Eliot's poem *The Waste Land* and O'Connor's self-admitted "preoccupation with belief and with death and grace and the devil," *Wise Blood* follows Hazel Motes's journey back home from war to a small Southern town, where he preaches on street corners a Christ-less church "where the blind don't see and the lame don't walk and what's dead stays that way." In the Church Without Christ, Haze preaches that "there was no Fall because there was nothing to fall from and no Redemption because there was no Fall and no Judgment because there wasn't the first two. Nothing matters but that Jesus was a liar." Soon he encounters, among other human oddities and grotesques, the fraud Asa Hawks, a Jesus-preaching preacher who pretends to be blind and pretends to have faith, and a would-be doppelgänger simply called the Preacher, played by William Hickey. Eventually, after murdering Hickey's Preacher, Haze will blind himself for real—no fraud for this truth seeker—and find his way back to the Jesus who had haunted him all his life. This was the Jesus who moved, in O'Connor's words, "from tree to tree in the back of his mind, a wild ragged figure motioning him to turn around and come off into the dark where he was not sure of his footing, where he might be walking on the water and not know it and then suddenly know it and drown."

Like Huston, Harry Dean was not religious, even atheistic—"Nobody's in charge," Harry Dean liked to say—but, like West Virginia native Brad Dourif, he knew the terrain of *Wise Blood*. He had seen the hard-shell Baptist preachers hurl fire and brimstone from the pulpits at camp meetings in rural Kentucky. His brothers Arch and Ralph were born-again Christians who worried about their older brother's soul and told him so frequently.

Huston would later tell interviewers that filming *Wise Blood* took him into a new and unfamiliar landscape, a backwoods South that takes its religion seriously. He saw O'Connor's novel as a critique of fundamentalism, a comedy about pathetic, misguided people. Such a view rendered the story's ending meaningless, and Dourif and the Fitzgeralds, Michael and his wife and fellow producer Kathy, had to convince him that redemption was the key to the story.

"He thought at the end Haze Motes has some kind of existential rebellion," Dourif said in an interview. "John Huston was a devout atheist. He didn't have anything to do with religion. I said it seems to me Haze Motes finds God, and he says, 'No, No!'" After a conference with the Fitzgeralds, Huston returned to Dourif and said, "Jesus wins."

Dourif and the Fitzgeralds helped save the integrity of O'Connor's story in the film. However, Huston's willingness to look at the story differently and rethink his own attitudes about it speak to the genius that made him a great filmmaker. Writer Francine Prose said O'Connor would have loved the notion of Huston's evolution in understanding Haze Motes. "In spite of himself, the director had made a film about a Christian in spite of himself, groping his way toward redemption."

Harry Dean and Dourif, the two Appalachians in the cast, would both later reach career heights with director David Lynch and with directors out of the New German Cinema, Harry Dean with Wim Wenders, and Dourif with Werner Herzog.

Harry Dean and John Huston remained close after *Wise Blood*. In fact, they became fellow poker players, and Harry Dean was at the table at Huston's last game before he died. They each lost $300. Harry Dean told that story at Huston's memorial service in 1987. After the story, he sang "El Revolucionario," an old revolutionary song from Huston's beloved Mexico. Maybe the song was a little much. "Jesus," Jack Nicholson could be heard saying under his breath as Harry Dean finished singing.

Monsters and Apocalyptic Gangsters

The same year *Wise Blood* came out Harry Dean would play bluegrass guitar picker Billy Ray in *The Rose,* starring Bette Midler as a rising singing star. He's in only one scene, but *New York Times* critic Janet Maslin called it "one of the most memorable scenes" in the film. Midler's character meets Billy Ray, her hero, in his dressing room and tells him she recorded one of his songs, "Huntsville Prison." "It didn't show me much," Billy Ray tells a deflated Rose. "I'd appreciate it if you wouldn't record any more of my tunes." Maybe the attitudes in the scene were too close to reality for Midler, who many years later told an interviewer that she wasn't prepared for how "tough" Harry Dean could be and that he wasn't supportive of her in the role.

Over the next few years, Harry Dean would more than tip his hat to the big production, sci-fi, and horror films that helped spell the end to the New Hollywood era, appearing in Ridley Scott's *Alien* in 1979 and John Carpenter's *Escape from New York* in 1981 and *Christine* in 1983. These were the years that "saw the same kind of upheavals that the film industry hadn't felt since TV shook its financial base in the early 1950s," Nat Segaloff wrote in his biography of screenwriter Stirling Silliphant. "The tremors begun by the blockbusters *Jaws* (1975), *Star Wars* (1977), and *Alien* (1979) rearranged the Hollywood landscape."

In addition to his roles as a space-traveling mechanic, a postapocalyptic gang thug, and a monster-car-chasing gumshoe in the Scott and Carpenter movies, Harry Dean also offered lighter fare as Sgt. Jim Ballard, the recruiter who convinces Goldie Hawn's Judy Benjamin in *Private Benjamin* (1980) that the New Army is just another country club. That same year he would play a gambling addict/veterinarian/dog kidnapper who, critic Roger Ebert observed, "talks like Robert Mitchum's mean kid brother" in *The Black Marble*. A year or so later, he played Moe in Francis Ford Coppola's disastrous flop *One from the Heart*, the film that lost more than $25 million at the box office, led to the downfall of Coppola's Zoetrope Studio, and marked the end of the New Hollywood. It also introduced Harry Dean to young actress Rebecca de Mornay, who played an understudy in the film and who, some say, became the love of Harry Dean's life.

Harry Dean came reluctantly to his role as Brett the mechanic in *Alien*, a combination science fiction and horror film about an interstellar freighter named *Nostromo* (after Joseph Conrad's 1904 novel) that's carrying a giant, practically indestructible stowaway monster.

"I don't like sci-fi or monster movies," Harry Dean told Ridley Scott at the audition.

"I don't either, but I like this one," Scott responded.

"I like real things. Authenticity. You so rarely see it. All we get is myths and morality plays."

"This film, it's a thriller, on the line of *Ten Little Indians*."

Ten Little Indians. The Agatha Christie classic. A whodunit with a spaceship instead of a house on an island or remote mountaintop, a murderous intergalactic monster instead a vengeance-seeking host.

"You got enough money to do it?" Harry Dean wanted to know.

"That's why I hired you," retorted Scott.

Harry Dean accepted the job and took home a paycheck that doubled anything he'd ever been paid before. "I wasn't attracted to it at all," he later said in an interview about the film. "It was Ridley's enthusiasm, actually, and his desire for me to be in the film that did it." Despite Harry Dean's initial hesitation, he went on to win new fans in the hugely successful film. In fact, one of the most memorable scenes in the film is his character's death scene, when he tries to rescue the *Nostromo's* pet cat, Jones. "Here, kitty," he calls out toward the plaintive meows he hears in the distance. "Kitty, kitty, kitty." Before Brett can get to the cat, however, he disappears into the deadly grasp of the monster, which had been lurking behind him.

It's a scene that forced Harry Dean to do some rethinking about his role versus the film as a whole. Why not inject some humor in the scene, he initially thought, and why would Brett go looking for Jones without a weapon to protect himself against the Alien? "I had some funny lines when I went looking for the cat. Which was, in a way, more believable, because I was pissed off at them for having told me to find it in the first place. I started out with lines like 'Kitty, kitty, kitty,' and worked my way to 'fucking cat,' and stuff like that. But it was only right they cut the funny lines because they economized in the editing as much as possible and I think that's why it was a successful suspense film. They didn't want any laughs in there because the suspense was building." The suspense element also "justifies the fact that I would even go looking for the cat unarmed in the first place. It was a fantasy and we used some old tried and true devices."

The "officially authorized" magazine of the movie predicted, "*Alien* may be the death knell for Stanton's anonymity with audiences." In an interview for the magazine, Stanton argued that he had earlier gotten star billing, if not necessarily first billing, in films like *Straight Time* and *Wise Blood,* but added that he mainly sought "believability" and "a total reality before the camera." He said he'd "love" to be a star so long as he was never "categorized." "I hate any kind of categorization, but it's unavoidable, I guess. I like to play people, not the same kinds of parts, from any point of view. Not playing a guy who gets killed all the time, not a loser all the time, or anything." Ultimately, he said, the film is more important that the actors who are in it. "I'm more interested in what a film says. . . . Does it move people? What kind of impact does it have? Any film, I don't care what it is. If it really touches people or moves people or changes their thinking somehow. Or, if they're seriously affected in a life-positive way. That's what I'm interested in. . . . I just want to be in a truthful film. And it it's really honest, it usually has something to say."

Writer Ian Nathan said Harry Dean was perfect as Brett because he played the role as a simple working stiff, not a futuristic space traveler. "He was way too earthbound for science fiction. Which was entirely the point with *Alien.* Stanton's Brett epitomized the script's 'truck drivers in space' dynamic: a mechanic in a Hawaiian shirt who has been soaking up fumes in the belly of this beast for years. Only a film as perverse as *Alien* would cast Stanton as comic relief—the below decks parrot to Yaphet Kotto's righteous sonofabitch Parker."

During the filming of *Alien*'s brutal "chestburster" sequence, Nathan wrote, "as offal was loaded into pumps, Stanton stood in the corridor, gently strumming on his guitar."

Harry Dean's disdain for sci-fi and horror films and his ideas about "believability" and the need for a film's having a "life-positive" effect on viewers were perhaps even more challenged in his work with director John Carpenter in the films *Escape from New York* and *Christine*. Carpenter built a career on horror films such as *Halloween* (1978) and *The Thing* (1974) and what he called the "cheap scare" of villains or monsters popping into view suddenly and just as quickly disappearing. Whether in his horror films or his sci-fi/apocalyptic films like *Escape from New York* or *Starman* (1984), he liked to cast actors and musicians from his "Carpenter's Repertory Group," including Kurt Russell, Donald Pleasance, and Isaac Hayes.

Carpenter and Harry Dean shared a Kentucky upbringing—Carpenter's father chaired the music department at Western Kentucky University in Bowling Green—and a love of basketball and especially music. Carpenter often composed the scores of his own films, and in the 1970s even formed his own band, the Coupe de Villes. Among his band members was Nick Castle, who cowrote the script for *Escape from New York*. He liked Harry Dean enough to offer him a lead as a private investigator in a television series. Harry Dean turned him down. "I could've been much more famous and richer," he told podcaster Mark Maron in 2014. "I didn't take it. Too much work. I didn't want it. [With television] it is twenty-four hours a day, twenty-four-seven."

In Carpenter's *Escape from New York,* Harry Dean plays Brain, who serves as a demolition guy for an underworld ruler, Isaac Hayes's Duke, in the futuristic prison camp that Manhattan has become. As *New York Times* critic Vincent Canby wrote, however, Brain is "emotionally unreliable" and works with Kurt Russell's tattooed, eye-patch-wearing Snake Plissken to try and free Duke's prize captive, the president of the United States, played by Donald Pleasance. Playing Brain's main woman, Maggie, is Adrienne Barbeau, Carpenter's real-life wife at the time, showing lots of cleavage but also enough loyalty to her man to die in a shootout with Duke after Brain is killed in an explosion.

With its depiction of Manhattan as "a sort of super Roach Motel," Canby, reviewing the film upon its release, called *Escape from New York* "a toughly told, very tall tale, one of the best escape (and escapist) movies of the season."

However, twenty years later, looking back at a film she once admired, *FlickFilosopher* writer Maryann Johnson said, "I remember it being a lot better than it actually is." Noting that "everything Carpenter has done with the exception of *Starman* . . . is shlock: pure, unabashed, unapologetic shlock," Johnson comes down hard on "Carpenter's heavy-handed comic-book irony" with "action that today . . . plays exactly like a first-person shooter video game."

Barbeau, in an email interview in September 2019, said she "knew nothing about Harry Dean's career prior to *Escape*" but learned to admire his "brilliance" on screen. During the filming of *Escape from New York,* she remembered Harry Dean "wanting to ad-lib some of his lines, and John putting the kibosh on that. John wanted the lines read as written. . . . It only happened once, and it must have been early on in the filming of our scenes together, because Harry Dean never ad-libbed again."

Harry Dean's next film with Carpenter, *Christine,* has him playing detective Rudolph Junkins, who's investigating the mayhem caused by a murderously possessive 1958 Plymouth Fury. Both *Christine* and *Escape from New York* scored big at the box office, grossing many millions of dollars over their budgets, even if neither has held up particularly well in the rearview mirror of some modern film critics. "Pretty shop-worn" was the dismissive assessment of *Variety* magazine in 2007.

Still, Harry Dean's "disheveled humanity and wiry wit" in both *Escape from New York* and *Christine* "made genre real," in the words of Ian Nathan.

One through the Heart

Francis Ford Coppola envisioned the first film out of the gate of his new American Zoetrope Studios "as a small, delicate porcelain figure of a film," one made entirely on a studio set, yet with the very latest in technology, a modest $12 million project that would mark a revival of the Hollywood musical tradition while being "the furthest remove from the excesses" of his three-years-in-the-making, $31 million blockbuster *Apocalypse Now,* Peter Biskind wrote in *Easy Riders, Raging Bulls.* The story line was fairly simple: a young couple go to Las Vegas to celebrate their fifth year together, and each partner ends up having an affair.

A director known for his ability to get the most out of his actors, Coppola was now focused on getting the most out of his technology. Basking in the success of films like *The Godfather* and *Apocalypse Now* (in which Harry Dean was cast, but his sequence ultimately was cut), Coppola had fallen in love with a high-tech aluminum trailer he called the "Silverfish." From his seat inside his mobile home–like control center, he could use monitors to see everything on the set. He could give actors directions via loudspeaker without ever leaving the trailer, as if the cast were hearing the words from God on high.

Zoetrope itself was envisioned as a "petri dish of creative talent, a repertory company, a sanctuary that would shelter talent cast off by the studios," Biskind wrote. Indeed, the greatest new and established filmmaking geniuses from Europe—Wim Wenders, Werner Herzog, Jean-Luc Godard—could be seen hanging around the set to learn what they could from one of the leading lights of the New Hollywood.

However, the New Hollywood was already imploding "from the blizzard of coke" and out-of-control egos that it had launched, plus the reassertion of executive control at the big studios, marking a kind of counterrevolution, wrote Biskind. "The American directors of the '70s, with few exceptions, burned out like Roman candles after an all-too-brief flash of brilliance, cut off in mid-career. Friedkin, Bogdanovich, Ashby, Schrader, Rafelson, and Penn, all went down."

One from the Heart grew from a $12 million to a $26 million project, which doubled the disaster when filmgoers eventually spent less than $400,000 to see it. Reviewers hated it, too, and Coppola had to bear much of the blame. The film was a musical, yet neither of his leading stars, Frederic Forrest and Terri Garr, could sing or dance, and neither had ever been in a musical. Forrest, nominated for an Oscar for his performance in *The Rose*, had been in earlier Coppola films, earning kudos for his Chef Hicks in *Apocalypse Now*. He would go on to do another Zoetrope film, with the title role in *Hammett*, another bust at the box office even though it was directed by rising star Wim Wenders. However, *One from the Heart* would prove as damaging to Forrest's career as it was disastrous for Zoetrope and Coppola, who filed for bankruptcy in 1982.

Coppola's direction from inside his Silverfish was a mistake. "By locking himself away from the set in a trailer to oversee the visual scope of his picture, there was little he seemingly could do to prevent the floundering of his two leads," wrote Jon C. Hopwood in his IMDb mini-biography of Forrest. "More concerned with technology than his actors, he lost his touch."

Contributing to the problem was Coppola's megalomania. His prior successes had turned him into someone whose dictates could not be challenged, who surrounded himself with yes men and women, according to Biskind.

Film critic Roger Ebert found that the film does offer "small pleasures," one of them being Harry Dean as Moe, the sidekick to Forrest's Hank. Even here, however, Coppola fails. "Coppola resists showing us Stanton's most effective tool," wrote Ebert: "his expressive eyes."

A number of coincidences mark the entire experience of *One from the Heart*. Forrest, who had worked with Harry Dean in *The Rose*, went on to star in *Hammett*, in many ways Wim Wenders's tribute to character actors. Based on a novel by Joe Gores about a return to the detective life for the famous writer Dashiell Hammett, the film was a financial bust, but it featured a wonderful cast of familiar faces, including old hands Elisha Cook Jr., R. G. Armstrong, Silvia Sidney, Royal Dano, and Hank Worden. Even hard-boiled director-screenwriter Samuel Fuller and writer Ross Thomas make appearances. Wenders's penchant for character actors would open a major door for Harry Dean a couple of years later.

In *One from the Heart*, Harry Dean's character, Moe, has to watch from the sidelines as Frederic Forrest's Hank has an affair with Nastassja Kinski's Leila. A few years later, in Wenders's *Paris, Texas*, Kinski's character, Jane, will be married to Harry Dean's Travis Henderson before he abandons her and their child.

Aside from his role in the film, Harry Dean got his one opportunity to direct during the shooting of *One from the Heart*. Coppola "did something on *One from the Heart* that was, especially for a 'big time' director, really wonderful," he would tell writer Alex Simon in 1997. "There was a scene with Teri Garr and Fred Forrest, and he came up to me and said, 'Harry Dean, you direct this scene.' No director has done that before or since with me. And I did. I helped him direct it. Of course, he had the final word on it, but for a director to do something like that is pretty special."

Perhaps the most important takeaway from Harry Dean's experience with *One from the Heart*, however, was that he met Rebecca De Mornay during his work on the film. *One from the Heart* was De Mornay's film debut, and she and Harry Dean would develop a romantic relationship that some argue was the most serious of Harry Dean's life. They would live together, and Harry Dean gave the much-younger De Mornay valuable advice and lessons in acting, and about life, too. "I met Harry Dean when I first came out to LA," she told the audience at the first Harry Dean Stanton Awards ceremony on October 23, 2016. "He was the first film actor I got to know. I was an acting student. I was twenty-one. He was fifty-four. The first thing he said to me was, 'Do you believe in magic?' I thought that was really cheesy, but it somehow stuck with me. We talked so much on the set. About movies. I got to see about what acting is. He told me about his little brother in Kentucky. They were playing, and his brother was crying. His brother would open his eyes wide, full of tears, and as he was telling it, his eyes filled with tears. And I said, gosh, his sensitivity. I had never seen a grown man cry. That really touched me. We wound up living together for a year and a half."

Although De Mornay had studied acting at Lee Strasberg's institute in Los Angeles, Harry Dean became her teacher as well as her lover. "I used to work on my auditions with him, and he would say, 'I don't believe you.' I had just read my line, and I was horrified. I kept saying the line again and again and again until he did believe me. His sense of truth, I am so glad of that. The thing that he understands about acting, it is almost impossible for him to say a line untruthfully. He used to talk about Max Reinhardt. You can't be something on stage that you don't inhabit off stage. Everything he is off stage he brings on stage, and vice versa. What strikes me about Harry Dean's acting is his ability to be in the moment. He goes with what is. He's more in tune with being in the moment than anyone I have ever seen."

Harry Dean's teaching indeed may have contributed to De Mornay's acclaimed performances in films such as *The Trip to Bountiful* (1985) and *The Hand That Rocks the Cradle* (1992). He also helped her make key connections that furthered her career. He made the contacts that helped get her a seminal role in *Risky Business* (1983), starring Tom Cruise. The film was a box-office hit, helped establish Cruise as the poster child of the post–New Hollywood era and future star of the high-tech, blockbuster films that marked that new era. *Risky Business* also led to a relationship between Cruise and De Mornay that edged Harry Dean out the door.

Harry Dean's affair with De Mornay was "the closest he had come to permanence," Ian Nathan wrote, adding that he was a "damn fool" for helping her get that role in Cruise's film.

"I got her in the movie with Tom Cruise, and she ends up with him," Harry Dean says in Sophie Huber's documentary on him, *Partly Fiction*. "I was heartbroken."

Out of a Death Watch to New Career Heights

On the day of the final shoot for *Death Watch,* actress Romy Schneider threw a party for the cast and crew. When the waiter brought five bottles of very expensive champagne to the table where Schneider and others sat, one of the producers expressed shock at the cost. "Are you sure, Romy?"

"The champagne is for Harvey, for Harry Dean, for Bertrand, Willie Glenn, and all the people for making an intelligent film," Schneider told the gathering.

With this she toasted lead star Harvey Keitel, Harry Dean, director Bertrand Tavernier, cinematographer Pierre William Glenn, and everyone else who had a part in making *Death Watch,* a film that today has a cult following but that was panned by critics when it first came out.

The *Death Watch* cast and crew needed a party, although Schneider made an early departure that evening. Eight weeks of intense, on-location filming had come to an end, and with it the problems that inevitably accompany every film, but that in this case had included frequent episodes of friction on the set between the two main stars, Keitel and Schneider. Keitel, a former Marine and roughhewn Jewish kid from Brooklyn's Brighton Beach, had come onto the set needing to prove something after several career misfires— roles in forgettable films like Robert Altman's *Buffalo Bill and the Indians* and Peter Yates's *Mother, Jugs and Speed*—and a critically lauded but personally unsatisfying Broadway performance as Happy in *Death of a Salesman,* with George C. Scott as Willie Loman. It had been four years since Keitel's excellent, if too seldom acknowledged, performance as the pimp Sport in Martin Scorsese's *Taxi Driver.*

Romy Schneider came to *Death Watch* after scoring big with her award-winning roles in *L'important c'est d'aimer* (1975) and *A Simple Story* (1978). However, she had her own demons—a painful and still remembered rejection by former lover Alain Delon, a subsequent unhappy marriage and then divorce, plus bouts with alcohol and drugs.

"Nobody wanted Harvey," Tavernier told me in an interview in August 2018. "I could never raise enough money [in the United States] because of Harvey. People wanted Richard Gere." Nevertheless, Tavernier wanted Keitel. "He was a stunning actor."

However, on the set with Schneider, "he did not have the social graces he did later on," Tavernier said. "He was not careful with somebody like Romy, who was not playing in her own language and for whom it was more difficult."

So, Harry Dean to the rescue—at Tavernier's request. "Please, Harry, help me with Romy," the director begged him. Harry Dean obliged, not only playing diplomat but also personal counselor to Schneider, encouraging her in her acting abilities. "You know, you are great," Harry Dean would tell her after watching some of the rushes. Schneider later told Tavernier how much that meant, that Harry Dean had given her the confidence Keitel's behavior tried to challenge.

"I love acting with him," she told the director about Harry Dean. "It is wonderful. I adore him." Tavernier said that, in a way, Schneider "fell in love with" Harry Dean.

So it was likely no accident that Harry Dean became the life of Romy Schneider's party for the cast and crew. Song after song he sang, as many as fifteen, playing his guitar, singing in both English and Spanish, particularly songs from the Mexican Revolution, songs like the one he would sing at John Huston's memorial service a few years later.

"Harry, can we have another revolutionary song?" cast member Max von Sydow would ask as he poured himself another glass of Romy Schneider's very expensive champagne, and Harry Dean would start strumming his guitar again.

At one point sometime after the party, the Swedish actor, still perhaps best known in his long, stellar career for his work with the great Ingmar Bergman, said to Tavernier, "That was one of the greatest evenings of my life."

Set and filmed in a futuristic Glasgow, Scotland, *Death Watch* tells the story of dying writer Katherine Mortenhoe, played by Schneider, whose last days are being filmed and recorded without her knowledge by a journalist named Roddy, played by Keitel. Under the supervision of his relentless producer Vincent Ferriman, played by Harry Dean, Roddy has a camera implanted in his brain so that he can secretly record Katherine's every painful moment in her slow decline for audiences to watch across the country. "Seventy-one percent of the audience share, seventy-four percent in Germany," Ferriman boasts at one point.

Death Watch is a powerful and even prophetic indictment of a particular brand of rapacious corporate journalism that has no qualms over sacrificing privacy if profits are to be made. The film also has become a kind of testament to a Glasgow that no longer exists. "It has become a fascinating documentary for Glasgow," Tavernier said. "Glasgow has been rebuilt. A lot of the buildings we filmed do not exist anymore. None of the British directors wanted me to film there. They said you will be mugged, attacked, that Glasgow was worse than Chicago in the times of Capone. The people were great. They helped us in many ways."

Dedicated to one of film noir's greatest directors, Jacques Tourneur, *Death Watch* is every bit a neo-noir film that takes viewers into Glasgow's lower depths, a society in decay where the poor fight for survival while a corporate world fights for ratings.

The novel by David Compton that inspired the film never names the city or town in which it is set. "I picked Glasgow," Tavernier said. "I was tired of having every science fiction story in the world where everything was plastic. No houses, a big dome." He chose centuries-old, working-class Glasgow with its many buildings that had stood the test of time because "it is more interesting to do something which is in the future with buildings of the past."

Tavernier said he had special memories of times with Harry Dean on the streets and in the bars of Glasgow. "In the street one day, we heard some music, and Harry was with us. It was with fife and drums . . . and they were protesting against drinking. . . . Harry called Jack Nicholson [back in Los Angeles], and he must have been waking him up because of the time difference, and he said, 'Listen to the fife and drums, all these slogans against drinking!'"

During those late evenings in Glasgow's bars, Harry Dean tended to get philosophical. "A bit stoned, he'd be asking you very difficult questions." Tavernier remembered one such evening in detail.

"Bertrand," Harry Dean asked after several drinks, "do you think we can verbalize the concept of Christ? The director looked at his friend and shook his head. "Harry Dean, maybe a little later, after several hours' sleep."

On and off the set, Harry Dean and Harvey Keitel got along well. They were very different to direct, however. "Harry Dean was a joy to work with," Tavernier said. "He was incredibly intelligent, fast, and sharp. . . . You didn't have to psychoanalyze the character. He loved the idea of playing someone who was educated. Harry Dean was always in character. He was never out of character. He did not have to do research. He was organic. I remember Jack Nicholson saying, 'If I could do one minute as organic as Harry Dean, I'd be happy.'"

Harry Dean's sense of humor finds itself into the film as well. In one scene, his and Keitel's characters discuss how to approach Katherine's estranged husband. Keitel's Roddy asks what the husband's name is.

"Harry," Harry Dean's Vincent says.

"Will he be trouble?" Roddy asks.

"Nobody named Harry is ever a problem," Vincent says.

"We did that line on purpose," Tavernier said in his interview with me.

Keitel's approach to his role was much more intense than Harry Dean's and very detail-oriented. "Harvey was asking a thousand questions every morning," Tavernier said, but in the years after *Death Watch*, "he has always been very loyal to the film. That was one of his best performances."

Death Watch may have been prophetic in ways other than its depiction of media and modern-day loss of privacy. Romy Schneider would die two years later at the age of forty-four (before the delayed US release of the film and after suffering the devastating loss of her son—who also appears in *Death*

Watch—to a freakish accident the year before). Tavernier challenged some suggestions that she committed suicide. "I don't think she committed suicide. I think that was a mistake on her part. She was taking medicine to sleep, then pills to be awake. I think she made a wrong mix. She wanted to live."

Keitel spent much of the rest of the decade working with European directors in Europe. "European directors tend to work more collaboratively with their actors than Hollywood directors," Marshall Fine wrote in his biography, *Harvey Keitel: The Art of Darkness*, "because, while budget is always a concern, there is not the same kind of devastating pressure to produce a hit."

Like Keitel, Harry Dean would turn to European directors as well and get the two major starring roles of his career in *Repo Man* and *Paris, Texas*. Keitel's years in Europe, however, largely produced films "that were never or barely released in the United States and hardly made a dent in their own countries." These included *Une Pierre Dans la Bouche* (1983), *Alleys and Crimes* (1985), and *Caro Gorbaciov* (1988). Harry Dean's work with British filmmaker Alex Cox in *Repo Man* and Wim Wenders in *Paris, Texas*, by contrast, solidified his status in America and beyond as an actor to be reckoned with, one with a growing cult status that would continue until his death and beyond.

The Stanton home and Harry Dean's birthplace in West Irvine, Kentucky. (Photograph of a drawing taken by Lula [Parsons] Kinder, courtesy of Jerry Eltzroth.)

Ersel with her three sons by Sheridan "Shorty" Stanton, circa 1930: (left to right) Arch, Harry Dean, and Ralph. (Photograph provided by Mrs. Patricia Wallace; thanks also to Stanley McKnight Jr.)

Sheridan "Shorty" Stanton (second from left, in white shirt and dark bow tie) in his barbershop in Irvine, Kentucky, circa 1930s. (Estill County Historical and Genealogical Society, with assistance from Jerry Eltzroth.)

Stanley McKnight Sr. and Ersel. (Courtesy of Stanley McKnight Jr. and Chad McKnight.)

Harry Dean in the US Navy. (Courtesy of Jim Huggins Jr.)

Harry Dean (seated, center) in a production of *The Last Mile* at the Pasadena Playhouse, October 1953. (Pasadena Playhouse Archive Collection.)

Rebecca De Mornay, 2010. (Wikimedia Commons.)

Harry Dean publicity shot for *Repo Man* (1984). Photograph by Martin Turner. (Universal Pictures/Photofest.)

Harry Dean in *Paris, Texas* (1984). (20th Century Fox/Photofest.)

Harry Dean and Hunter Carson in *Paris, Texas* (1984). (20th Century Fox/Photofest.)

Harry Dean and Dean Stockwell in *Paris, Texas* (1984). (Argos Films/Photofest.)

Harry Dean and Michelle Phillips at the 2014 Harry Dean Stanton Fest in Lexington, Kentucky. (Courtesy of Lucy Jones and the Harry Dean Stanton Fest.)

Lucy Jones in Lexington, Kentucky, May 2017. (Courtesy of Joseph B. Atkins.)

Jamie James and Tom Thurman. (Courtesy of Joseph B. Atkins.)

HD doormat at his Mulholland Drive home. (Courtesy of Jim Huggins Jr.)

8

A Repo Man and His "Tense Situations"

The relationship between Harry Dean Stanton and director Alex Cox during the filming of *Repo Man* in the summer of 1983 was about as amicable as that between a repo man and a fellow who just got his car repossessed: lousy. Harry Dean was a fifty-seven-year-old veteran character actor already well known for his attention-getting supporting roles and who just three years before had scored his largest role yet as Vincent the amoral television producer in Bertrand Tavernier's *Death Watch*. For that movie, he received billing just under lead stars Harvey Keitel and Romy Schneider. The British-born Cox, not long out of film school at the University of California in Los Angeles, was twenty-nine and making his first feature-length film.

Harry Dean grumbled about his salary—roughly $70,000, a deal for Cox after losing his earlier choice for the role of Bud the Repo Man, actor Dennis Hopper. When Hopper demanded $100,000, $30,000 more than executive producer and former Monkee guitarist Michael Nesmith wanted to pay, they went with Harry Dean. Harry Dean pitched the idea of playing both Bud and crazed scientist J. Frank Parnell in the film but, when that idea got nixed, suggested the actor who ended up with the Parnell role, Fox Harris. Harry Dean was slow to learn his lines and told Cox he wanted to use cue cards like Warren Oates did in *Two-Lane Blacktop*. Cox warned him that "refusal to learn one's lines was a breach of the Screen Actors Guild contract." Harry relented.

When Harry Dean suggested his character Bud wear a fedora, Cox said no and Bud went hatless. When Harry Dean's rival for Rebecca De Mornay's affections, Tom Cruise, showed up on the set and hints surfaced about getting Cruise into the picture, Harry Dean was not happy and indicated he might quit. Cruise was out of the picture.

A near break in the relationship occurred the very next day during film-ing, when Harry wanted to give costar Emilio Estevez's character a baseball signal to show him where to park his car. Cox again said no.

"I've worked with the greatest directors in the world, including Francis Ford Coppola," Harry Dean shouted at Cox. "And you know why they were great? They let me do whatever the fuck I want!"

The two even got physical during the filming of a fight scene between Harry Dean's repo men and their enemies, the notorious Rodriguez brothers. When Harry Dean began swinging a real baseball bat instead of the plastic prop provided, Cox tried to take it away. "Harry Dean Stanton only uses REAL baseball bats!" the actor told his director, at which point the two wres-tled for control of the real baseball hat. Assistant director Betsy Magruder and her assistants had to intervene, confiscate the wooden bat, and allow filming to proceed.

Cox would later acknowledge that many of Harry Dean's points were sound. "Arthur Penn didn't get a great performance out of Harry in *The Missouri Breaks* by putting him in a straightjacket," Cox wrote in his 2008 book *X Films: True Confessions of a Radical Filmmaker*. "Harry needed the tension of these emotional outbursts; like a repo man, he was addicted to 'tense situations' in order to do his work. But this made for a difficult process, if you weren't one of the world's greatest directors."

Repo Man is a film full of memorable quotes, and one of them is Harry Dean's advice to young Emilio Estevez's Otto as they snort cocaine in Bud's car. "An ordinary man spends his life avoiding tense situations," Harry Dean's Bud tells repo man novice Otto. "A repo man spends his life getting into tense situations."

From Bud's indictment of ordinary people—"Look at those assholes, ordi-nary people. I hate 'em"—to Otto's question after repo man Miller (played by Tracey Walker) shares his views about "cosmic unconsciousness" ("You eat a lot of acid, Miller, back in the hippie days?") to Bud's appropriation of Mexican revolutionary Emiliano Zapata's famous "I'd rather die on my feet than live on my knees," the script to *Repo Man* is a virtual film-quote dictionary.

Repo Man is today considered a classic, "the quintessential cult film," in the words of writer Dante A. Ciampaglia. "A low-budget, high-concept tear-down of early '80s consumer culture, Reaganism, nuclear fears, and surbur-banism inspired by the death of cities and the birth of punk . . . so weird and so angry that it . . . connected with kids (and adults) who felt alienated and marginalized by an increasingly conservative society." The film is finally "an

American punk touchstone," he wrote, with a soundtrack that included punk icons like Iggy Pop and the Sex Pistols' Steve Jones.

"I think it is a great American film," Michael Nesmith told me in an October 2018 interview. "*Repo Man* was about something that was ineffable, a cultural sea change for America and much of the world, a punk rock movie."

The film made lots of money for Universal Studios, Cox, and Nesmith—Cox estimates earnings to be $30 million to $40 million—and Cox said he hopes to make a sequel, since US film rights reverted to him in March 2019.

However, even today residue remains from the frequent acrimony between Cox and Harry Dean during filming. In an interview for the Criterion Collection edition of the *Repo Man* DVD, film producer Peter McCarthy asked Harry Dean if he had ever worked with a director who "didn't have his shit together" but still made a good film. Harry Dean's response: "Yes, Alex Cox." After the interview, Harry Dean told McCarthy to tell Cox, "I love him." Harry Dean was prone to contradict himself from time to time. He told journalist Sean O'Hagan many years later that Alex Cox was a "nut" and an "egomaniac" but also "brilliantly talented and a great satirist."

In an interview with the author in November 2018, Cox said he had only limited contact with Harry Dean after the completion of *Repo Man*. "I don't like hanging around people who are rude and don't like me," Cox said. "That's the thing. As an individual, I found him selfish, disgruntled, and unpleasant. As an actor I thought he was fantastic."

Cox chose Harry Dean for the role as Bud in part because of the "Old West–cadaver look" that seemed a perfect match for the chief repo man, wise to the ways of the world, particularly a world where one's job was to repossess the cars of people who had gotten delinquent in their payments, all of them "assholes" but also those "who elected, sometimes through no fault of their own and sometimes through their own volition, not to pay," in the words of real-life Los Angeles repo man Mark Lewis. Lewis's work was the inspiration for the film, and he served as an advisor and guide to Cox into the repo world.

Harry Dean "had a particularly world-weary, exhausted, saddened face" that appealed to Cox, a face that lit up "when he smiled" and made "his eyes glitter with delight." It was also "the perpetually sad face of someone who had been yelled at by successions of tough-guy directors and actors who were bigger and more brawling than him," Cox wrote in his 2008 book *X Films: True Confessions of a Radical Filmmaker*.

Yet in Harry Dean's previous major film, *Death Watch,* he worked with a director, Bertrand Tavernier, who not only admired his work but also saw in him potential to help keep the film on track by, among other things, smoothing the edgy relationship between stars Harvey Keitel and Romy Schneider. "I don't know that anyone can say they were close to him," Tavernier told me in my interview with him. "He was very much enigmatic, but everybody on the set loved him, loved him."

Harry Dean didn't get the lead in *Death Watch,* but it was the meatiest role of his career up to that point. With *Repo Man,* he shared the lead with Estevez, but he was in his late fifties, working with an inexperienced twenty-nine-year-old director on a limited budget, and he had to share top billing with a novice actor who was only twenty-one and had graduated from high school three years before.

The roots of *Repo Man* can be traced back to the 1955 film noir *Kiss Me Deadly,* directed by Robert Aldrich and transformed from Mickey Spillane's hard-boiled novel by legendary screenwriter A. I. Bezzerides into a tale of atomic-age paranoia. A locker filled with a deadly cache of glowing radioactivity is the sought-after prize of foreign agents and detective Mike Hammer. Alex Cox, a committed film buff even if a novice filmmaker, kept thinking of *Kiss Me Deadly* as he plowed through the first fourteen drafts of *Repo Man,* envisioning the 1964 Chevy Malibu that is his film's sought-after prize as the potential equivalent of the apocalyptic locker in Aldrich's film.

Writer Sam McPheeters found another important link in the two films. The protagonist in *Kiss Me Deadly,* Mike Hammer, "is a brutal, misogynist lunk with no patience for other humans. Otto [the novice repo man played by Emilio Estevez] shares this misanthropy, floating through the story as an upwardly mobile cipher, mimicking empathy when convenient, never rising to true brutality only because it would require too much effort. He's not an antihero, just a beautiful jerk."

Or, as Alex Cox put it, "Otto is a blank page, endlessly influenced by events around him."

It is Harry Dean's Bud, veteran of the repo shop called the Helping Hand Acceptance Corporation, who at least attempts to instill in Otto a code of conduct in his newly chosen field of endeavor. "Not many people have a code to live by anymore," he tells Otto, and this is the code of the repo man: "I shall not cause harm to any vehicle nor the personal contents thereof, nor through inaction let the personal contents thereof come to harm."

A $20,000 bounty on the mysterious Chevy Malibu launches a scramble that will include the Helping Hand Acceptance Corporation, the Rodriguez brothers, government agents, UFO scientists, and even a televangelist to get to the car, the trunk of which, Otto learns, contains radioactive aliens that have already vaporized a policeman (in the opening scene) and led to the death of the scientist, J. Frank Parnell, who was driving the car before radiation exposure killed him.

In the glorious end of the film, the entire car glows bright green with Bud sitting in the driver's seat. After Bud gets shot, he is replaced by Miller (veteran character actor Tracey Walter nearly steals the film), who is then joined by Otto. Together they ride off into the night with the flying, glowing Chevy as it rises up and soars over the LA skyline.

"All great narratives start with a great story," Michael Nesmith told me. "That story gets put out there early. If you're waiting for the nub of the storyline and the substance of it till the middle of the book, you start to lose interest. You lose your focus on it. *Repo Man* didn't do that. It was a stunner from the first page I read. When I was finished with the first page, which as I recall, ending with 'You don't want to look in the trunk, officer,' I was into it. Like 'What's in the trunk?' A classic movie trap."

Oddly enough, this "stunner" of a story began as a comic strip drawn by Alex Cox. "I'd planned to draw the whole script as a comic book of some thirty-six pages," he wrote in *X Films: True Confessions of a Radical Filmmaker.* "But I realized after only four pages that drawing a comic book is a lot of work. I gave it up."

Inspired by Spanish filmmaker Luis Buñuel and Japanese filmmaker Akira Kurosawa, Alex Cox came out of film school at UCLA with a firm belief that "feature film was the original art form of the twentieth century" and that "an independent filmmaker is a revolutionary fighter in a prolonged popular war." Just as Bud declared the repo man code, Cox provided a short manifesto of the independent filmmaker and his war in the introduction to his book *X Films:* "This is the same war that Free Software and GNU/Linux activists fight against Microsoft; that independent musicians fight against the RIAA (Recording Industry Association of America) and the Apple Music Store; that Fairtrade activists fight against WalMart and the WTO; that the Zapatistas fight against patriarchal systems of control in Mexico."

Even today Cox sees *Repo Man* as an indictment of "things that don't go away," such as "government surveillance, the ever-present threat of nuclear annihilation." He would pursue his leftist politics further in films after *Repo Man,* such as the one he considers his magnum opus, *Walker* (1987).

The dilemma a leftist, independent filmmaker faces is the question of how to finance one's film. "Independent filmmakers are apt to be political, angry, and scornful of the rich people/trust-fund babies who might support their films," he wrote in *X Films*. "Artists can easily turn into notorious sycophants in the company of the rich. It's best to avoid them, if possible." Thus Cox initially envisioned *Repo Man* as a low-budget film produced by the small independent production company he and his UCLA pals created, Edge City. In the prospectus they prepared for potential financiers, a projected budget of $160,000 was presented, with $40,000 coming from UCLA and $50,000 in crew, actors, and editor's fees and expenses deferred. So the capital contribution actually needed to finance the film was only $70,000. With ten investors contributing $7,000 each, the film could be made. Even with the low projected budget, however, the script got rejection after rejection. No one, it seemed, liked its "unsympathetic" characters.

Then a UCLA student, Abbe Wool, managed to get the script into the hands of producer Harry Gittes, who in turn handed it to ex-Monkee Michael Nesmith, the most musically talented member of that band and someone who had built a solid post-Monkee reputation as a songwriter, film and television producer, and creator of the concept of twenty-four-hour music television that became MTV. He won the first-ever Grammy Award for a music video, and he had composed songs recorded by the Paul Butterfield Blues Band and the Stone Poneys with Linda Ronstadt in addition to many of the Monkees' biggest hits. John Lennon invited him to be on hand when the Beatles recorded the classic "A Day in the Life."

When Cox learned Nesmith had the script, he began checking out the ex-Monkee and discovered an old screenplay for the Monkees television show. It was written by Bob Rafelson and Jack Nicholson, who had spent part of the 1960s rooming with Harry Dean in Laurel Canyon. Nicholson was also cowriter and coproducer of the Monkees' first film, *Head*.

The Texas-born Nesmith liked Cox's script but felt the future film needed a bigger budget if it was ever to be made successfully. "I didn't want more money; I wanted to make the film as cheaply as possible," Cox wrote in *X Films*. "Nesmith wanted *Repo Man* to cost a lot more, and for someone else to pay for it."

"Alex thought they'd find a wind-up camera in the glove box of the Malibu, everybody would go out happy and high and make this film, like *Easy Rider*," Nesmith told me in an interview. "I would invariably stop him and say, 'Alex, we don't have the money for that.' . . . Alex didn't understand a lot of vicissitudes of budget filmmaking." With a larger budget is gained is "a set of professional tools."

Nesmith sent the script to Universal Studio head Robert Rehme and fellow studio executive Thom Mount, and both rejected it. Then a chance meeting with Rehme at a restaurant changed the film's fate. Nesmith had gone to the restaurant, Morton's in Beverly Hills, with a friend, singer Kenny Rogers's manager, Ken Kragan. Rehme happened to be there, too, dressed in a cowboy-style leisure suit, and when he passed their table, Kragan, eyeing Nesmith as a potential client, asked the Universal boss, "What about *Repo Man?* You've got a great thing on your desk."

Rehme, wanting to please a mover and shaker like Kragan, left the restaurant and gave the script a second look. "That's a good script," he later told Nesmith. "Let us make that movie."

The deal Universal offered Nesmith was for a $1.8 million film, but with a "negative pickup" arrangement. This allowed the studio to pay at the end of filming, not before, and thus lower costs by circumventing union and guild agreements. "So my first professional directing gig was a union-busting enterprise," Cox wrote in *X Films*. "Not that we leftist independent filmmakers thought about that. We just wanted to make our film, and we were glad that— since Universal was also a major distributor—it would also get a proper commercial distribution. We had much to learn."

Universal's involvement would prove troublesome in the days ahead— the filmmakers' fears the company would pull out as a result of the changing of the script's ending from the original apocalyptic destruction of Los Angeles to the glowing Malibu's flight over the city skyline, the studio's failure to promote the film, and even its efforts to sabotage it once it was finished. Cox and Nesmith still wrestled over funding—Cox insisted on simply renting a Malibu for the filming, Nesmith said at least two were needed just in case something happened. In fact, the first Malibu used on the set disappeared, either stolen or squirreled away to force a decision. They found it after purchasing a second.

"I don't think it was legitimately stolen," Nesmith told me. "It was a setup."

So who took the first Malibu, forcing Cox to get a second? "These were guerrilla filmmakers," Nesmith said. "Not larcenists or thieves, but looking for a way of getting something on a screen."

Assembling cast and crew was the next big challenge. Cox secured legendary cinematographer Robby Müller to be director of photography, and he would later go on to serve in that role in Harry Dean's next film, *Paris, Texas.* The Dutch native had impressed Cox with his work on an earlier Wim Wenders film, *The American Friend,* and he would go on to make classics for

Wenders, Jim Jarmusch, and others, including films such as *Down by Law* (1986), *Barfly* (1987), *Mystery Train* (1989), *Buena Vista Social Club* (1999), and *Ghost Dog: The Way of the Samurai* (1999).

Universal's backing meant more money for casting, but not enough for Dennis Hopper in the role of Bud. Cox went for Harry Dean, an actor he had always admired. "Harry Dean was authentic and sincere," Cox told me. "The first time I noticed him was in *Missouri Breaks*. In one early scene—he was one of Jack Nicholson's gang members—he was getting a haircut, and he had one of those pudding pots on his head and getting this awful haircut that way. I thought this is a guy who takes his work seriously."

When Cox met with Harry Dean's agent—whom he identified at the Harry Dean Stanton Fest in July 2019 as Rick Nicita of Creative Artists Agency (CAA)—the agent shocked him by suggesting Mick Jagger of the Rolling Stones for the role of Bud. "This was an eye-opener. I spent twenty minutes chatting to Harry's agent about what a great actor Harry was, the wonderful work he'd done. The agent listened and then said, 'Harry Dean's okay, but he's past it. You need someone younger, more up-and-coming. I also represent Mick Jagger. Why don't you offer Mick Jagger the part?'"

Cox was flabbergasted. "This gobsmacked me. First, Jagger was completely wrong for the role of the grizzled, burned-out LA repo man. And second, the guy was out of line. We'd offered Harry the part, and here his agent was trying to do him out of the job. It was immoral, surely a breach of contract, and stupid. I replied that Harry's age, experience, and nationality made him the best choice, made my excuses, and left." (Efforts to contact Nicita for this book were unsuccessful.)

Within a year of *Repo Man*'s release, *Variety* magazine reported Harry Dean had left CAA and signed with Toni Howard of the William Morris Agency. Ironically, CAA was created in 1975 by former agents with the William Morris Agency. However, Harry Dean's later longtime agent, John Kelly, told this author that he and partner Sandy Bresler, also Jack Nicholson's longtime agent and a former junior representative with William Morris, began representing Harry Dean in 1982—after the shooting of *Repo Man*—and Kelly remained his agent until Harry Dean died in 2017.

This wasn't the only agent issue that came up during casting. Emilio Estevez's agent and manager discouraged the actor from taking the role of Otto because *Repo Man* was a "small film." Estevez overruled them because he liked the script so much. Then the agent insisted Estevez get top billing. Once filming got underway and friction arose between Harry Dean and Cox, these issues remained secrets. "The thing is I couldn't tell Harry things because he was already so furious," Cox told me. "I couldn't tell Harry about his agent, about those who wanted Emilio for first billing [as lead]. It would have made him even more angry."

Cox believes his issues with Harry Dean stemmed in part from the actor's Method approach to acting. "It was never an easy relationship. Part of the problem with people who come from the Method school, they kind of forget what Laurence Olivier told Dustin Hoffman when they were working on *Marathon Man*. Dustin said he was going to get his tooth filled without an anesthetic to know how his character felt. Olivier said to him, 'Ever tried acting?' I said that to Harry Dean in various ways every day. I was trying to push him in that direction."

The two clashed in other troublesome ways as well. Cox was struck by Harry Dean's comments about Jews. "Harry Dean was apt to get into a longish diatribe about the Jews, not that Harry was anti-Semitic—he thought the Christian culture every bit as bad and stupid as the Jewish one—but he did tend, given a trapped interlocutor, to go on about the Jews." Harry Dean's own Zen Buddhist–Krishnamurti–Eckhart Tolle–Alan Watts–imbued philosophy of life didn't particularly impress Cox, an atheist. "Harry was like a lot of those Hollywood actors who imagine themselves to be Buddhist," Cox told me. "He was terribly confused—Buddhism and Calvinism, utter mishmash. In Hollywood they all think they're Buddhists living in the moment. What are they going to do tomorrow? Live in the moment."

Universal, which enjoyed a reputation of being more willing than other major studios to back low-budget films, had largely lost faith or interest in *Repo Man* by the time it was finished. When an early screening of it before studio executives elicited only silence, a young woman in the small audience stood up and said, "What is wrong with you people? Don't you realize this is a great movie, what we have here?" She was fired a week later. Neither Nesmith nor Cox remembers her name.

Even though *Repo Man* won praise at the Berlin Film Festival, Universal pulled it a week after its US opening in Chicago. After much delay, producer Jonathan Wacks finally convinced the studio to screen the film in Los Angeles. However, the film didn't earn enough to please the studio, which then sent it to cable and later video. *Repo Man* might have slowly descended into obscurity at that point had it not been for its LA punk soundtrack. An album of the music in *Repo Man*, released by MCA through its sublabel San Andreas Records, began to pick up sales, and eventually punk music lovers bought more than 50,000 copies. When MCA head Irving Azoff asked, "Is there a movie to go with this?" Universal official Kelly Neal pushed the studio to open the film again, this time in New York City's Eighth Street Playhouse on Bleecker Street in the heart of Greenwich Village. The film began to rake in millions.

"They put the music out and it took hold," Nesmith said. "It was a respectable record accepted by the punk community. As it got some traction, the film was playing at a theater in Cambridge or Boston. It went on for a few months. Next thing you know it had been playing at the one theater for a year and sold out every night. That is a bellwether of the best sort."

Repo Man will be remembered as Alex Cox's most successful film, an iconic punk look at early 1980s America, and for featuring Harry Dean in his first lead role. "I think there was a kind of droopy dog sensibility about him that he understood about himself," Nesmith told me. "He was able to play it. 'Nobody ever gets killed for a car,' delivered with the compassion of a stage actor. That line does not work, but when Harry Dean said it, it becomes a throwaway, like 'What did you just say?' He just dismantled the American capitalistic motor system in one phrase. That's why when Harry Dean rolls off on the Repo Creed, it becomes absurdist in the extreme. . . . It gets to be hilarious. It exposes a value system that is absolutely corrupt."

Nesmith said the film is so much a testament to its times that he isn't sure a true sequel can be made. Cox, however, hopes to make one. "It is too good of an opportunity not to do it," contends Cox, since US rights reverted to him in March 2019. Some tentative efforts have been made over the years, including Cox's 2008 graphic novel *Waldo's Hawaiian Holiday,* but none has been considered a true sequel. Harry Dean did reprise his role as a repo man in a 2010 appearance on the NBC show *Chuck.*

Despite all his disagreements with Harry Dean, Alex Cox said he never doubted him as an actor and knew that Harry Dean helped make *Repo Man* the cult classic it is today. He also helped Cox in another significant way more than a year after *Repo Man* was completed. Cox was in Rotterdam for a film festival. The largest cinema in town, the Luxor, was playing *Repo Man.* "I went over for the opening and in the bar of the hotel across the street from the Luxor ran into Harry Dean Stanton, who had been invited to attend. Harry was chatting with a bearded guy. He introduced us."

The "bearded guy" was noted screenwriter Rudy Wurlitzer, who'd written the scripts for past Harry Dean films, including *Two-Lane Blacktop* and *Pat Garrett and Billy the Kid.* Wurlitzer and Cox hit it off and remain lifelong friends today. Wurlitzer went on to write the script for the film that Cox considers his best, *Walker*.

As for Harry Dean, he thought enough of his experience with *Repo Man* to name one of his bands after the film. "Harry Dean Stanton and the Repo Men" played on the stages of clubs across Los Angeles.

More than a decade after the film was made, Harry Dean had this to say to writer Alex Simon: "I thought *Repo Man* was a brilliant satire on the whole culture, on everything, violence, religion, desperation of the whole society trying to make it. How a man's got to have a 'code.' Some wonderful lines in that. Alex Cox did a wonderful job."

9

To Paris, Texas, and Beyond

The music confronts you with the same intensity as the desert seen through Robby Müller's cinematography and, of course, the lone figure of Travis Henderson emerging out of that desert on his journey to reconcile his past. The music you're hearing is Ry Cooder's solo slide guitar playing Blind Willie Johnson's "Dark Was the Night," a searing, wordless gospel that the Texas street singer recorded back in 1927.

"The most transcendent piece in all American music" Cooder calls it.

Blind Willie Johnson lost his sight at seven when his angry stepmother threw lye at his father and hit him instead, in the face. He grew up to be a guitar-playing, sandpaper-voiced preacher, and he performed on the streets of Dallas and Waco, in camp revivals and country churches, singing to passersby as well as the faithful the need to get right with God. He used the blade of a pocketknife to make his guitar wail with the same conviction that was in his voice. He would die of pneumonia, caught from sleeping amid the charred remains of his fire-destroyed home and being refused treatment at a local hospital.

The nearly sixty-year-old gospel tune worked for Wim Wenders's *Paris, Texas* because it echoed what was going on inside Travis Henderson: the cry of a soul that's suffering, wrestling with itself, needing help. Here is where Blind Willie Johnson and Travis Henderson meet. Johnson, however, turned to God. Travis Henderson had no God to save him.

In the liner notes to a CD of Johnson's music, Cooder called the singer "one of those interplanetary world musicians—and there are only a few. Blind Willie Johnson is in the ether somewhere. He's up there in the zone." In a way, so is Travis Henderson, now a part of the American iconography, like the European-made film that told his story.

In an October 2019 interview via email, Wenders said, "it never crossed my mind for a second to have anybody else do that score but Ry Cooder."

Cooder's playing and musical explorations have provided the backdrop to films ranging from Herbert Ross's *Steel Magnolias* (1989) to Wim Wenders's

Buena Vista Social Club (1999). In *Paris, Texas,* perhaps more than in any of his films, he caught the spirit of the composer, the battle that can rage even in a man sure of his God. Travis Henderson wants redemption but knows he may be beyond it. So how does he deal with the guilt he feels for letting jealousy and anger destroy the love of his life, for abandoning a wife and child? He needs a cleansing of the soul, but how? He's not as much a desert monk as a desert fugitive, the most desperate of fugitives because his is the impossible task of escaping himself. He is silent because he has no words for his predicament, nothing that can explain, excuse, or forgive.

As we witness the "shell-shocked intensity" of Travis Henderson's struggle, we hear Cooder's score, which "seems somehow to have burned itself into the landscape of the Southwest, to the point where footage of that dry red terrain, with its wind-eroded mesas, can hardly appear on an editing console before someone reaches for the Cooder button" for music that brings "yearning to the bleakness of the landscape," Nick Roddick writes in an essay that accompanies the Criterion Collection edition of the film.

"Ry Cooder was so much in harmony with what we wanted to portray," Wenders would later say. "Nobody else could have created that sound so exactly like we wanted. . . . He was playing directly into the images, like his guitar was directly related to the camera."

Cooder said the music had to be in harmony with Travis Henderson. "If he doesn't talk, convert that into melody. With Harry Dean, it's all in his face."

A Bar in Santa Fe

The story that became *Paris, Texas* was very much circling in Sam Shepard's head as he sat in a bar in Santa Fe, New Mexico, one night in 1983. The bar was crowded with movie people and fans in town for the film festival that had brought him there. It wasn't called *Paris, Texas* then. It was *Motel Chronicles,* the same title of the patchwork of sketches, ideas, characters, and memoir he'd published in 1982. Ideas from that book, more than characters or scenes, became the seeds of *Paris, Texas,* and he'd turned them over to his friend Wim Wenders to develop into a screenplay.

One sketch from the book, however, does come close. A man looks down at his few belongings in a "smashed suitcase" on a hot desert highway, and he asks himself whether he "should try to bring her something back. . . . Some memento so at least she'd think he'd been doing more than nothing. Just drifting all these months." He sees there's nothing there "worth saving." He even pulls off the clothes he's wearing, leaves all of it, and walks naked "straight out into open land."

"There was an alchemy between Sam and myself," Wenders would later say. "Sam had never written a script before. . . . We had no story at all. We talked about what we'd like to do, and everything overlapped. Sam and I worked together like twin brothers."

The first kernel of the story became Travis Henderson, "a stubborn, catatonic, strange man who comes out of another world and seems to be going nowhere," Wenders said. "When Sam and I sat down in 1982, this was our first idea." At one point during the story's development, as they traveled back to Los Angeles from Texas, he and Shepard fueled their imaginations by listening to another blues singer, Mississippi's Skip James, whose "Devil Got My Woman," "Hard Luck Child," and "Hard Time Killin' Floor Blues" are some of the most eerie and woebegone roots music ever sung.

When Shepard had to leave to work on another film, Wenders continued to wrestle with the story, particularly with how to end it. He got writer L. M. Kit Carson on board to help him work on it. Even after filming started, they didn't know how to finish the story. Travis, thanks to his brother's intervention, reunites with his abandoned son. They knew that much. Wenders and Carson finally got the story to where Travis meets his estranged wife, Jane, in a Houston peep show. "For two weeks I sat in the hotel, and I had to figure out how to continue the story," Wenders said. "I wrote ten pages of a rough treatment and sent it to Sam." Shepard called Wenders at six in the morning and read him the dialogue for the scene line by line. Wenders, in his German accent, dictated to Carson the lines of what would become the film's most famous scene.

Shepard "turned it into what became the rest of the movie," Wenders said. "Before, the film kind of meandered. Here everything fell into place, thanks to Sam."

Ending a story had always been a problem for the German director. "I've never been able to imagine the end of any story," he said. "I can come up with ten beginnings and maybe a middle."

Working without a finished script was familiar territory for Wenders. His earlier film *Wrong Move* (1975) had followed line for line noted German playwright Peter Handke's script, something that made Wenders feel too restricted, so his next film, *Kings of the Road* (1976) was made entirely with "no script, only an itinerary," Wenders later said.

With *Paris, Texas*, when Shepard was away, Wenders and Carson worked hard to stay true to the writer's unique sense of the West, a boundless, iconic fixture in the American imagination that embodied both guilt and innocence as well as endless possibility and ruined opportunity, a rapidly-changing-and-not-for-the-better region that had haunted him since Shepard's early days as a stable hand and sheep shearer on the family farm in California.

Both Wenders and Shepard were poets of alienation. The son of an alcoholic father, Shepard probed the broken dreams and promises of family life as much as he did man's failed stewardship of the land. He was at the top of his powers as both a writer and an actor in 1983, winning an Oscar nomination for his performance as test pilot Chuck Yeager in *The Right Stuff* that year. Shifting from the wildly experimental writing of his early days to more conventional dramatic forms, he had earned a Pulitzer Prize for his play *Buried Child* five years before.

Wenders had grown up in war-destroyed Düsseldorf, Germany, surrounded by the carpet-bombed ruins of what had once been a leading city in Germany's Industrial Revolution. Like many Germans, only more so, Wenders developed a complicated relationship with America. As one of the leading voices in the German New Cinema that would shake the world of film in the 1960s and 1970s, he deeply admired the American iconography of John Ford's great Westerns and the dark, brooding world of film noir that was so uniquely American in the hands of directors such as Nicholas Ray and Samuel Fuller, but that also ironically was the bequeathal to Hollywood of German and Austrian émigrés including Fritz Lang, Billy Wilder, Robert Siodmak, and Otto Preminger. Yet Wenders resisted America's postwar pull on German culture and ideas, particularly in film. "The Yanks have colonized our subconscious," Hanns Zischler's Robert Lander tells Rudiger Volger's Bruno Winter in *Kings of the Road*. Wenders yearned for a revitalized German cinema that could connect his generation of filmmakers with the Golden Era of Lang, G. W. Pabst, F. W. Murnau, and the other German Expressionist filmmakers of the 1920s without dragging along with it the embarrassment of the cinema of the Nazi years.

The challenge that faced the New German Cinema is clearly stated in the young filmmakers' initial declaration of independence, the Oberhausen Manifesto of 1962 (Wenders, only seventeen at the time, was not one of the original signatories): "We declare our intention to create the new German feature film. This new film needs new freedoms. Freedom from the conventions of the established industry. Freedom from the outside influence of commercial partners. Freedom from the control of special interest groups. . . . The old film is dead. We believe in the new one."

Wenders was one of those European film talents who "prowled the lot" at Francis Ford Coppola's American Zoetrope Studio in the late 1970s and early 1980s, and Coppola gave him the opportunity to direct his first American film. He had already distinguished himself in Germany and Europe with his noirish *The American Friend* (1977), starring his perennial favorite actor, Bruno Ganz, and the New Hollywood's most notorious bad boy, Dennis Hopper. His brooding, existential road trilogy, *Alice in the Cities* (1974), *Wrong Move* (1975), and *Kings of the Road* (1976), had made him rival Rainer Werner Fassbinder as the leader of the New German Cinema.

Filmmaker Michael Almereyda, in an essay that accompanies the Criterion Collection edition of the three films, called the trilogy "Hitchcock, Anthony Mann, Nicholas Ray, Walker Evans, Edward Hopper, blues-based rock and roll"–influenced films that "seem at once minimal and romantic, austere and lyrical, and "at a remove from the ferocity, the expressive frenzy" that one sees in the work of the other great New German Cinema filmmakers like Werner Herzog and Rainer Werner Fassbinder."

"A road movie for me is a way of life, an itinerary," Wenders told German writer Roger Willemsen, "and like all itineraries, I hope I get somewhere, a linear form, and there's always something waiting at the end of the road," perhaps "a crossroads where you have to make a decision."

With *Hammett,* based on Joe Gores's novel about writer and former detective Dashiell Hammett's return to the gumshoe life to help an old buddy, Wenders had an opportunity to plumb his beloved Americana at its most scintillating—the hard-boiled, mean-streets world of writers like Hammett, Raymond Chandler, and James Cain—and recruit some Old Hollywood–era veterans to help him do it. With Frederic Forrest as the detective and Marilu Henner as his heroine neighbor, Wenders assembled one of the greatest collections of character actors ever in a movie—led by Elisha Cook Jr. (who had played Wilmer Cook in John Huston's 1941 classic *The Maltese Falcon,* based on Hammett's novel), who, as the gun-toting, former radical cabbie Eli in *Hammett* gets to utter one of the film's most delicious lines. Asked by Marilu Henner's Kit Conger if he truly was a former IWW Wobbly, Eli tells her, "Naw, that's just Hammett talkin'. What I am now is sort of an anarchist, with syndicalist tendencies."

What Wenders ran into, however, was the buzz saw of Coppola's post–*The Godfather* and *Apocalypse Now* ego, yet unfazed by the coming failure of *One from the Heart* and demanding obeisance from those who had contracted with The Genius. Neither Coppola nor Wenders could know that *Hammett* would contribute to Zoetrope's bankruptcy. The film took five years to make, and, when it was finally released, met with a slew of negative reviews and failure at the box office. Wenders had wanted Shepard to write the screenplay. The studio said no. "The studio only saw that he'd never made a screenplay," Wenders later said. Wenders had also wanted Shepard to play the lead role. The studio said no. He even made two versions of the film, the first filmed on location at various points in Hammett's San Francisco, the second entirely on a sound stage. Nothing remains today of the first version. He lamented a process that he considered "impersonal" in which "the story and the images don't belong to me. The story and the images belong to the studio, the producer."

For all its troubles, *Hammett* has tons of charm—and a loyal fan base today that includes this writer—with its Old Hollywood cast members and the campy-but-rich and noirish atmosphere that befitted its detective-turned-writer namesake. It is a strange outlier from much of the rest of Wenders's films, a body of work that tends toward the open road, the great beyond, such as in his road movie trilogy and in *Paris, Texas*. He even named his production company Road Movies Filmproduktion.

For Wenders, the next film was going to be different. "I had come to America and did *The State of Things, Lightning on Water* (a 1980 documentary about filmmaker Nicholas Ray), *Hammett*, and I hadn't done what I wanted to do. I couldn't go back to Europe without this." He was going on the road again with Sam Shepard's story. He traveled to Texas. So did Shepard. Wenders remembered Monte Hellman's 1978 Western *China 9, Liberty 37*—Hellman's last film with Warren Oates and one that also starred Sam Peckinpah as a Ned Buntline–like dime novelist—and visited the two east Texas towns of China and Liberty as he scouted locations. "Wenders knew of the movie I made," Hellman told me in a March 2018 interview. "He knew the title was based on two towns, so he made a pilgrimage to those towns and sent me stationery that had the names of the towns on them." Wenders also checked out nearby Port Arthur, partly because he was a Janis Joplin fan and that was her hometown. This would become the location for the film's peep-show scene. Much of *Paris, Texas* would be shot in remote southwest Texas around Terlingua, in the Big Bend region near the Mexican border—a place that was "difficult to get there, to say the least," Wenders described it—as well as in other locations, including Los Angeles and Houston.

In some ways, *China 9, Liberty 37*, though an inferior film, anticipates *Paris, Texas*, as does the oft-cited John Ford film *The Searchers*, the 1956 John Wayne classic that's also about a desert wanderer and a lost woman. Hellman's

Western is another journey through the Texas landscape with protagonists haunted by their past. As does Travis, Fabio Testi's Clayton Drumm will leave his love behind because he knows he can't give her what she needs. Plus, as Wenders will do in *Paris, Texas,* and as many German directors have had a penchant to do, Hellman makes skillful use of mirrors in his film to probe a "landscape . . . [that] is essentially an interior one" where "personal dilemmas can be confronted and eventually resolved," in the words of Hellman scholar Brad Stevens.

Wenders wanted Shepard to play the lead in *Paris, Texas.* With his lean, handsome, yet world-weary face, Shepard looked the part. However, this time Shepard said no. He would be too close to the part, he told his friend. In Travis Henderson, he saw too much of Sam Shepard with his upended sense of family and its long trail of pain, disaffection, self-destruction, and guilt. Travis is a Shepardian character, to be sure, adrift in a strange, surreal West, an in-between world where he can't figure out how to reconcile the past with the present but searches vaguely for roots, the place where he began, where his parents first made love: Paris, Texas. "I started out there," Travis says at one point. What that return will resolve or mean to him, he doesn't know.

These were some of Shepard's thoughts as he sipped his tequila that night in Santa Fe. Then at one point he looked across the bar and spotted a familiar face in the crowd, a face that was more than familiar, a face that was lean like his but older, as etched and lined and life-hardened as the outcroppings in Monument Valley: the face of Harry Dean Stanton.

"His face is the story," Shepard would later say.

Sure, Harry Dean was a Kentuckian—and later in life Shepard would himself move to Kentucky to tend his thoroughbreds, and it's where he would die, too. However, Harry Dean was a Kentuckian who had swallowed enough trail dust in all those *Gunsmoke, Rawhide,* and *Laramie* episodes to claim a stake out West. Before long, the two were drinking tequila together.

Those TV Westerns, police procedurals, and cops-and-robbers shows over the years had earned Harry Dean a good living, but his more recent roles in *Straight Time, Wise Blood,* and *Death Watch* had given him a taste for something better, more substantial.

"I want to play something of some beauty or sensitivity," Harry Dean said into his glass that night as Shepard listened. "I'm sick of the roles I've been playing."

The two downed a few more tequilas. A Mexican sang from a nearby stage. They were getting drunk, but the writer was studying his friend's face as they tipped their glasses. He had the role Harry was searching for in mind. All he had to do was clear it with Wim.

Wenders, with his partiality toward character actors, knew Harry Dean's work, and he admired it. He'd seen him in Monte Hellman's *Two-Lane Blacktop* and that same year as Dr. Oliver Ludwig in *Young Doctors in Love* (1982), as well as in other films "when he didn't have to do anything." Even "the worst movies with Harry were always good and constantly remarkable," he said. Harry Dean had been in Coppola's disastrous *One from the Heart* with Wenders's *Hammett* star Frederic Forrest and with Nastassja Kinski (in her first American film), whom Wenders would cast as Harry Dean's lost wife, Jane, in *Paris, Texas*. Still, Wenders had some concerns. All those years in Hollywood, and Harry Dean had never played a lead role. "People questioned whether he could play lead after thirty years of playing supporting parts."

Shepard pushed hard and successfully for Harry Dean, however. "Every actor who ever sees him admires him for his craftsmanship, what he does," he'd later say in Sophie Huber's documentary about Harry Dean, *Partly Fiction*.

Two weeks after they drank tequila together at that Santa Fe bar, Shepard gave Harry Dean a call. "I want you to play the lead in this film," Shepard said.

No completed script existed yet for what would become *Paris, Texas*, but Shepard sent what he had. Harry Dean was intrigued, but he had one serious question. He got in touch with Shepard.

"Why aren't you doing it?" Harry Dean asked him.

"It'd be too indulgent," the writer responded.

Harry needed more assurance. He was fifty-seven, Shepard was forty. Nastassja Kinski would play Travis Henderson's wife, and she was twenty-two. "I want to know if you both [Shepard and Wenders] are totally convinced that I'm right for the part," Harry Dean wanted to know.

"We want you for the part," Shepard told him.

"Then yes."

Casting the right actor for a role is crucial to the art of filmmaking. "You have to have an eye who is going to be good on screen," Werner Herzog, Wenders's fellow leader of the German New Cinema, told me in September 2017. "It is something you cannot learn in film school. You learn it in life. You learn it from very profound experiences, solitude, hunger. . . . To know the heart of man . . . what is deep inside somebody that can be made visible on the screen."

For Harry Dean, Travis Henderson would become the role of a lifetime. As he told Sean O'Hagan of the *Guardian* in 2013, "After all these years,

I finally got the part I wanted to play. If I never did another film after *Paris, Texas* I'd be happy."

Cast and Crew Come Together

Wenders began putting his team together. He knew the work of Nastassja Kinski well. He'd cast her in her very first feature him, *Wrong Move,* the second in Wenders's Road trilogy. Kinski, the daughter of the notorious wild man of German film, Klaus Kinski, was discovered by Wenders's wife in a Munich disco when she was only twelve. She was just thirteen when she made *Wrong Move,* a film based on Goethe's 1795 bildungsroman, *Wilhelm Meister's Apprenticeship.* She plays Mignon, a mute street urchin/pickpocket/acrobat who is bound to an exploitative grifter and former Nazi and who subtly seduces the film's main character, the wandering writer Wilhelm, played by one of Wenders's perennial lead stars, Rüdiger Vogler. Kinski, strikingly beautiful with her pouting lips and deep-set eyes, fit naturally into the role of Jane in *Paris, Texas,* her German nationality well concealed under her impressive Texas accent. In her own life, Kinski had been abandoned by her father, a violently passionate and emotional German actor once described by his frequent director Werner Herzog as "pestilence personified" and best known to American audiences for his work with Herzog and for supporting roles in films like *Doctor Zhivago* (1965) and *For a Few Dollars More* (1965). Estranged from her mother as well, Kinski brought real-life experience to her role as a woman who had been abandoned by her husband. In fact, as writer David Jenkins has pointed out, abandonment is a recurrent theme with the characters Kinski has played throughout her career—from *Tess* (1979) to *One from the Heart* and *Paris, Texas* to *The Claim* (2001). "Over Kinski hovers the fearful cloud of her aberrant father and his abandonment of her."

With *Paris, Texas,* Wenders would later say, Kinski "reinvented herself" after the failures of *One from the Heart* and *Cat People* (1982), both major money losers and clear signs of the decline of the New Hollywood.

Playing Travis Henderson's brother, Walt, in *Paris, Texas* was veteran actor Dean Stockwell, who began his career in 1943 at the age of six on a Broadway stage and went on to countless television appearances as well as noteworthy films such as *The Boy with Green Hair* (1948) and award-winning and award-nominated roles in *Gentleman's Agreement* (1947), *Compulsion* (1959), *Long Day's Journey into Night* (1962), and *Married to the Mob* (1989).

Several years after *Paris, Texas*, he would score with a new generation of fans as costar of the television series *Quantum Leap* (1989–1993).

An artist and music lover as well as an actor who was once considered James Dean's rightful successor, Stockwell had hung out with the writers of the Beat Generation in the 1950s, lived in San Francisco's Haight-Ashbury in the mid- to late 1960s, befriended people like musician Neil Young and actor Dennis Hopper, and a couple years after *Paris, Texas* would join Hopper in the cast of David Lynch's *Blue Velvet* (1986). In the early 1960s, he was briefly married to actress Millie Perkins, who starred in Monte Hellman's *The Shooting, Ride in the Whirlwind,* and *Cockfighter.* She was also matron of honor for Sandra Knight at Knight and Jack Nicholson's wedding in 1962, with Harry Dean as Nicholson's best man.

By the time *Paris, Texas* came along, however, Stockwell had become discouraged with acting and the parts he was offered and had even obtained his real estate license in order to begin a new career. Stockwell was eyed for a role in *Paris, Texas* even before Harry Dean, and he, like Sam Shepard, encouraged Wenders to cast his friend as Travis. They often would talk together over coffee during filming.

The other major cast members in *Paris, Texas* included eight-year-old Hunter Carson, son of writer L. M. Kit Carson and actress Karen Black. Carson played the son of Travis and Jane Henderson, whose abandonment by both parents is a key element of the story. French actress Aurore Clément played Walt's wife, Anne, who's French and thus adds a twist to the film's title; and Austrian actor and director Bernard Wicki played Dr. Ulmer, the physician who checks Travis after his four-year sojourn in the Mohave Desert. Young Hunter, whose father also worked on the film's script, even helped a little with the script himself.

In the commentary to the Criterion Collection edition of the film, Wenders said, "Hunter himself came up with the idea of saying 'Goodnight, Dad' to both his dads"—Walt, his surrogate father, and Travis, his real father—after Walt brings Travis back home from the desert.

To complete his team, Wenders hired his old reliables Peter Przygodda, a fellow German, to do editing and Dutch cinematographer Robby Müller to handle the camera. Both had worked with Wenders on the road films, *The American Friend,* and other work. Müller had just finished shooting Alex Cox's *Repo Man* with Harry Dean.

With Müller, Wenders once said, "we would dream it up a little bit, the atmosphere of the film, and then I would leave it completely to Robby to find the light." Director Jim Jarmusch, some of whose best work featured Müller behind the camera, said Müller "is like some kind of Dutch interior painter from the Vermeer or de Hooch kind of school, that just got born in the wrong century."

Jarmusch, a young production assistant on Wenders's 1980 documentary about dying director Nicholas Ray's last days, *Lightning over Water,* later worked with Müller in *Down by Law* (1986), *Mystery Train* (1989), *Dead Man* (1995), and *Ghost Dog: The Way of the Samurai* (1999). "He doesn't really light from the outside in like most people," Jarmusch said. "He doesn't think of try-ing to light the characters at a dramatic moment or line. He lights instead, in a way, from what he interprets the emotional content of a scene to be, dis-cussing it with me—which I found rare and interesting."

Paris, Texas showed audiences "Müller at his most entrancingly poetic," writer Ryan Gilbey of the *Guardian* said in his obituary of Müller in July 2018. Müller, who had grown up in Indonesia and studied at the Netherlands Film Academy, was a master of the long take and the medium shot, preferring it to close-ups, and above all sought to get the best lighting for his shots. Müller's use of "the magic of the Polaroid filter" and of bifocal, or split focal, lens for hard-to-get shots helped make *Paris, Texas* the film it became, Wenders said.

Müller liked the pace Wenders set in working on a film. "I never had the impression that we are going for something that we have to get. No one is impatient. We have all the time to think how we're going to do it."

For Wenders, the music was as important as the cast or crew, something true in all his films. His first film was dedicated to the 1960s rock group The Kinks. His film *Alice in the Cities* was inspired in part by Chuck Berry's *Memphis, Tennessee,* a tale of an estranged father and daughter, and Berry is featured in the film singing the song at a rock concert. "The music is never added to a film," Wenders said. "It's as important as what happens to the char-acters. It is a main character." As for *Paris, Texas,* "there is only one music in the film, only Ry Cooder."

Although some rumored that Wenders initially considered Bob Dylan to compose the film's score, the director maintained that Cooder was always his choice. "From the first time I heard Ry Cooder's music I wanted to work with him. I dreamed of working with him."

"He calls me and says, 'I'm making a movie,' and I said okay," Cooder recalled. Then Wenders's second sentence was, 'I'd like for you to do the music." Cooder showed up at the studio the next day and had the music recorded within thirty-six hours.

Filming Begins

The story that took years to evolve and remained unfinished even after the cameras began rolling is a simple one. Travis Henderson has been wandering the desert for four years after drink and jealousy led him to abandon his wife, Jane, and their son, Hunter. He's trying to find Paris, Texas, "where I started out." After the abandonment, Jane left the boy with Travis's brother, Walt, and his wife, Anne, in Los Angeles. Walt leaves home to find Travis and, when he does, convinces Travis to come back with him. Travis reunites with Hunter, and both leave to find Jane. Travis spots her in Houston and tracks her down to a sleazy peepshow, where they encounter each other on opposite sides of a trick, see-through mirror. He tells Jane where Hunter is, and as she finds the boy Travis disappears again, this time forever.

Filming took place in the fall of 1983, and problems inevitably arose with multiple locations, restricted timing, and budgetary woes. The film was a German-French coproduction with no US funding. Kinski only had a week to shoot, and she became pregnant by Egyptian film producer Ibrahim Moussa toward the end of production, once even fainting on the set. Troubles with the Teamsters began when they realized Wenders was using nonunion crew members from France and Germany. Plus, the workers were in the country with only tourist visas, not work permits. "They didn't blow the whistle on us, which was cool after all," Wenders told me in my interview with him. "They only demanded we employed a maximum amount of their drivers for the shoot." These wranglings, however, shortened the shooting schedule to five weeks. Then the Teamsters noticed Wenders was driving his own car and insisted he hire a Teamster driver. "That was a condition I couldn't possibly agree to," Wenders said. "I needed to drive myself in order to be able to make this film." So they reached a compromise: Wenders would join the Teamsters in order to be able to drive his own car. "I accepted and gladly paid my dues. After all, I proudly presented my Teamster card some-times on American freeways when I was stopped for speeding. It always had the most amazing effect that the highway patrols saluted me and let me go without a fine."

Writer-director-professor Allison Anders, who served as production assistant for *Paris, Texas,* said Wenders was impressive in handling the stand-off. "I'll never forget watching Wim, who is tall, talking with these big Teamsters. Those union bosses looked seven feet tall. He held his own, and we got back up running again."

With the film's ongoing financial and other struggles, Anders joked with Wenders that he was living in real life what he had depicted in his previous film *The State of Things* (1982), which deals with a director who runs out of money and film. Wenders told her, "The production reflects what the film is about," and that this was true of every film ever made.

For Wenders, it was important to shoot the film on location and in chronological order. On location meant suffering through 110 degrees Fahrenheit in the southwest Texas heat, and chronological order meant shuffling back and forth between southwest Texas, Los Angeles, and Houston in east Texas. Anders remembered those shifting locations. "I was a young assistant, we shot first in Texas, then road-tripped to Los Angeles, and then I went back to Texas, in story sequence—rather than doing what most producers would insist on: shooting all the Texas stuff at once, then doing the LA chunk out of order."

Wenders, who would do much the same for his other films, going back to *Alice in the Cities* in 1973, said that filming in chronological order helps the actor in developing the role. "It was crucial for Harry to shoot this in chronological order, to build his relationship with his brother" and the other characters, he believed.

Harry Dean faced challenges he'd never faced before in more than three decades of acting. He says nothing the first twenty-six minutes of the film, forcing him to rely only on facial expressions or body movements to communicate. His first word in the film is "Paris," and it's a word that becomes key to the mystery that he is. Going from silence to speech, Harry Dean has to navigate Travis's tentative reentry into the world, no easy task. Then he has to navigate a kind of rapprochement with his son. Wenders's approach was to step back and let the actors do what comes naturally to them for the scene. "Let them do the scene first, and then we'd figure out the shots," Wenders said. "It liberated me."

Travis's inscrutability was itself a challenge. Production assistant Allison Anders's major task was to run lines with Harry Dean, something she had never done with any professional actor before. "Harry was in the trailer, and Dean Stockwell, and Harry was frustrated. What was going on in Travis's head? Is he catatonic? I burst out that I had been catatonic when I was a young girl. I wrote a poem about it, and I just happened to have had that poem with me. I don't know why. Harry grilled me. 'When you weren't talking, what was going on in your head?' I told him my experience. Harry said, 'When you talked after your voice came back, what was it like? Was it shaky?'

I said, no, it just came out. I learned that an actor can take an experience I went through and use that. It happened so organically."

Another frustration was the lack of a finished script. "It was shocking for Harry Dean and the crew not knowing what was going on," assistant director Claire Denis said. "Wim took advantage of it. He felt free, a sort of special call for Wim not knowing what was going on. I would freak out."

When Shepard finally called in the lines for the peep-show scene and the conclusion—what Wenders called the equivalent of two one-act plays—time was short because of Kinski's limited days on the set, and twenty pages of lines had to be learned fast. "Nastassja had forty-eight hours to drum the lines into Harry Dean," Wenders told interviewer Roger Willemsen. "He had a lot of lines. Harry Dean had never learned more than two sentences together his entire life."

Harry Dean complained. "I can never learn this in a matter of days," he told Wenders. "It's completely out of the question." Kinski, who herself had pages of lines to learn, prodded him. "We can do it, Harry. We can do it together!" Day and night they went over the lines, and when Kinski needed sleep, Allison Anders filled in for her. "In the end, when we just had to resume shooting and I couldn't possibly delay the scenes any longer, Harry had interiorized those huge monologues completely," Wenders told me.

At that point Harry Dean "was so enamored with the text" that he insisted they shoot his two scenes "in one go." Wenders said he agreed, even though it was a costly request requiring multiple rolls of additional film. "I agreed to this insane approach to honor the incredible effort on the part of the actors to memorize these dialogues by heart."

Dealing with a child actor can also be a test for an older actor, and Harry Dean and Hunter Carson had to figure out a working relationship. "He brought the kid in and we did this scene," Harry Dean later said. "The kid said it was boring. I wanted to say 'Fuck off.' I don't talk down to a kid. There was this cup, a Styrofoam cup, full of water, and the kid says, 'Will you pour this cup of water on your head?' I poured half of it on my head and left some, and I said, 'You pour the rest on your head.' He looked around to see where his father was, didn't see him, and then he threw the rest of it in his face. It was like blood brothers, like a contract. We trusted each other from then on."

Even after Wenders and Shepard finally came up with an ending, Harry Dean had problems. "When Wim said you're not going back with your family, I fuckin' wanted to kill him." Eventually he understood the point of Travis's final departure. "The character was just like that, not altogether, like myself, not ready to accept the responsibility of dealing with her or his romantic obsession with her or with the tenderness he would have had to give to the kid."

In my interview with Wenders, the director recalled lengthy discussions with Harry Dean about the ending, and even 20th Century Fox got involved. "Harry felt that Travis had deserved this family. I felt he had made up for the past, but that his son and wife had a better chance alone, just the two of them, than with him. I felt that Travis leaving them was a heroic act, and that this act would take much more courage than trying to reestablish that little family. The happy ending, in my book, would have been phony. Harry later on saw my point. 20th Century Fox, who released the film, made another effort to convince me. They wanted me to do 'just one more shot': Travis making a U-turn in the end. I declined that, much to their dismay."

What resulted from all the back-and-forth was a layered performance that arguably is the best of Harry Dean's long career. As they went from scene to scene, Wenders began to see Harry Dean and Travis Henderson merge into one person. Everything in Harry Dean's life, from his difficult parentage to his failed relationships with women and his own uncertainty as to whether he himself was a father, became a kind of biography of both Harry Dean Stanton and Travis Henderson.

Wenders recalled a poignant moment with Harry Dean as they were wrapping up their work on the film. "At the very end of the shoot, one night Harry opened his heart and told me that he had identified so entirely with the part of Travis as he himself had a son that he had abandoned. He told it to me in tears, and it dawned on me how much of his life Harry had really invested in his performance."

Harry Dean often talked about the possibility of a son, and a quarter century after *Paris, Texas* even had dinner one evening at Ago with a man named Jeremy who had changed his last name to Stanton and claimed to be that long-lost son. Harry Dean said little at that dinner, however, but denied that the man was his son. His relatives Sara Stanton and Jim Huggins Jr. were there, and so was Jeremy's wife. Harry Dean "sat at the opposite end of the table and never made conversation with them," Sara Stanton said. Huggins agreed. "It was a strange and awkward dinner. If Harry Dean ever had kids he never claimed them."

The great stage, film, and television writer Paddy Chayefsky once wrote eloquently about the kind of performance Harry Dean gave in *Paris, Texas,* although the performance he described was by the actor Eddie Albert in his role as Charlie in Chayefsky's *The Bachelor Party* in 1953. "Under Eddie

Albert's casual performance lie layer upon layer of meticulous thinking," Chayefsky said. "It is much easier to play an articulate character than an introspective one, for in the latter case the actor has to achieve his effects by silent relationships. . . . I watched Eddie Albert carefully build his part, thought by thought, gesture by gesture. . . . Piece by piece he reconstructs the moment just as it would be if it were happening to him."

Harry Dean's silence for the first half-hour of *Paris, Texas* forces the audience to study his face even harder, "his lean face and hungry eyes" and the "sad poetry" they create, as Roger Ebert wrote. *New York Times* writer Manohla Dargis also wrote about that face. "As the years tugged at Mr. Stanton's face, pulling down the corners of his mouth and further hollowing out his cheeks, his face became a fantastic landscape. Mr. Wenders understood its power beautifully."

Walking for the first time into the eye of Robbie Müller's camera along that desolate landscape, "on foot and wholly alone save for a watchful eagle, wearing a red cap and an inexplicable double-breasted suit, Travis looks like a former cowboy or maybe a businessman who took a wrong turn," Dargis wrote. "He looks like someone Dorothea Lange might have photographed during the Great Depression. He looks like the American West, all sinew, dust and resolve."

Silence was long one of the powerful components in Harry Dean's acting. In his personality, too. His friend George Hatzis, an actor and musician from San Francisco, recalled that trait in Harry Dean when they would go to his favorite restaurant, Ago in West Hollywood. "He would tell me, 'When you learn to be still and quiet, this is the most powerful thing you will have in life.' He would bet that I couldn't say anything for a half-hour, and we would go out, and people would look at the clocks." Hatzis said a cousin told him once that a friend of hers watched the two of them at Ago and said, "It was the strangest thing. They just sat there and did not talk to each other for forty-five minutes."

"I think everybody talks too much," Harry Dean said in an interview about *Paris, Texas.* "Everybody knows that." He recalled something about silence Marlon Brando told him during the filming of *Missouri Breaks.* "He told me about these Indians in the Southwest who'd come to town and stand at this corner, and maybe someone would join them and they'd not say a word for twenty minutes. There's no need to talk."

As powerful as that silence was, Wenders said, "it was so good to finally hear Harry Dean speak, so good to hear Harry Dean with his tender voice. Such a beautiful voice." Nastassja Kinski's Jane will tell Travis later when they meet on opposite sides of that mirror in the peep show, "Every man has your voice." Harry Dean–Travis Henderson was indeed a kind of Everyman, the lone wanderer of the classic fifteenth-century morality play who loses all that he has, save what good he can do for others. It would not be the last time Harry Dean played Everyman.

Paris, Texas gave Harry Dean opportunities to show his ability as an actor in a variety of ways. It was a film that stretched him beyond what he had learned at the Guignol Theatre and the Pasadena Playhouse, and in Jeff Corey's and Martin Landau's acting classes. No class lesson prepared him for the scene in which he found himself high on the scaffolding of a billboard. "Harry Dean was scared of heights," Wenders said in his commentary on the Criterion Collection DVD of the film. "When he was on the billboard scaffold he couldn't look down." In another scene, Harry Dean and Walt's family are watching an old video of them with Jane when they were all much younger. "Harry had to look a lot younger for the family film, and he did and it wasn't makeup," Wenders said about that scene.

A German Bares the American Soul in Paris

As Wenders exposed what writer Ian Nathan called "the bared American soul" in *Paris, Texas,* he left along the trail a few signposts of his own journey in understanding America. Among his favorite writers is William Faulkner, who probed the "bared American soul" as deeply as any other American writer ever did, and when Travis and Hunter travel to Houston and first spot Jane in a red car, a copy of Faulkner's 1932 novel *Light in August* is in the back seat. In that tale from Faulkner's mythical Yoknapatawpha County in northern Mississippi, where generations of families wrestle with the burden of history, their own and their region's, pregnant young Lena Grove searches for the missing father of her child. In his *Kings of the Road*, Wenders has protagonist Bruno Winter reading Faulkner's 1939 novel *The Wild Palms* through much of the film. That book, like the film, features two protagonists on a journey together, although in the book they're convicts allowed to travel up and down a flooded river in search of stranded victims.

After finding where Jane works, Travis goes to the peep show, where customers hire women to talk with them privately in separate rooms outfitted with a walkie-talkie–like telephone and a one-way mirror that allow the customers to talk with and see the women without the women being able to see the men. The meeting between Travis and Jane is a long, heartbreaking scene that reveals the pain and suffering of both, the tragic destruction of the love that created Hunter, a scene of long monologues, particularly from Travis, that Sam Shepard wrote and that Wenders allowed to be filmed without interruption.

"People become so impatient today, so fast-paced," Wenders has said about his shooting of that scene. "I still think it was the right decision to leave it with the actors and the dialogue and not rely on my editing for the rest of the scene. The only thing that is happening is a slight camera movement."

Wenders's use of the one-way mirror in that scene as well as the rearview mirror in Travis's 1959 Ford Ranchero in an earlier scene of *Paris, Texas* reflected his own roots in German film. German filmmakers love mirrors, the great historian and film writer Lotte H. Eisner once wrote. She dedicated an entire chapter of her classic 1952 book on German Expressionist film, *The Haunted Screen,* to shadows and mirrors. "In their trips through the looking-glass the metaphysically-inclined Germans go much deeper than Alice (that essentially very materialistic little girl), and of course much further than Cocteau," she wrote. "Life is merely a kind of concave mirror projecting inconsistent figures which vacillate like the images of a magic lantern, sharp-focused when they are small and blurring as they grow." From Paul Wegener's *The Student of Prague* (1913) and Fritz Lang's *The Spiders* (1919) to F. W. Murnau's *The Last Laugh* (1924) and G. W. Pabst's *The Joyless Street* (1925), the German Expressionist filmmakers made much use of mirrors and mirror-like distortions.

With her groundbreaking work on German film, its traditions, and its contributions to world cinema, Eisner was a major inspiration for the film-makers of the New German Cinema. In fact, Wenders dedicated *Paris, Texas* to her. His colleague Werner Herzog, who in 1974 walked 425 miles from Munich to Paris to visit the ailing Eisner, waxed eloquent about her in a 1982 tribute. "You have enabled us to find a link with our own history, and more important than that: because you have given us a legitimacy."

German Expressionist film had great influence on American film, particularly film noir after World War II. Many of the directors of film noir—Fritz Lang, William Dieterle, Robert Siodmak, and Edgar G. Ulmer—came out of the Expressionism era in Europe and migrated to the United States as Hitler rose to power in Germany and Austria. Even with all its desert sun, *Paris, Texas* qualifies as a noir—in the presence of Harry Dean himself—whom Roger Ebert described as an actor who "long inhabited the darker corners of American noir"—and in Travis Henderson's existential struggle, his alienation from the world around him. At the end, as Jane and Hunter unite in the hotel room where Travis told Jane the boy was, Travis stands below in a parking lot suffused in a shadow-crossed green light, utterly alone, near the car that will take him away forever, as much a ghostlike silhouette as an actual person. In the dark night behind him loom rows of dark buildings watching him through their eye-like lit windows, the brooding, even monstrous gateway through which he must pass to leave. In the center of this final mise-en-scène is a lamppost, brilliantly white, a cross, and it, too, stands between him and the world that awaits him—all of it as pure a noir ending as anything Fritz Lang ever made.

Praised at Cannes, Panned in America

Claire Denis will never forget the reaction of the crowd at the Cannes Film Festival in France that May of 1984 as they watched *Paris, Texas.* "The film had such a grace that it transported people. I could feel the breathing in the room, and the people crying. This is something, of course, very rare." Wenders still remembers sitting on the front row near legendary director John Huston, whose film *Under the Volcano* was in competition with *Paris, Texas* for the prestigious Palme d'Or. When Wenders's film was announced the winner, Huston looked at the German and shrugged with an appreciative smile. Wenders never forgot that either.

Despite the worldwide acclaim a victory at Cannes brings, *Paris, Texas* struggled at the box office in the States, where critics panned it and its limited release hurt as well. It won fans in faraway places like Japan, but a botched release by the distributor Filmverlag der Autoren in West Germany led to limited audiences there, too. Wenders fought a losing legal battle over the release with the distributor, which ironically was created in 1971 as a way to push the work of the independent filmmakers of the New German Cinema.

The reaction in the United States was fierce, and sometimes still is. Richard Brody, film critic for the *New Yorker,* wrote in 2017 that *Paris, Texas* "sold Harry Dean Stanton short," as did Harry Dean's final film, *Lucky.* Harry Dean "had the misfortune of becoming a star in a bad movie," Brody wrote. *Paris, Texas* "is a series of reprocessed moods and tones in which [Wenders] filters his mythologized America back onto American characters and places, resulting in a cinematic echo chamber that also echoes Hollywood's clichéd sentimentality and offers no contrasting practical complexity. . . . Stanton, at the moment that he was ready to soar, was weighed down with an iconography that was neither his own nor as rich as the inner life that he pressed into its service."

Wenders said one reason for such a reaction is that "Americans don't like others showing them themselves. They've always told their stories." Allison Anders said the film dealt with subjects that US filmmakers typically avoid. The idea of a mother leaving her child with her estranged husband's family, as in *Paris, Texas,* or a mother leaving her child with a total stranger, as in Wenders's *Alice in the Cities,* would never be in an American film. "People would have too much to say about it," Anders said. "Yet what happens is a very powerful thing."

Certainly Harry Dean didn't agree with Brody's assessment, and neither did many other critics. "The movie lacks any of the gimmicks used to pump up emotion and add story interest because it doesn't need them," Roger Ebert wrote. "It is fascinated by the sadness of its own truth." *Paris, Texas* "is a love letter to America and American cinema," Nick Roddick wrote. "It now also has something of the feel of a farewell. The world to which Wenders pays homage is vanishing fast: not the desert, which is close to eternal, but the pay phones and diners and motels that used to line the approach to every small US town, now replaced by cell phones and McDonald's and multistory Doubletree Hotels and Quality Inns."

The film has gone on to develop a loyal following—rock singers Kurt Cobain and Elliott Smith called it their favorite film, the Scottish band Texas took its name from the film—and Wenders looks back at it with pride. He sees it as the fulfillment of a long artistic struggle to tell a certain story about the road and about America. "I was able to do everything I've been wanting to do for a long time. I'm very proud of this film. Everything I know how to do I put in this film."

Anders goes so far as to say that *Paris, Texas,* along with Alex Cox's *Repo Man* that same year, set the stage for an entire new era of independent filmmaking in the United States. "*Paris, Texas* and *Repo Man* are the beginnings of the American independent film movement. Those films influenced Jarmusch, us, everyone."

If this assessment is true, Harry Dean, the costar in *Repo Man* and the star in *Paris, Texas,* helped launch a new film movement in America. He had survived the collapse of the New Hollywood and turned to European directors to help carve a future for serious filmmaking at a time when a new generation of Hollywood moguls were mainly interested in the big-buck potential of blockbusters and action-film heroes. Let the moguls and Tom Cruise do their thing. Harry Dean was finally a star. What would his future be?

10

Harry Dean the Punk Icon

Sean Penn's first impression of Harry Dean Stanton was way off base. It was in 1980, and both the then-unknown-but-soon-to-be-rising young star and the quarter-century-older veteran actor were hanging out at the Sherman Way roller-skating rink, an upscale celebrity haunt in the San Fernando Valley where Jack Nicholson, Leonard Cohen, Ringo Starr, and Harry Dean buddy Ed Begley Jr. were often among the clientele.

The Sherman Way rink "was like a roller-skating Studio 54 with lights on and a mirror-ball over the skating floor," Penn told writer Richard T. Kelly in *Sean Penn: His Life and Times*. "I wasn't going to get out on fucking roller skates. . . . I was a wallflower at those things. I used to see Harry Dean, and he was doing *The Black Marble* at the time—I know, because he had a perm. The perm made me think he was gay. Later I saw the movie and reoriented myself." In director Harold Becker's romantic comedy, Harry Dean plays a chain-smoking veterinarian named Philo Skinner who becomes a dog kidnapper to pay off his gambling debts.

A few years later, Penn connected again with Harry Dean, along with actor Mickey Rourke, who was in New York during filming of *Nine and a Half Weeks*. The three spent the week hitting the bars and nightclubs, with Harry Dean and Mickey Rourke helping Penn get over his recent breakup with actress Elizabeth McGovern. By this time, Penn was getting a name for himself after playing a military cadet in *Taps* (1981) and stoned-out surfer Jeff Spicoli in *Fast Times at Ridgemont High* (1982). Back in Los Angeles a couple weeks later, Penn ran into Harry Dean at On the Rox, a private club and another celebrity hangout perched just above the Roxy Nightclub on Sunset Boulevard. It was an hour before midnight, and Harry Dean was drinking alone at the bar.

"So I sat and talked to Harry, and he didn't remember me at all," Penn told Kelly. "No idea who I was. I'd just spent a week as a roommate with him two weeks ago." Harry Dean later talked about the encounter. "He told me he'd been a big fan of mine, watched movies of mine when he was in high school. I'm always glad to be appreciated—like everybody else. I've always been kind of aloof, probably too aloof at times, too standoffish. But I realized—I was affected by the fact—that he regarded me highly. And I was intrigued by him."

As Julie, the On the Rox bartender, served them drinks, Penn found out that Harry Dean was leaving the next day to travel to Cannes, France, to attend the famous international film festival there. *Paris, Texas* would win its highest prize that year, the Palme d'Or.

"Can I go with you?" Penn asked.

"Uh . . . OK," Harry responded.

"I had a passport from going to Mexico to work on *The Falcon and the Snowman*," Penn later told Kelly.

So Harry Dean and Penn flew to France, and Harry Dean let the young actor also stay in his hotel room. Harry Dean was fifty-seven at the time, and Penn was twenty-three. "All he brought with him was a passport and a toothbrush," Harry Dean recalled.

The two stayed together in the room for five days, at the end of which Harry Dean was ready for some private time. "Maybe you should find somewhere else to stay," he told his young admirer. Penn found refuge with actors Joe Pesci and Robert De Niro, both of whom were at Cannes for Sergio Leone's film about Jewish mob bosses in New York's Lower East Side, *Once Upon a Time in America*. De Niro got him a room at the Hotel du Cap.

The "Patron Saint of the Edgy Set"

It was Harry Dean's performance as Bud in *Repo Man* that opened wide the eyes of young Hollywood to an actor who had been making movies since 1956. That role "elevated him to the position of punk icon," Steve Oney wrote, "and thereafter he became one of the few Hollywood old-timers easily embraced by young actors, particularly Sean Penn."

Ian Nathan put it another way. "In the '80s he was ordained as the patron saint of the edgy set, living in a frugal cabin on Mulholland Drive—mattress for a bed and fridge stocked only with beers—nestled between the fortified estates of Nicholson and Marlon Brando. The location served as a metaphor for his place as actor and icon: a humble rebel."

It didn't start with Sean Penn.

Harry Dean had been part of the edgy set ever since the mid-1960s, when a newly separated Jack Nicholson moved into Harry Dean's bachelor pad, what writer Patrick McGilligan called "party central" for the hip crowd in Laurel Canyon. Folks like Cass Elliott and Michelle Phillips of the Mamas and Papas would drop in and turn on. The orgies, booze, and good times eventually got to the point where perennial loner Harry Dean had to bow out. Still, he remained an enigmatic presence, a Zen philosopher in the middle of all the action, yet somehow above it, too. The growing mystique around Harry Dean became evident in Nicholson's quirky Western *Goin' South* in 1978. As horse thief Henry Lloyd Moon, played by Nicholson, sits in jail awaiting the gallows, on the jail cell wall behind him is scrawled the name "H D Stanton," obviously a previous resident.

Harry Dean himself wasn't in the cast of *Goin' South,* but *Saturday Night Live* star John Belushi was, and he, too, was part of the edgy set, and a Harry Dean pal. Four years after *Goin' South,* Harry Dean would be one of several hard-partying celebrities checking in on Belushi the night before he died of a drug overdose at the upscale Chateau Marmont on Hollywood's Sunset Boulevard.

Writers Bob Woodward and Shawn Levy have detailed the events of the fateful evening that stretched from the late hours of Thursday, March 4, into the daylight hours of Friday, March 5, 1982. "De Niro was bopping around town with actor Harry Dean Stanton, and the two kept phoning Belushi to get him to come out and join them, first at Dan Tana's, an Italian restaurant favored by movie people, and then at On the Rox, the exclusive nightclub on Sunset Strip where famous folks could get up to just about anything," Levy wrote in a *Hollywood Reporter* excerpt from his 2019 book *The Castle on Sunset.* "Failing to raise him, they drove over to the Chateau to see if they could coax him into a bit of play. Instead, they found him—and his bungalow—in an awful state. The living room was in shambles—not sloppy, but actually trashed, as if in a rage." Belushi, overweight, disheveled, and in a continual cocaine-, heroin-, Quaalude-, and booze-induced fog those days, emerged from the chaos of his bungalow to tell them to come back later, after they'd partied at On the Rox.

At On the Rox, Harry Dean and De Niro ran into comedian Robin Williams, and they all agreed to meet at Belushi's after Williams finished a performance at the Comedy Store. When Harry Dean and De Niro returned to the Chateau Marmont, however, they were with women, and they went to De Niro's suite, not Belushi's. When Williams called to check on plans, De Niro told him they were busy. Both Williams and De Niro would later swing by Belushi's trashed place but quickly leave. Hours later, Belushi's personal trainer and bodyguard found the thirty-three-year-old actor-comedian in the fetal position in his bed with a pillow covering his head. Repeated efforts to revive him failed. He was dead.

Holding Court at Dan Tana's

When Harry Dean and De Niro tried to coax John Belushi out to Dan Tana's the night before he died, they didn't pick the place at random. The West Hollywood bar and restaurant on Santa Monica Boulevard had been a Harry Dean haunt since the 1960s. For him and many others, it would eventually become Hollywood's equivalent of London's Turks Head Tavern, where Dr. Samuel Johnson, Oliver Goldsmith, Edmund Burke, and the other members of London's eighteenth-century literati met, or the Rose Room in New York's Algonquin Hotel, where Dorothy Parker, Robert Benchley, and other Big Apple bright lights of the so-called Algonquin Round Table met after World War I. In later years, a typical night on the town for Harry Dean was dinner at Ago, an upscale Italian restaurant on Melrose Avenue in West Hollywood partly owned by De Niro, then drinks at Dan Tana's.

Opened in 1964 by its namesake, Dan Tana, a former Yugoslav soccer star, refugee from Marshal Tito's Communist takeover of his country, and part-time actor, the bar and restaurant, with its distinctive plush red walls and cushioned seats, quickly became a favorite haunt. Movie stars and music lovers would stop by before or after a visit just down the street to the historic Troubadour, the venue where comedian Lenny Bruce's performance on October 23, 1962, got him arrested on obscenity charges, where Buffalo Springfield, Joni Mitchell, Neil Young, and James Taylor did key debut performances in their careers in the 1960s, and where Harry Dean and buddy Kris Kristofferson also would make crowds happy with their performances.

"The food is the best consistently of any restaurant I have ever been in my life, the best steaks and lamb chops," actor Dabney Coleman and long-time Harry Dean friend told me in a January 2018 interview. "A great saloon. You ever been to Elaine's in New York? Dan Tana's is the best New York saloon in Los Angeles."

Veteran Dan Tana's bartender Mike Gotovac, like the place's founder a native of old Yugoslavia, said Harry Dean was one of his first customers when he started there in 1968. He often came in with fellow Kentuckian Warren Oates, and sometimes with singers and musicians, including Linda Ronstadt and Kristofferson. Gotovac, a Croatian, said Harry would sometimes break out in song, and would sing in Croatian while sharing with the bartender a

Slivovitz brandy. Then they would go outside and have a cigarette. "I remember one situation that was so funny. One of his friends came in with a woman and said, 'Harry Dean, this is my girlfriend. Can you keep her company till I get back?' Harry Dean's having a drink, she's having a drink, the friend comes back an hour later, and he [Harry Dean] never once opened his mouth, never said one word to the lady, and she said, 'Nice talking with you, Harry.'"

Eventually Harry Dean would become the leader of a growing group at the bar or at a table that would include fellow actors and musicians who would become lifelong friends. Actor Ed Begley Jr., who'd been in the cast of *Cockfighter* along with Harry Dean and Warren Oates, was one of them. "We'd be sitting there, and Buck Henry would walk in, Don Henley, Jack Nicholson, Joni Mitchell, hanging out at the table. Dabney Coleman," Begley told me in August 2018. "He had these friends, and they loved him. He would hold court. It was always just a treat. He was such an icon, even then back in the '70s, working as an actor in Westerns, *Cool Hand Luke.* He was an icon to all of us. He was central to the gathering."

As much as Harry Dean prized hanging out with veteran actors like himself and veterans from the late 1960s, he also enjoyed the respect and admiration he was getting from charter members of the "Brat Pack"—a term coined by *New York* magazine writer David Blum in 1985 and one Harry Dean hated with something of the same passion as "character actor." Among his Brat Packer friends were Belushi and Sean Penn and his superstar wife, Madonna. He hung out with Penn and Madonna in New York and LA restaurants, dance clubs, and movie theaters, and he was a venerated presence at Penn's bachelor party at On the Rox in August 1985. "There were three 'old guys' there: me, [actor Robert] Duvall, and—though he would bristle to be so described—Harry Dean," theater and television director Art Wolff told Penn biographer Richard T. Kelly. "We just sat and commented wryly on all the activity."

Penn's high-school buddy at Santa Monica High School, composer Joseph Vitarelli, remembered Harry Dean and Duvall being a center of attraction at the party. "Someone had arranged for about twenty-five Playboy Bunnies to show up. And the interesting thing is that none of the men were schmoozing with the Bunnies at all. . . . Frankly it was more interesting to talk to Harry Dean and Robert Duvall. So all these beautiful girls were sitting around kind of bored."

The party was a comparatively calm prelude to Penn and Madonna's wedding extravaganza at a friend's home in Malibu (just down from Johnny Carson's house). The Wolfgang Puck–catered wedding featured a half-dozen or more media helicopters buzzing overhead to cover the proceedings, driving a frustrated Penn to write in the sand "FUCK YOU" to the paparazzi snapping photo after photo from overhead and from out of the bushes bordering the grounds. The guest list included Andy Warhol, Diane Keaton, Tom Cruise, and Christopher Walken, who compared the event to "a Fellini movie."

That a nearly sixty-year-old actor with a quarter century of films under his belt fit in such a world was perfectly natural to Sean Penn and Madonna. "Behind that rugged old cowboy face, he's simultaneously a man, a child, a woman—he just has this full range of emotions I really like," Penn told writer Steve Oney. "He's a very impressive soul more than he is a mind, and I find that attractive."

"Harry Dean has got a rebelliousness in him, a freedom, a youthfulness, that even most young people don't have," said Madonna, whom Harry Dean once interviewed with surprising journalistic skill for *Interview Magazine*. "At the same time he has the wisdom of the ages, an Eastern philosophical point of view." Oney went on to say this himself about Harry Dean: "In other words, Stanton is 60 going on 22, a seeker who also likes to drive fast cars, dance all night, and chain-smoke cigarettes with the defiant air of a hood hanging out in the high school boy's room."

Harry Dean once explained why he might have appealed to young people. "I find younger people less conditioned and therefore more alive. I don't take a paternal or authority position with them. I don't play mentor. I try to relate to them on a peer level. I'm trying to function totally in the moment." Harry Dean's readings of philosophers such as Eckhart Tolle echo in such comments, but maybe, too, the fact that he never had to father a child or be an authority or a mentor of one.

"I know he's lonely sometimes," Madonna told Oney, "but I think he's reconciled himself to being a lone figure in the universe."

True, perhaps, but he had not reconciled himself to remaining in a second-tier acting career.

The Frustrations of a Saint

Even a patron saint and a punk icon may want more out of life. Harry Dean was an actor, and getting starring roles in *Repo Man* and *Paris, Texas* had whetted his appetite for better parts. He wanted a new turn, a bigger piece of the pie. He wanted to cast off the toll that decades of languishing in the supporting cast had taken. "Harry always had so much hostility and resentment," producer and casting agent Fred Roos told Steve Oney in 1986. "There was a long period where he couldn't get anything but bit parts, and the frustration level was very high. You read interviews with other character actors, and they're proud of their work, proud of being able to bring a touch of authenticity to a small part. He kept saying, 'I have to get out of this.'"

He thought *Repo Man* and *Paris, Texas* would be the door to more lead roles and a new, higher-level stage in his career. These movies had even earned him a couple of spots on *Late Night with David Letterman,* the first on October 16, 1984, when Letterman introduced him as "the world's greatest character actor." On the show, Harry Dean told a story of an early career role he had in an US Air Force documentary and having to purchase a quick publicity photo, his very first, from a nearby "four for a quarter" photo booth. He appeared again on Letterman's show two days before Christmas in 1985 wearing a hunter's camouflage jacket. He sang a rendition of "Canción Mixteca" from *Paris, Texas* as Letterman and the crowd chuckled.

"The role for Harry Dean really is still out there," Roos said in 1986. "I've been in his corner so long that I'd like to be the one to give it to him, so I'm looking, waiting."

So was Harry Dean. Good roles came, but no lead roles.

Repo Man and *Paris, Texas* were followed by *The Bear,* a biopic of University of Alabama football coach Paul "Bear" Bryant. Gary Busey played Bryant, and Harry Dean played Coach Thomas. Next came *Red Dawn,* which *Repo Man* director Alex Cox once called "the big 'official' youth picture" of the day. Directed by John Milius and starring rising young stars Patrick Swayze and Charlie Sheen (the brother of *Repo Man* costar Emilio Estevez), the film depicts a futuristic world on the brink of World War III, when the Russians and their Cuban and Nicaraguan allies have invaded the United States. Swayze and Sheen play underground guerrillas who call themselves the Wolverines after their school's team name. Their dad, played by Harry Dean, languishes in a reeducation camp awaiting execution. Again Harry Dean is only briefly on screen, but he has the lines many people most remember from the entire movie. "Boys, avenge me!" he tells his sons through the prison fence that separates them. "Avenge me!"

UFOria appeared the year after *Paris, Texas* won the Palme d'Or at Cannes, although the film had been made in 1981. It had languished on the shelves of Universal and 20th Century Fox for years due to their lack of faith in its box-office appeal, a fate somewhat similar to that of *Repo Man.* When it was finally released in 1986, it won critical approval and played to sold-out crowds in New York and did well in Boston, San Francisco, and Los Angeles. The film featured *Laverne and Shirley* television star Cindy Williams as a deeply religious, UFO-obsessed supermarket checker named Arlene who lives in a desert town and meets a cynical drifter named Sheldon, played by Fred Ward. Harry Dean is a car-thieving, revival-tent preacher named Brother Bud, who is an old buddy of Sheldon's. Peter Stack of the *San Francisco Chronicle* called Bud "arguably his [Harry Dean's] most accomplished comic role . . . a bitingly funny performance as a charlatan preacher . . . a lout, heavy on guile, light on scruples. . . . When Bud isn't selling hellfire-and-brimstone in his big tent, he's dealing in stolen cars for Jesus."

The same year as *UFOria*'s release also brought *One Magic Christmas*, a Walt Disney picture with Harry Dean as the guardian angel Gideon, whose task it is to bring poor, worn-down Ginny Grainger, played by Mary Steenburgen, back into the loving-Christmas fold after a series of family trag- edies. Critic Roger Ebert praised the acting, but ultimately panned the film as a "tactical miscalculation" that forced holiday audiences through ninety min- utes of family misery before good triumphed. Ebert, generally one of Harry Dean's biggest fans, questioned his casting in the film. "I'm not sure what to make of Harry Dean Stanton's archangel. . . . He looks like the kind of guy that our parents told us never to talk to."

None of these films was as important for Harry Dean's career as *Fool for Love*, also released in 1985, director Robert Altman's translation of Sam Shepard's play and screenplay onto the big screen. The tale of incest and for- bidden love in a remote Texas desert town starred Shepard, Kim Basinger, and Harry Dean as a harmonica-playing "old man" who hangs around the backwater motel where Basinger's character, May, works. Randy Quaid played May's current boyfriend, Martin. Ultimately the audience learns that the old man is father to both May and her recently returned former lover, Eddie, played by Shepard. The dialogue-heavy film stumbles plotwise on several fronts, but Pierre Mignot's neon-lit cinematography is brilliant and the great strength of the film. "We feel we might be looking at the characters in a story by William Faulkner or Erskine Caldwell," Roger Ebert wrote in his review, "and the visual compositions look inspired by the lurid covers of 1940s paperback novels. The deliberately trashy surface, however, conceals deeper levels of feeling, and by the end of 'Fool for Love' we have witnessed some sort of classic tragedy, set there in the Texas backlands."

In the film, Harry Dean's old man mostly stands around and watches from a distance, but he again scores a memorable line of dialogue when he tells Sam Shepard's Eddie at one point, "I'm actually married to Barbara Mandrell in my mind." Still, it was a film that nearly got made without Harry Dean's participation. Director Altman said Harry Dean and his agent, John Kelly of the Sandy Bresler and Kelly firm, pushed so hard for more money and benefits that he almost lost the part.

"I think Harry Dean's a victim," Altman told Steve Oney in 1986. "He's 60, and he's been doing this all his life, and now he wants adulation and respect. He's so thirsty for it. Not only does he want the acclaim, but he wants the things that our industry uses to confer worth—more money, a bigger makeup trailer. As much as I wanted him in *Fool for Love,* he almost didn't get the part because his agent was gouging us for these things, making outrageous demands. I hope Harry Dean gets beyond this."

Kelly, in an email exchange with this writer, said he has no recollection of what Altman is describing. However, he had this to say about the making of *Fool for Love:* "I represented both Harry and Randy Quaid in that film so the deals were probably made in concert with one another, but there is nothing that stands out as memorable in that process. I think they both earned the same salary, but I can't remember for sure. I do recall that *Fool for Love* was a film produced by Menahem Golan's company, which was often difficult to negotiate with because it was notoriously cheap. It churned out most movies inexpensively, with action films and 'Happy Hooker' type movies being its typical fare. . . . I think working with Mr. Altman and Sam Shepard was an attempt to raise the 'respectability' aspect of Mr. Golan's reputation." He added that he would have remembered the details of the deal if the negotiations had been contentious: "If I ever made a demand about a 'bigger make-up trailer,' I'm certain I would remember! It was never my style nor Harry's."

Harry Dean in the Mainstream

The second half of the 1980s saw Harry Dean go mainstream in many ways. His next film after *Fool for Love* was director John Hughes's *Pretty in Pink,* a $9 million production that grossed $40 million at the box office and made Molly Ringwald a star. A classic coming-of-age tale centered on the strict class system that has forever dominated high-school experience, Ringwald played Andie, a teenager who's smart and loves pink but is from the wrong side of the tracks and yet has a terrible crush on popular rich kid Blane, played by Andrew McCarthy. Her forever friend Duckie, played by Jon Cryer, secretly loves her, but she only has eyes for Blane.

Harry Dean plays Andie's loving but hapless father Jack, underemployed and still pining away for Andie's mother, who dumped him and their daughter three years before. It's the role many moviegoers remember when they think of Harry Dean, the lifelong bachelor cast as loyal single parent. "His most iconic mainstream performance," Zach Vasquez wrote in *Crooked Marquee*. "As Molly Ringwald's depressed but unfailingly supportive father, Stanton manages to elevate John Hughes' thinly sketched material, crafting a truly heartbreaking performance that in a better world would have earned him an Oscar."

Even with its unlikely ending that has Andie finally connecting with Blane at the senior prom and not Duckie, the film has become something of a classic, with a wildly popular soundtrack that featured the title song by the Psychedelic Furs. The 2019 Harry Dean Stanton Fest in Lexington, Kentucky, included an "'80s Prom" after a screening of the film and a costume contest for the person wearing the best *Pretty in Pink*–style clothes. When Harry Dean died in 2017, Molly Ringwald wrote how much working with him meant to her. "Having the chance to work with Harry Dean has been a highlight of my career. In everything he touched, Harry radiated soulfulness and complete authenticity."

Harry Dean returned to television in 1987 after a four-year hiatus—his last TV appearance had been on a segment of the sitcom *Laverne and Shirley* in 1982—this time to star in an hour-long segment of *Shelley Duvall's Faerie Tale Theatre*, the twenty-sixth and final segment of that 1982 to 1987 series. The award-winning series, inspired by the TV show *Shirley Temple's Storybook* in the late 1950s and early 1960s, featured some of the top actors and stars in the business—Art Carney, Liza Minnelli, Alan Arkin, Vanessa Redgrave, Robin Williams, Helen Mirren, Roger Vadim, James Earl Jones, Teri Garr, even Mick Jagger—bringing to life famous fairy tales by the Grimm Brothers, Hans Christian Andersen, and others, including "Rumpelstiltskin," "Sleeping Beauty," "Pinocchio," and "The Pied Piper of Hamelin."

Francis Ford Coppola directed Harry Dean in the title role in "Rip Van Winkle," with Coppola's sister, Talia Shire, playing his wife and Harry Dean's *Paris, Texas* costar Hunter Carson playing his son. Also in the segment were Ed Begley Jr. and Sean Penn's brother, Christopher. Coppola's father, Carmine, provided the music.

Based on the classic Washington Irving tale about a mid-eighteenth-century farmer who wanders into the Catskill Mountains to escape his nagging wife only to fall asleep for twenty years after drinking a mysterious brew, Coppola's rendition cost roughly $650,000—miniscule compared to the $58 million budget of the feature film he'd just finished, *The Cotton Club*—and took six days to shoot. It was the director's first foray into television, and he saw it as possibly an opening to a new and more profitable phase of his career, one that might help him climb out of the $40 million hole left by the failure of his Zoetrope Studios. "Rip Van Winkle" was also an opportunity for the tech-prone director to use video technology and the computer matting technique known as Ultimatte. He brought in Japanese designer Eiko Ishioka to employ Japanese stage techniques, such as creating a human mountain, a canvas covering five people and thus able to magically move and change shape. "I'm more interested in impressionistic films that require fantastic images to be invented," Coppola told Stephen Farber of the *New York Times*. "In 'Rip Van Winkle' we're working with a surreal vision of America in Revolutionary times."

The result has received mixed reviews over the years. In the user reviews section of IMDb's breakdown of the segment, one called it the "black sheep" of the series. Another praised Harry Dean's depiction of Rip. Still another, Julien Houle of the website *Pop Culture Thoughts*, praised Harry Dean as a "terrific character actor" but one who is "definitely not leading man material, which is reinforced here as he seems unwilling to abandon himself to the silliness of the material."

Looking back from the vantage point of thirty years, Mark Curtis of the online film journal *The Directors Series* wrote, "Stanton and Coppola really give their all to the charmingly cheesy children's show. It has aged terribly in the time since—its handcrafted set designs don't hold up against the hyperbright colors of LCD televisions—but what remains is a fascinating look at how far children's programming has become, if not saying much in the way of Coppola's directorial development."

Also in 1987 Harry Dean appeared in Wayne Wang's *Slam Dance,* which some labeled a "punk movie" but which others lamented as an unsuccessful $4.5 million reach into the mainstream for independent filmmaker Wang. In the film, an underground cartoonist, played by Tom Hulce, is falsely accused of killing his girlfriend, played by Virginia Madsen. Harry Dean plays a perfectionist police detective named Smiley, who never smiles. The cast also includes musicians Adam Ant and John Doe in dramatic roles.

Veteran Los Angeles punk rocker Doe, who played a police investigator, talked about the *Slam Dance* experience during the 2017 Harry Dean Stanton Fest in Lexington, Kentucky. "Wayne Wang was in a little over his head, maybe. He listened to the cinematographer too much. All the shooting and fighting, no constraint, no natural flow to the scene. There was so little actual emotion."

However, Doe said he learned much from working with Harry Dean. "The few scenes we had together, it was so clear to me I was getting left in the dust. He's doing this thing that seems to be nothing. He is so high above me, and I am sucking so bad."

Critics panned the film. "*Slam Dance* is like junk food," *Variety* magazine said. "It's brightly packaged, looks good, and satisfies the hunger for entertainment, but it isn't terribly nourishing or well-made." Vincent Canby of the *New York Times* said Wang's "first mainstream movie" was "complete confusion, a movie without any identity whatsoever."

Another major mainstream production came the next year with *Mr. North,* which for Harry Dean must have seemed much like a family affair, or least a time with old friends and colleagues. Directed by John Huston's son Danny, the film was based on a Thornton Wilder story about a curious stranger in a Rhode Island town who seems to have healing powers and helps an elderly shut-in reenter the world. Eighty-year-old John Huston, who had directed Harry Dean in *Wise Blood* back in 1979, had planned to be executive producer and costar in the film, but his decades-long battle with emphysema and related ailments caused him to back out early in production.

"I called Bob Mitchum to have him stand by just in case I didn't feel well, but I feel great," Huston told Harry Dean in July 1987 as the cast assembled at a rented house in Newport, Rhode Island, for the first reading of the script. The next day Huston and Harry Dean played poker, which turned out to be the great director's last poker game. A couple of days later, he checked into a hospital at Fall River, Massachusetts, suffering from pneumonia. Huston died on August 28, a little more than three weeks after his eighty-first birthday.

Huston's friend Robert Mitchum, who had worked with Harry Dean in *Farewell, My Lovely* in 1975 and who was on a break in the production of *War and Remembrance,* agreed to step in and take over Huston's role as the elderly shut-in Mr. Bosworth. Danny Huston wanted either Timothy Hutton or Tom Hanks for the lead role as Theophilus North, but both were too busy, and he settled on Anthony Edwards. Lauren Bacall played Mrs. Cranston, and Danny Huston's half-sister Anjelica Huston, just coming off another breakup with Jack Nicholson, played Persis Bosworth-Tennyson. Also in the cast was young Hunter Carson, his third project with Harry Dean. The film had limited box-office appeal and got a mixed critical reaction. Roger Ebert called it slow-moving, but *Playboy* reviewer Bruce Williamson wrote that it provided "reassuring evidence that the Huston dynasty lives on."

Ending the Decade with *The Last Temptation*

As the 1980s drew to a close, Harry Dean gave one of the most striking performances of his career as the Apostle Paul in Martin Scorsese's *The Last Temptation of Christ*. The project had been simmering in Scorsese's mind since 1971, when he was making his second feature film, *Boxcar Bertha*, and actress Barbara Hershey gave him a copy of *Zorba the Greek* author Nikos Kazantzakis's novel of the same name. Nearly two decades later, when she read in a trade publication that Scorsese was finally turning the novel into a movie, Hershey asked him to let her play Mary Magdalene, which she does.

The story depicts a deeply conflicted Jesus Christ, who is all too human and who also wrestles with the divinity within him that gives him the power to cast out demons and perform other miracles. At his crucifixion—the very moment when he cries to God, "Why hast Thou forsaken me!"—he is tempted by the devil in the form of an angel and falls into a reverie, a dream or possible alternative fate that has him married to Mary Magdalene. They make love, and he becomes a father and resumes his life as a carpenter, only to be later confronted by his erstwhile followers for his failure to die on the cross in the cause of mankind. Ultimately, he returns to that fate and indeed dies as Christ the Savior.

The film starred Willem Dafoe as Jesus, David Bowie as Pontius Pilate, Harvey Keitel as Judas, and Hershey as Mary Magdalene. Veteran actor Nehemiah Persoff plays a rabbi at the temple, who scolds Jesus for chasing away the money changers.

Filmed in the deserts of Morocco, the $7 million, 152-day production was a project of the heart for Catholic-bred Scorsese, who has again and again wrestled with Christian images and themes in his films. This film, however, won him the scorn of conservative Christians, attacks from television evangelists, and death threats. He took a great chance in even doing such a film after scoring box-office duds with three previous films, *New York, New York* (1977), *Raging Bull* (1980), and *The King of Comedy* (1982). Fear of Christian reaction made studios nervous about *The Last Temptation of Christ*. Paramount pulled out, and so did MGM before Universal brought it back to life. Scorsese won critical praise: Roger Ebert, while conceding that the film is "indeed technically blasphemous" argued that it also "grapples with the central mystery of Jesus, that he was both God and man, and uses the freedom of fiction to explore the implications of such a paradox." Scorsese received an Oscar nomination for directing, but in the United States the film grossed less than a million dollars more than its production costs.

For Harry Dean, the role of Paul, the sinner turned saint, gave him an opportunity to tap into his rejected Southern Baptist roots. He had heard the tent-revival preachers, the Bible-thumping sermons. His Paul is a calculating realist who conspires with Judas and even kills Lazarus to destroy proof of Jesus's greatest miracle. Judas is depicted as the disciple ironically closest to Jesus and the one whose ultimate betrayal is necessary for Jesus to fulfill his mission as savior. In the scenes following Jesus's descent from the cross into marriage with Mary Magdalene, Harry Dean's Paul tells him that the people's "only hope is in the resurrected Jesus. . . . I created the truth out of what people needed."

Jesus, now at a distance from his divinity, responds to Paul, saying, "I'll tell them the truth."

Paul fires back, "They won't believe you. You don't know how much people need God." Then he gives Jesus some credit, but with a dose of his own truth. "It was a good thing I met you," he concedes, but "my Jesus is much more powerful."

Harry Dean's Paul in some ways evokes the Grand Inquisitor in Dostoevsky's *Brothers Karamazov*. In that classic story, Jesus returns to earth during the Inquisition in Spain and is confronted by the Grand Inquisitor, a Torquemada-like figure who rules mercilessly as a vicar of the Roman Catholic Church, and he has no patience for a returned Christ who could destroy his and the church's power. After imprisoning Jesus and telling him he will burn at the stake the following day, the Inquisitor tells a silent Jesus that he as Messiah abandoned his work when he died on the cross and left the rest to the church. "Do you know that centuries will pass, and humanity will proclaim through the mouth of their wisdom and science that there is no crime, and therefore no sin, there is only hunger! 'Feed men, and then demand virtue from them!' That's what they'll write on the banner, which they will raise against you."

Scorsese's film dares to probe the mystery of Jesus, his presence, and his message in ways that prohibit tucking both him and his message neatly away on a shelf or in an empty church. The director and the cast he chose to tell the story of Jesus's "last temptation" opened forbidden doors, which angered many but made many others think, and think profoundly, about what lay behind those doors and its meaning in their lives.

The Lynchian World of the 1990s

Director David Lynch waxed eloquent about his longtime friend and colleague Harry Dean Stanton in Sophie Huber's documentary about the actor, *Partly Fiction*. "He's got this innocence and naturalness that's really rare," said Lynch. "He says a line and it's just real. It's so phenomenal, and what he does between the lines is incredible."

Lynch and Stanton would be deeply linked throughout the 1990s, a decade in which the director would reach the apex of his career for his strange, mystifying films and their challenge to what is "real." Harry Dean would see his cult status continue to grow, in part due to his association with Lynch, while experiencing some Lynchian episodes in his personal life. The decade itself was Lynch-like, with a Democratic president's triangulation of traditional left-versus-right politics in Washington and his subsequent impeachment, and in Hollywood a shift from studio to talent agent power as audiences increasingly stayed home and watched videos rather than go to the movies.

Harry Dean appeared in four David Lynch projects in the 1990s, beginning the decade with *Wild at Heart* (1990) starring Nicholas Cage, Laura Dern, Diane Ladd, Isabella Rossellini, and Willem Dafoe and ending the 1990s with *The Straight Story* (1999) starring Richard Farnsworth and Sissy Spacek. Between these Lynchian bookends to that decade came *Twin Peaks: Fire Walk with Me* (1992) and *Tricks,* the first segment of the television trilogy *Hotel Room* (1993).

They would reunite again in the next decade in *Inland Empire* (2006) and in the television series *Twin Peaks: The Return* (2017).

The 1990s also brought Harry Dean several notable roles in non-Lynch films, including as inmate Toot-Toot in *The Green Mile* (1999), starring Tom Hanks as chief prison guard Paul Edgecomb, Michael Clarke Duncan as the kindhearted and mysteriously gifted inmate John Coffey, and David Morse as prison guard Brutus Howell. One of Toot-Toot's duties is to help test the prison's electric chair. Asked for last words during one of the rehearsals, Toot-Toot tells Howell, "I got to have Mae West sit on my face because I'm one horny mutha-fucker," prompting a round of laughter from the guards. To prepare for the role, Harry Dean traveled to a prison in northern California and sat in the electric chair there.

Harry Dean was also the fiery judge with an axe as a gavel in *Fear and Loathing in Las Vegas* (1998), starring Brat Pack alumnus and guitar-picking buddy Johnny Depp.

Another key role was Harry Dean as Tony "Shorty" Russo in the powerful film *She's So Lovely,* directed by Nick Cassavetes and written by John Cassavetes. The film starred Sean Penn, brilliant as the volatile Eddie Quinn; Robin Wright, Penn's then real-life wife, as Eddie's wife, Maureen; and John Travolta as Joey, the man Maureen marries after Eddie is sent to a psychiatric institution. Harry Dean plays Shorty, Eddie's friend and drinking buddy.

Still, the 1990s was largely a Lynchian world for Harry Dean, and he became an important resident of that world in the eyes of many filmgoers.

"Lynchian" is a term defined in film writer and curator Dennis Lim's book *David Lynch: The Man from Another Place* as "the sublime, the uncanny, the abject . . . abysmal terror, piercing beauty, convulsive sorrow." Lim quotes the late writer David Foster Wallace, whose essay "David Lynch Keeps His Head" is a key text in Lynch studies: Lynchian is "a particular kind of irony where the very macabre and the very mundane combine in such a way as to reveal the former's perpetual containment within the latter."

That Lynch and Harry Dean would find in each other kindred spirits is no accident. Like Harry Dean, Lynch came from a small town, Missoula, Montana, and moved to the big city, first Philadelphia, then Los Angeles. Both were chain-smoking musicians and music lovers, and both possessed a philosophical bent and tilt toward mysticism. Transcendental Meditation (TM) became, and remains, a major focus in Lynch's life, much as Harry Dean's own Zen-like probings and musings became a fundamental part of his persona.

"I'd always been impressed with David's films, and we had a natural bond," Harry Dean said about the director. "We understood each other. We talked about Taoism, Buddhism, and meditation and have a rapport based on our shared interest in Eastern thought."

Still, Lynch, whose TM interests would lead him to create the David Lynch Foundation for Consciousness-Based Education and World Peace, never could convince Harry Dean to become a disciple. "I could sit next to him for hours," Lynch said about the actor, "because everything that comes out of him is natural, no pretense, no bullshit, just beautiful, and he's the kindest, gentlest soul. He's got a melancholy thing, and he's got his own spiritual thing going, too."

However, "he would never do TM. His meditation is just life, he says."

Back in the mid-1980s, Lynch had asked Harry Dean to play Frank Booth in *Blue Velvet* (1986), a seminal film in Lynch's career, a neo-noir about a young man, played by Kyle MacLachlan, who finds a severed human ear in his hometown of Lumberton, North Carolina, and whose subsequent investigation leads him into a strange, sexually deviant, and violent underground world led by Booth, one of the most malevolent psychopaths in the history of film. Harry Dean said no.

"I didn't want to go on that violent trip," Harry Dean would explain. By the end of the 1990s, however, he regretted his decision. "I think I was afraid of it," he told writer Alex Simon. "That was a big mistake, though. I wish I'd done it and just seized the bull by the horns. The older I got, the more I didn't want to go [to those dark places], which is a mistake for an actor."

Dennis Hopper, who'd gone from acclaimed costar with James Dean of *Rebel without a Cause* (1955) and free-spirited, motorcycle-driving hippie in *Easy Rider* (1969) to persona non grata due to his drug-induced wild and uncontrolled personal life, was eager to reestablish himself in Hollywood, and he told Lynch, "I have to play Frank because I am Frank." He did, and it became one of the most unforgettable roles of his career.

That same year Hopper would also perform in *Hoosiers,* for which he earned an Oscar nomination, and the acclaimed *River's Edge.* In both films, Harry Dean was offered, but turned down, the roles Hopper ended up getting. "Dennis and I have laughed about it before," he said.

In 1988, Lynch asked Harry Dean to costar in a French production, a short film for the television miniseries *The French as Seen by. . . .* Harry Dean agreed, and, in a segment written and directed by Lynch called *The Cowboy and the Frenchman,* played a cowboy who has to deal with a beret-wearing, cheese- and baguette-eating Frenchman, played by Frederic Golchan, on a dude ranch.

Harry Dean said yes again to Lynch two years later and agreed to play the role of detective Johnny Farragut in *Wild at Heart,* based on the novel by Barry Gifford, a road movie in which young lovers Sailor, played by Cage, and Lula, played by Dern, travel from the North Carolina–South Carolina border to New Orleans and then west through Texas toward California to escape Farragut and the sinister hit man Marcelles Santos, played by J. E. Freeman. Both were hired by Lula's mother Marietta, played by Diane Ladd, also Laura Dern's real-life mother. Santos goes after Farragut, too, because the detective is on to his criminal past. Even though Marietta tries to save Farragut, her former boyfriend, he is captured by some of Santos's henchmen, then tortured and murdered. Sailor will go on to hold up a feed store with thug Bobby Peru, played by Willem Dafoe, and wind up in prison. Lula, pregnant with their child, waits for him, and they ultimately reunite and live happily ever after.

The film won the Palme d'Or at the Cannes Film Festival. *Rolling Stone* film critic Peter Travers called it "a triumph of startling images and comic invention" that "confirms [Lynch's] reputation as the most exciting and innovative filmmaker of his generation." However, Roger Ebert penned a devastating critique from Cannes that dismissed *Wild at Heart* as "a cinematic act of self-mutilation, a film that mocks itself" with its "cynical shorthand formula for commercial success—sex, drugs, and rock 'n' roll," a film that's "too long, slow-moving and soporific" and a poor update of Russ Meyer's sex- and violence-filled films of decades earlier.

The violence in the uncut version of *Wild at Heart* caused hundreds of viewers to walk out of the theater in early test screenings and forced Lynch to delete a scene where Harry Dean's Johnny Farragut "gets shot in the head and his brains splatter against the wall, then the two characters who kill him laugh manically over the stump of the neck, stick their heads down into it, then come up and do this frantic wild kissing," in the words of film editor Duwayne Dunham. "The second that scene went up on the screen, a hundred twenty-five people walked out of the theater."

Lynch's other major project at the time was the ABC television series *Twin Peaks*, which was midway through its first season when *Wild at Heart* had its world premiere. The groundbreaking show about the mystery of small-town homecoming queen Laura Palmer's death "didn't break the rules of dramatic television so much as subtly derange them," Dennis Lim wrote. It also made Lynch even more famous. Fans became as obsessed with it as earlier TV fans had been with *Star Trek*, even though ABC—or its conservative owner Capital Cities—became so nervous about the show that it moved *Twin Peaks* to Saturday night, the television viewing equivalent of a dead end. Halfway through the show's second season, the network demanded that the writers give audiences the answer to the question that had been the driving force of the entire series: "Who killed Laura Palmer?" Once audiences learned the answer—Laura was murdered by her father, Leland, who was possessed by a demon called BOB—many stopped watching.

The plot of the show was relatively simple, even if the trappings that surrounded it were anything but. FBI Special Agent Dale Cooper, played by *Blue Velvet* star Kyle MacLachlan, comes to the Pacific Northwest town of Twin Peaks, Washington, to investigate the murder of fast-living teenager Laura

Palmer. The investigation leads into a maze of weirdness and mystery that even has supernatural forces at play.

In 1992, just as the television series was losing critical and audience support Lynch brought out a feature-film prequel, *Twin Peaks: Fire Walk with Me,* which starred MacLachlan again as Special Agent Cooper, plus Sheryl Lee as Laura Palmer, Chris Isaac as Special Agent Chester Desmond, and Grace Zabriskie as Laura's mother, Sarah. Also in the cast were Kiefer Sutherland, Ray Wise, and David Bowie. Harry Dean played Carl Rodd, caretaker of the "ends of the earth dump" known as the Fat Trout Trailer Park. "I've already gone places," Carl Rodd says at one point. "I just want to stay where I am."

Although criticized for trying to profit on the television show's early success, Lynch said he merely "wanted to go back into the world before it started on the series and to see what was there, to actually see things that we had heard about." He also wanted to see a living Laura Palmer on the screen. "I was in love with the character of Laura Palmer and her contradictions, radiant on the surface, dying inside. I wanted to see her live, move, and talk." Lim defended Lynch, saying that making a prequel in which the end was already known by audiences was hardly a good strategy to make money at the box office.

Critics savaged the film. *New York Times* writer Vincent Canby wrote, "It's not the worst movie ever made: it just seems to be." Director Quentin Tarantino said, "David Lynch has disappeared so far up his own ass that I have no desire to see another David Lynch movie until I hear something different." However, future critics and audiences saw the film very differently, and *Twin Peaks: Fire Walk with Me* has attained cult status. "Few movies have undergone so complete a rehabilitation," Dennis Lim wrote.

Harry Dean's Carl Rodd became one of the actor's best-known roles, something attested to in the poster I have in my office of Carl in his red plaid housecoat with a cup of "Good morning, America" coffee in his hand. In the film, he was a tiny island of near normalcy in an ocean of weirdness. Harry Dean would return to the world of Twin Peaks fifteen years later when Lynch and cocreator Mark Frost brought *Twin Peaks: The Return* to the television screen. This time he even got to play his guitar and sing "Red River Valley."

Just one year after *Twin Peaks: Fire Walk with Me,* Harry Dean was involved in another David Lynch project, the three-part television series *Hotel Room.* This time he got the starring role in the first segment, titled "Tricks," written by Barry Gifford. He played a sad-sack john named Moe who brings a prostitute named Darlene, played by Glenne Headly, to Room 603 in the Railroad

Hotel and is unable to have sex with her. Soon a friend of Moe's, Lou, played by Freddie Jones, shows up, has his way with Darlene successfully, and leaves. In his wake arrive the police, who think Moe is Lou and arrest him for murdering Moe's wife, Felicia.

Harry Dean was excellent as Moe, the ultimate loser who early on falls on his knees before joint-smoking Darlene. "The White Knight is about to undertake a tenuous journey to the dark forest," he tells her.

"You think too much, man, is what I think," she responds. "Before the White Knight takes out his sword, he has to pay tribute to the Fair Maiden."

As the twentieth century drew to a close Harry Dean found himself in yet another David Lynch film, *The Straight Story*, one of the most atypical of the Lynch canon. A Walt Disney film with a G rating (this in itself signifying its uniqueness), *The Straight Story* was based on an Associated Press and *New York Times* story about seventy-three-year-old, vision-impaired Alvin Straight's nearly 250-mile journey across Iowa and Wisconsin on a John Deere riding lawnmower to visit his long-estranged and ailing brother, Lyle.

Portraying Alvin Straight was seventy-eight-year-old veteran stunt man and actor Richard Farnsworth, who won an Oscar nomination for his performance. Seven months after the awards ceremony Farnsworth, sick with cancer, would take his own life. Sissy Spacek played his mentally challenged daughter, Rose. Harry Dean as Lyle only appeared at the very end of the film, but his appearance was poignant and important.

The Straight Story is the only Lynch-directed film that he didn't either write or cowrite, and as different as it is from much of the rest of his work, Lynch called it "the most experimental film I've made. . . . You gather pieces you think are correct, but you never know if they're right until you actually combine them. You've got to have image, sound, music, and dialogue going in a really delicate balance to get the emotion."

In his book of interviews, *Lynch on Lynch*, writer-editor Chris Rodley called *The Straight Story* "pure David Lynch" and a film that marked a "real continuum" between it and *The Elephant Man* (1980), a poignant tale that showed "the other side of David—it's like an Irish, lyrical, poetic side that is emotional without being sentimental, and full of grace." A road movie that was in some ways the polar opposite of *Wild at Heart* and *Lost Highway* (1997), *The Straight Story* did expose "a tear-jerking, sentimental side" of Lynch, according to Dennis Lim. Lynch himself once told the *New York Times* that "tenderness can be just as abstract as insanity." The film was a critical success, but it lost money, grossing only $6.2 million to cover a $10 million estimated budget.

Envisioning Farnsworth, who served as Kirk Douglas's double in *Spartacus* (1960) and drove one of the chariots in Cecil B. DeMille's *The Ten Commandments* (1956), as Harry Dean's brother in the film was easy, Lynch said. "The word 'natural' is them. Harry is as pure as can be and Richard's that way, too, and you can feel that" in their scene together. Alvin and Lyle hadn't spoken in ten years, a deep rift due to alcohol and the speaking of "unforgivable things." Still, "no one knows you better than your brother," Alvin says at one point.

Alvin finally reaches Lyle's old wooden shack out in the country. When Lyle, aided by a walker, comes outside, the two brothers take a seat on the porch. Lyle sees the John Deere and says, "Did you ride that thing all the way out here to see me?" And his eyes fill with tears as he realizes how much it meant to his brother to see him. It's an unforgettable scene that ends the film.

Harry Dean told the story of how he worked up those tears. "A while back Sean Penn gave me a copy of a speech by Chief Seattle, who was the first Indian to be put on a reservation, and I always cry when I read it, so David had me read some lines from the poem prior to shooting my scene. And it worked."

It was typical of their working relationship. "David's sets are very relaxed and he never yells at anybody—he's not a yeller—and he gives me the freedom to improvise as long as I don't mess with the plot," Harry Dean once said. "We always have a good time working together."

The Weirdness Touches Home

Harry Dean would enter the twenty-first century still a supporting actor, but also a punk icon and more. The bizarre, even violent Lynchian world that he had inhabited in David Lynch's films regrettably seemed to have touched his own private life. On a Saturday night in January 1996, the son of his housekeeper and two partners forced their way into his Mulholland Drive home, shoved a pistol up against his face, tied him up in his bedroom, and went through his house stealing cash, a VCR, a CD player, various other items, and also his 1995 Lexus. "I was lying there, thinking how it's going to feel when [my] head explodes," Harry Dean said afterward. "I got robbed, and thought I was going to die. Aside from that, everything is great." Although they didn't threaten his life, he said, "a pistol in your eye is enough of a threat."

Activating a security device in the Lexus, police later found the abandoned car on a North Hollywood street, staked it out, and when suspects pulled up to reclaim it, began a car chase that resulted in the crashing of the

Lexus and the arrest of two suspects, eighteen-year-old Jose Enrique Rivera and twenty-year-old Alberto Guerrero.

Friends quickly showed up at Harry Dean's house to help, including Ed Begley Jr. "It was something of an inside job. He was very shaken up, of course. I had given him a Sony Watchman television as a gift, he loved it, wanted to know how much it had cost. That was not recovered. I tried to give him some advice about being more secretive. Harry was such a trusting guy. He had money there he kept for poker. Thousands of dollars. He didn't hide it from anybody. I said, 'Harry, you can't do that. You don't know.'"

Mary McCormack, an actress and Harry Dean's neighbor on Mulholland Drive, told me in an April 2018 interview that the break-in hit Harry Dean hard. "It was someone who knew him, disguised himself, wore a mask. It was horrible, the cleaning lady's son. It was heartbreaking for him. He had watched that little boy grow up. Harry was so generous and trusting."

Harry Dean's trusting nature also extended to some poker-playing friends who cheated him out of $250,000, said his cousin James Huggins Jr., an FBI agent who would become one of Harry Dean's closest friends as well and have power-of-attorney responsibilities during his illness and subsequent death. Huggins had warned Harry Dean about the gamblers. Another close friend, fellow musician Jamie James, remembered those poker games. "Until he found out he was being cheated, they cheated him over a period of two and a half years—probably got a couple hundred thousand. . . . He'd say, 'No, they're my friends.' Then one night there's this guy on TV. He was a reformed convict and he was telling people this is who you watch out for in your neighborhood card games. From that time on, he got hip. He didn't want to be believe they were cheating him."

Harry Dean's financial manager, Bill Wine, also cheated him. Wine spent time in jail after being caught embezzling his client's funds of as much as $2 million. Harry Dean "trusted people," Huggins said. "He was talking about this investment guy, Bill Wine was his financial manager. 'I got a couple million with him,' Harry said. He handed me his financial statement. I said this could be fraud. He was embezzled."

Huggins, with help from Harry Dean's old flame Rebecca De Mornay and backing from the FBI, looked deeper into the case, and in 2005 it was determined that Wine indeed had cheated the actor. He was convicted in federal court and put behind bars. "He had taken almost everything from Harry," Huggins told me. Harry Dean was "saved financially" by his subsequent involvement in the television series *Big Love*.

"I think I'm blessed with a pretty tough psyche," Harry Dean told reporters after the robbery at his home.

The robbery and the swindles tested Harry Dean the philosopher as he reconciled these events to his view of life and people. Perhaps, too, these experiences gave an even deeper resonance to his art, including the music that was so important to him. He could always sing the blues because he knew the blues. He knew them even better now.

11

The Musician and Philosopher

If you listen closely, you can hear in Harry Dean's voice a faint echo from the clapboard churches and tent revivals of his youth as he sings "Just a Closer Walk with Thee" in the prison yard scene in *Cool Hand Luke*. The young Harry Dean may have squirmed and rolled his eyes as the preacher waved that big Bible in his hand from the pulpit, but he was all ears when the choir started singing.

He would later talk about Brother Gibson and the other evangelists who came through Irvine, pushing him through the line after church or at church picnics as they glad-handed the congregation's biggest contributors to the collection plate. "Shook hands with me and moved me on, like something's wrong with this picture," he told podcaster Marc Maron.

Not that Harry Dean was particularly surprised after sitting through what he called Brother Gibson's "based on fear, fear of God, father figure, bullshit" sermons.

They may have been "bullshit" to little Harry Dean, but when the forty-one-year-old actor, playing the guitar-picking prison inmate Tramp in Stuart Rosenberg's first completed big-screen feature, sang and played "Just a Closer Walk with Thee," he did it with the kind of conviction that only a born-again Christian, or a really good actor, can muster.

I am weak but Thou art strong
Jesus, keep me from all wrong
I'll be satisfied as long
As I walk, let me walk close to Thee.

Harry Dean never talked much about Jesus, although, as told in an earlier chapter of this book, he did probe French director Bertrand Tavernier's thoughts on the topic late one evening at a bar in Glasgow, Scotland, during the filming of *Death Watch* (1984). "Bertrand, do you think we can verbalize the concept of Christ?" he asked. "Harry Dean, maybe a little later after several hours' sleep," the director responded.

So the old atheist was thinking about Jesus that night in that distant bar.

"Deep down I think he was saying a lot of stuff, but I think he had more questions than answers," his nephew Ralph Stanton Jr. told me. "He always came across like he was an authority. It all is nothing. He had all the answers. Yet, at the same time, he was really searching for something."

From Harry Dean's childhood on, he loved music, and he wondered about life much like a young, emerging philosopher or preacher might. In Sophie Huber's documentary *Harry Dean Stanton: Partly Fiction,* he talked about the terror he felt at the age of fourteen at the notion that "there was nothing out there" and that "I was alone." As he grew older and rejected the fundamentalist ideas of Brother Gibson and the other Southern Baptist preachers of his childhood, he eventually rejected Christianity altogether. In the void that rejection left he came to accept that perhaps indeed "there was nothing out there." Incorporating such a worldview into one's life, however, makes necessary a corresponding search for what truly is valuable and worthwhile in life. He would muse about the transitoriness of life—"It's all going to go away," he goes on to say in *Partly Fiction.* "Everything disappears. I'm not Buddhist. I'm nothing. When you're nothing, there's no problem." Still, Harry Dean did place great value on certain aspects of his life—his friends, his acting, and his music. As important as music had always been for him, it became even more important in the 1980s.

"He did think he would be a leading man after *Paris, Texas,* and then it did not happen and it did hurt his ego," Sophie Huber told Marc Maron. It was at that point that he began to turn more seriously to music. In fact, she later told me in my interview with her, the only way she could even convince him to do *Partly Fiction* was to emphasize the music rather than the acting or even the man. "Let's not think of it as a documentary," she told Harry Dean. "I come to the house, we film a song and go and talk."

"When I said it was not about him but the music, he was willing to do it," Huber told me in August 2018.

Harry Dean's music was good. He could inhabit a song just like he could inhabit a role. "He loves to bring that wounded beast to the table," Michelle Phillips, formerly of the 1960s Mamas and Papas rock group, told Tom Thurman in his documentary about Harry Dean, *Crossing Mulholland.* "He knows where to find that in his heart. When he sings, you're afraid he's going to burst into tears any minute."

"I've Got a Dream"

Jamie James, veteran musician, longtime Harry Dean friend and fellow band member, former front man for the Kingbees, and current lead guitarist with Dennis Quaid and the Sharks, got to know Harry Dean in the 1980s through actor Dabney Coleman. James was dating Coleman's daughter Kelly at the time. During a July 4 gathering at the Coleman house, Harry Dean walked in wearing a jacket "with a sheen on it, really gnarly," James recalled in my March 2018 interview with him. "He had a tendency to look like a rubby-dub. He wore that jacket, never got it cleaned, like his sofa.... I didn't know he was an actor, a millionaire, or any of that stuff."

At one point, a conversation began between James and Harry Dean. "I told him, 'I didn't know the buses ran on July 4 in Los Angeles.' He looked like a bum." Harry Dean "started to roar" with laughter at the comment. "Dabney," he called out to his friend the host. "Your future son-in-law is a riot. He just told me the buses don't run on July 4."

The two began to run into each other at nightclubs and bars where music was playing—the Lighthouse down on Hermosa Beach, the Central (which later became Johnny Depp's club, the Viper Room) on Sunset Boulevard, and On the Rox, also on Sunset Boulevard. They'd talk music, sometimes play together. Like Harry Dean, James loved roots music, Buddy Holly, the blues. "Late one night he called me. He knew I was up late. It was maybe three in the morning. He was half in the bag. It was rare because he had certain rules he'd learned in the Navy. You don't drink at home. You don't drink in the daylight. You don't drink alone." James recalled the conversation.

"Jamie, I have made it as an actor. I got money put away. I'm a millionaire."

Harry Dean, the small-town Kentuckian, liked saying he was a millionaire.

"I don't have money like Jack [Nicholson], but I'm a millionaire. I've got a dream. I really want to have a band and play shows, and go out and perform. Maybe you can help me."

James agreed to work with him, and they started practicing together every Thursday and Sunday evening. Harry Dean had a PA system set up at his house with microphones and amplifiers. Early on, the sessions were a challenge for the professional musician in the duo. "Harry just couldn't come in at the right place. I remember trying to think how some of the old blues guys would miss a bar. Harry would come in at two-thirds of a bar, or half a bar. He was approaching singing like an actor. . . . He's got a great voice, not just a normal voice, a great voice, a natural vibrato to die for, and perfect pitch, and an excellent ear, but his timing was way bad. I would start to watch his lips."

When Harry Dean pulled out his harmonica, James noticed another idiosyncrasy. He'd play it backwards—with the high notes on the left instead of on the right. Still, "he played harmonica beautifully. He was an excellent harmonica player. He played melody harp, old school."

Harry Dean's tastes in music ranged widely, but not without limits. "I love all kinds of music—country, folk, rock 'n' roll if it's not loud," he once said. "I hate blast-out rock 'n' roll, which most of them make the mistake of doing. They start way up here at a volume, and they've got no place to go. As far as artists, I like Phil Ochs, Dylan, Kristofferson, Creedence Clearwater Revival. I love John Fogerty. Their lead singer is great. Muddy Waters, Jimmy Reed, all the black blues singers. Like roots rock, pretty much everything."

The repertoire Harry Dean would develop with Jamie James and other fellow musicians ranged from the Great American Songbook to rockabilly and the blues to Mexican corridos and ballads like Roy Orbison's "Blue Bayou." His song list included neighbor Marlon Brando's favorite tune, "Limehouse Blues," and personal favorites, including Fred Neil's "Everybody's Talkin'," Willie Nelson's "Blue Eyes Crying in the Rain," the old Irish classic "Danny Boy," and "Canción Mixteca," which he sang in *Paris, Texas.* He could perform silly songs like "Wooly Bully" and heartbreakers like "Love Me Tender," "He'll Have to Go," and "Just Because." Over the years, Harry Dean had learned Spanish and could croon in Spanish as well as occasionally in other languages, including Italian and even Croatian.

Curiously missing from Harry Dean's song list was a song he once told nephew Ralph Stanton Jr. was his favorite, Cole Porter's "Begin the Beguine," a tale of tropical memories and lost love.

Like Frank Sinatra and Elvis Presley, Harry Dean didn't write songs; he interpreted them. For Harry Dean, music could be rehearsed and performed on a stage in front of a large crowd or be spontaneous in an alley or on the street, as long as it was natural and real. Ralph Stanton Jr. tells a story from around 2007, when Harry gathered with a couple of friends for a smoke outside Dan Tana's in West Hollywood. "We were out that night, and this black homeless man came by. He just kind of saw us and said, 'A dollar for a song.' Harry said, 'What you got?' The guy pulled out some spoons and started singing. Harry was intrigued by him. 'This guy has got some talent,' he told us.

Harry asked if anybody had a guitar, and someone had one in a trunk. He wound up out there till almost dawn, on the street."

Harry Dean the actor wasn't shy about audiences, and Harry Dean the musician had been performing music in front of them since he was a young man. He'd crooned "By the Light of the Silvery Moon" in barbershop quartets with his brothers, and he'd sung with the American Male Chorus all over the country. With Jamie James and other assorted band members, however, he was able to realize his dream of having his own band playing his kind of music. Over the years, these bands had several different names, from the Harry Dean Stanton Band and Harry Dean Stanton's Orchestra to Harry Dean Stanton's Repo Men (after his 1984 film *Repo Man*). They performed at various Los Angeles venues, such as the Mint on West Pico Boulevard, Jack's Sugar Shack on Hollywood and Vine Street, the Moonlight Supper Club on Ventura Boulevard, and of course the Troubadour, near Dan Tana's on Santa Monica Boulevard.

It was at the Troubadour where Kris Kristofferson made his LA debut, opening for Linda Ronstadt. Harry Dean helped launch Kristofferson's movie career by recommending him for the title role in *Cisco Pike,* the 1972 film that featured the singer-songwriter as an ex-con musician who's trying to rebuild his life. Harry Dean played his speed-addicted former bandmate Jesse Dupre. The film also included a scene in the Troubadour. In 2013, the two actors joined to kick off a screening series of Kristofferson films at the Cinefamily theater in Los Angeles with a showing of *Cisco Pike* and a Q&A session.

Once Harry Dean gained traction as a musical performer, star-studded audiences came to the small clubs around Los Angeles where he performed. "Bono was there, asking 'How do you guys make it so natural?'" Jamie James remembered. "Ike Turner, Steve Cropper. We did 'Mustang Sally.' Harry's version was a lot different from Wilson Pickett's. Steve said, 'You guys are great.' Joni Mitchell sat in with us." One night at a cigar club before a mainly male audience, James got worried the crowd was not right for the soulful ballads like "Blue Bayou" that Harry Dean wanted to sing. "Harry, it's all guys. We're dying here," James told him. "Men are sensitive, too," Harry Dean reassured him.

Like any old pro, Harry Dean could be jealous of the limelight. At Jack's Sugar Shack one night—Grammy Award–winning singer Chaka Khan was in the audience—a man pulled on James's sleeve and asked if his young son could come up on the stage and play harmonica with the band. James turned to Harry Dean, who said, "Sure." "I see this eight-year-old, blond-haired, blue-eyed kid, and he's really a virtuoso," James said. "Now this kid just starts wailing. Everybody is on their feet. The kid gets an applause you wouldn't believe." Later in the evening, the father again tugs on James's sleeve and asks if his son can play another tune. James turns to Harry Dean, who's not smiling. "Fuck him," he tells his lead guitarist.

"I had to go back and say sorry to the father," James recalled with a chuckle. "There was no upstaging Harry Dean Stanton. So much for 'There is no self.'"

Harry Dean even got invited to perform at the Royal Festival Hall in London, England. On the night of the performance some friends came into his dressing room and offered him marijuana. "The worst thing Harry Dean could do before a show was smoke some weed," James said. "I said no, and he said, 'None of your goddamn business.' He smoked up, and we went out there bombing. Harry was awful. I went over to him and said, 'Let's go in with the Mexican songs.' He could sing those stoned. We won the audience over with 'Canción Mixteca.'"

Some time later, James got the opportunity to perform with Dennis Quaid's band, the Sharks. Quaid was another actor who loved music and whom Harry Dean had mentored. "Harry wasn't crazy about it," James said.

"How can I lie down with this knife in my back?" Harry Dean asked James.

"He was really overly dramatic," James told me, smiling.

Harry Dean forgave him, however. "Harry was a very understanding and forgiving guy. In his own way, he was the Americanization of a self-made guru. . . . He was a forgiving, altruistic, genteel pure soul."

The Philosopher

They had the crowd in their hands. People were enjoying their drinks and each other. They were into the music.

"Jamie, have you ever thought about doing nothing on stage?" Harry Dean said to Jamie James during a break between songs.

Jamie looked at Harry Dean like he was crazy.

"What do you mean?"

Harry Dean's lean, grizzled face grew serious. "Just try it. Try to do nothing."

They kept playing that night, but on another night at the Mint on West Pico Jamie figured he'd see whether his friend and bandleader meant what he said. In the middle of a song, Jamie said to Harry Dean, "I'm going to do nothing."

And then Harry Dean's lead guitarist stopped playing. He went silent. Did nothing.

"Come on! What are you doing?" the bandleader demanded.

"Nothing."

Harry Dean smiled.

James looks back on such moments often. "I gained more from Harry than I could ever repay. It is like having a teacher with you all the time. He said some profound things on stage."

San Francisco–based musician and actor George Hatzis said music and philosophy often combined during evenings with his friend Harry Dean. "Some of the first people [in Hollywood] I met were Dabney Coleman and Harry Dean. They were just yin and yang. I was more like a Texas wild guy, Harry the Zen Buddhist Kentucky guy. Dabney would turn and say, 'Turn the music up,' and Harry would say, 'Turn the music down.' It was a natural relationship. Somehow I landed between the two."

Over the years, Hatzis and Harry Dean would get together and make music. "It was quality time. We would play guitar for a half hour, then we would read from Eckhart Tolle. Then we'd say we can focus on something," and, with each new revelation, "say, 'Whoa!'" Eventually, the philosophy became more important than the music when Hatzis, a born-and-bred Catholic who had turned to Krishnamurti and Yogananda, came to Harry Dean's house. "I would go to his house at daytime. I would bring a couple of my books, and we would turn it into a book fest. We would just break out these incredible books and pick each other's brains. It just happened."

In his book *Zen Guitar*, musician-writer Philip Toshio Sudo says that music transcends our separateness as it goes from musician to listener, that it moves people toward the oneness that lies at the heart of Zen thinking. He also notes that good music, like all art, can come out of a point in life "when things fall apart." Things hadn't fallen apart for Harry Dean, but he had gotten his heart broken in the early 1980s and knew he'd likely never marry. He'd ended the 1990s with a robbery and begun the new century with a swirl of betrayals from poker buddies and a financial advisor. And despite the promise of *Repo Man* and *Paris, Texas*, he knew he'd never be a lead star.

Sudo goes on to write that a musician should "play what you are meant to play." Harry Dean did. In a way, his song list reconciled him to the roots he had rejected in other aspects of his life. Hank Williams tunes like "Cold, Cold Heart,"

Jimmie Rodgers's "T for Texas," and old traditional folk songs like "Midnight Special" don't evoke much Zen philosophy, but they do rural Southern roots. Even Harry Dean's beloved "Canción Mixteca," as far away as Mexico is from Kentucky, is a song of longing and homesickness, the kind of suffering from which Siddhartha Gautama sought release when he left his family and his father's palace to become a wandering ascetic five centuries before Christ.

Harry Dean sang those songs, but the rebel in him would never allow him to accept the Christian world out of which they came. He had turned a fateful corner away from that world that day at the Pasadena Playhouse when he found a worn copy of a Ralph Waldo Emerson book. "I was at the Pasadena Playhouse and found this book just lying in the dust one day," he told magazine writer Alex Simon. "Somebody had dropped a book of Emerson and I picked it up."

That book "got me started questioning the whole traditional concept of religion."

"That was no accident that you found that," Simon responded.

"No," Harry Dean said. "There are no accidents."

Emerson was a kindred spirit. Events such as the death of his wife and a destructive fire at his home had turned Emerson away from the staunch Christianity of his younger years. When he questioned the Christian faith and established church in public, he was attacked as an atheist. Certainly he didn't share the same idea of God his critics did. He studied Indian philosophy as well as German idealism and viewed nature, creativity, and the inherent "oversoul" within the mind of each individual as the closest to true divinity man can know. This triad became the foundation of Emerson's philosophy of Transcendentalism. Emerson encouraged each person to use his or her creativity, sense of freedom, and powers of introspection to build his or her own world.

In key ways, Emerson's ideas reflect the thinking of ancient writers such as Lao Tzu, traditionally recognized as the author of the 2500-year-old *Tao Te Ching*, and they foreshadow the future writings of Indian philosopher Jiddu Krishnamurti and German thinker Eckhart Tolle. "These roses under my window make no reference to former roses or to better ones," Emerson once wrote. "They are for what they are; they exist with God to-day. There is no time to them. There is simply the rose. It is perfect to every moment of its existence." Close to such thinking is Tolle when he writes, "the present moment holds the key to liberation.... the present moment is all you ever have. Make the Now the primary focus of your life."

Harry Dean bridged the worlds of the 1950s Beat Generation and the 1960s "Flower Power" generation—from Jack Kerouac road novels, jazz, and the Zen poetry of Allen Ginsberg and Gary Snyder to Timothy Leary and psychedelic rock. By the time he was living in Laurel Canyon with Jack Nicholson and getting neighborly visits by Cass Elliot and Joni Mitchell, he was already approaching elder-statesman age in comparison to his younger friends and admirers. However, he absorbed much from both worlds, and what he absorbed remained with him the rest of his life.

"The '60s were great," he told writer Alex Simon in 1997. "They ought to re-run 'em. A lot of people didn't get it. The whole revolutionary concept is the consciousness revolution against the whole system. The state, government, religion, everything. A lot of eastern religion started having an effect on the culture, too, at that point. Alan Watts, Kerouac, Ginsberg. Leary, of course, who leaned a little too heavily on LSD saving the world, but I understood exactly what he was doing. On LSD the ego just goes out the window. It's all tied in to eastern philosophy and Buddhism, although they certainly wouldn't recommend LSD because that's not the answer to it."

Harry Dean was with Leary in Beverly Hills in late May 1996 as he was dying. Jamie James was there, too. "I remember Harry and I were standing at his bedside. He was excited about departing this life. It was sincere. He said he looked forward to the next adventure. He was energetic about it. Harry was very moved by that."

Making room for the new ideas and ways of thinking Harry Dean encountered required a wholesale rejection of old ideas. "I can't relate to the Judaic-Christian concept at all," he continued with Alex Simon. "It's a fascistic concept. All fear-based. All about there being a boss. Someone in charge. A creator. As far as we know, infinity is reality. There's no beginning and no end. So [the Judeo-Christians] made it, 'Okay, after you die you're gonna live forever, but not before.' But with a positive eternity, there's no ending and you also have to realize there's no beginning, which blows the creationist theory totally out the window."

Although Harry Dean rejected Christ as the son of God, he kept a sense of him as a significant figure in history and in human consciousness, one he wrestled with that night in that Glasgow bar during the filming of *Death Watch*. Harry Dean told Alex Simon, "I'm convinced that Christ was a Buddhist," adding, "They always talk about there were years they didn't know where Christ was," and that he actually "went to India because everything he talks about is Buddhistic. . . . The Jewish hierarchy and certainly the Romans didn't want any part of that, because that would blow their whole trip." Thus, they nailed Jesus the subversive to the cross.

Here Harry Dean's ideas reflect those of a major Eastern thinker of the first half of the twentieth century, Indian-born spiritual leader Paramahansa Yogananda, one of the premier advocates of Yoga meditation, who believed that Christ's teachings linked him closely with the original Yoga teacher, Bhagavan Krishna, and that these principles form the foundation of all religion.

Throughout its history Hollywood has always had an open-door policy toward all kinds of religious and spiritual thinking—from Yoga masters to astrologers, soothsayers, and Ouija-board mediums. An openness to Eastern Buddhist thinking goes back at least as far as D. W. Griffith's 1919 film *Broken Blossoms,* in which an idealistic young Buddhist travels from China to London's gone-to-seed Limehouse district to spread the gospel of peace in post–World War I Europe.

The Hollywood penchant for the occult and all kinds of spiritual exploration was nowhere more evident than in the life and death of one of its first major stars, Rudolph Valentino, the "Great Lover" of *The Sheik, Blood and Sand,* and *The Four Horsemen of the Apocalypse.* He was such a sex symbol and superstar that his death at thirty-one and subsequent funeral, which was attended by tens of thousands of fawning, many hysterical, fans in 1926, launched a new revolution in the spiritualism industry, one aided by Valentino's former wife, costume and set designer Natacha Rambova (her real name was Winifred Shaughnessy). Rambova and mediums claimed to have communicated repeatedly with Valentino in heaven, where he and the late Italian tenor Enrico Caruso were even said to have attended a celestial opera performance together!

Even the much tamer spiritual side of modern-day Hollywood is sometimes a bit too much for some Angelenos. Harry Dean's nephew Chad McKnight, who heads a casting company in Los Angeles, remembers going with his uncle to a session conducted by Eckhart Tolle in the late 1990s or early 2000s. "This was before Oprah got hold of him [Tolle] and made him into a thing. He was very much under the radar, Tolle was. There were these agape centers. Harry Dean and [actor] Owen Wilson and me would go. It was basically two hundred or three hundred people sitting in this conference room—nothing but celebrities, Dennis Quaid, Meg Ryan. It felt a little obnoxious." However, over time, McKnight said he began to hear the message behind what Tolle, Harry Dean, and others were preaching. "It helped me in my life. He turned me on to what he loved—Eckhart Tolle, Hinduism, and Buddhism."

Of course, Harry Dean sometimes used his philosophical side to get nonphilosophical benefits. "He would use the language of it to pick up women. They loved him for it. It was like minitherapy," McKnight said.

Repo Man director Alex Cox dismissed Harry Dean's philosophy as a confused "mishmash" of Buddhism and Calvinism, an atheistic brand of fatalism on one hand and the need "to live for the moment" on the other.

Actor Ed Begley Jr. has an entirely different take on it. Harry Dean "changed my life in some meaningful ways," he said. "I learned a great deal about being relaxed on camera with Harry. Different paths and philosophies. It was transformative, allowed me to appreciate the moments as they were happening, not worrying about the next acting job. I was never really enjoying things as they were happening. I made things out of wood, woodworking, chest of drawers. I would go buy the wood and sand the wood, et cetera, [making] the finished wood, making it smooth, just right. Because of Harry Dean I would actually enjoy each part of that process. I did that with the acting, the preparation. I started enjoying the little games of memorizing the lines, not just the drudgery, the process of doing it."

Begley said he and Harry Dean often discussed Alan Watts's book *This Is It* and the notion that the present moment is "it" and "not just the next acting job." "If you can enjoy that and savor that, it leads to a great deal of serenity and enjoyment."

Harry Dean's views, however, made him also fatalistic at times. "He certainly loved nature," said Begley, an ardent environmentalist. "He was like everything was part of a master plan, not to a God or something like that. He just felt that what is just is. Smog just is. I argued we can change that, and he would say, 'You're baying at the moon, Begley.' I said, 'Harry, you've been here longer than I have. Millions more people now, and there is a fraction of the smog that used to be. You can make a difference. Some battles you can fight and win.' He agreed. He seemed to admire that."

Harry Dean could be as preachy at times as his brothers Arch and Ralph. As they got older, they would ask you about your soul and whether you'd given your life to Jesus Christ. These were not questions Harry Dean would ask, but he wasn't shy about his own beliefs and how the truths that lay within them applied to everyone just as much as to himself. "He was such a rebel," his cousin Jim Huggins Sr. recalled. "I don't know where all that [philosophy] came from. He was doing a movie in Hazard, Kentucky, *Fire Down Below*

(1997). I went up and picked him up on a Friday. He came home with us. He started giving me his philosophy on Buddhism, Zen. He talked nonstop for about thirty miles. He said, 'Jim, do you understand what I'm saying?' I said, 'Harry, I haven't understood a word you said since I picked you up.' He said, 'Okay, I'll keep trying.'"

Maybe Harry Dean got preachy at times because he saw his ideas work in his own life. Certainly a philosophy that teaches the importance of valuing the now instead of worrying about the past and future would appeal to an actor. "The actor's life is one of the hardest lives," David Lynch told his biographer, Dennis Lim, in 2015. "They only have themselves and they are mostly waiting and hoping, and you see how fate plays such a role in who rises and who falls."

The value of silence as taught in Zen philosophy also was important. "Where there is silence, one finds peace," the poet-philosopher Lao Tzu wrote. "Where there is silence, one finds the anchor of the universe within himself." D. T. Suzuki, whose books helped introduce Zen Buddhism to the Western world, had this to say: "The silence is not that of the desert shorn of all vegetation, nor is it that of a corpse forever gone to sleep and decay. It is the silence of the 'eternal abyss' in which all contrasts and conditions are buried." Krishnamurti also wrote about this: "You can see something clearly only when your mind is silent."

Harry Dean utilized the power of silence in both his acting and his life. As he said in Sophie Huber's documentary on him, "Silence is very powerful. Just not saying anything is already a powerful statement."

The bohemian, even licentious, lifestyle Harry Dean and friends like Jack Nicholson led during chunks of their lives probably wouldn't have been any more acceptable to the self- and ego-eschewing Zen Buddhist monks in China, Myanmar, or Tibet than that of Kerouac and his fellow Beat writers. "Beat Zen is a complex phenomenon," Alan Watts, a thrice-married, chain-smoking hard drinker who hardly exemplified ascetic discipline, wrote in *This Is It.* "It ranges from a use of Zen for justifying sheer caprice in art, literature, and life to a very powerful social criticism and 'digging of the universe.' . . . When Kerouac gives his philosophical final statement, 'I don't know. I don't care. And it doesn't make any difference'—the cat is out of the bag, for there is a hostility in these words which clangs with self-defense."

Podcaster Marc Maron once suggested to Sophie Huber that this might be Harry Dean's attitude. "There's a fine line between Buddhism and fuck it," Maron said. "The whole Buddhist thing, he is not entirely believable in it.

Parts, yes. He clearly has an ego, a funny way to interpret the whole Buddhist philosophy, to say, 'Well, I really don't care about anything.'"

"There is no self," Harry Dean would say. "You've got to get beyond consciousness."

Maybe an answer to the Harry Dean riddle lies in the Kris Kristofferson song that gave Sophie Huber her title for her documentary on Harry Dean, *Partly Fiction*. "I didn't have the title until the last week of the edit," Huber told me. "Suddenly I hear these words, 'He is a walking contradiction, partly truth, partly fiction.' That is Harry. . . . I think he was very intrigued by his philosophy. He tried to be in the moment as much as possible, to get away from the idea of an ego, but he was a man who had as much of an ego as you."

Truth is, Harry Dean never claimed he was a Buddhist. In fact, he said he wasn't anything. He hated labels. However, he clearly saw truths in Buddhist teaching. "It's all a movie anyway" he would say about life, essentially paraphrasing the first-century Buddhist text the *Dhammapada,* which says that "all forms are unreal" and that knowing this makes one "passive in pain" and "leads to purity." Shakespeare hinted at such a view in one of Harry Dean's favorite quotes from *The Tempest:* "We are such stuff as dreams are made of."

Harry Dean also found himself living out another of the *Dhammapada*'s teachings. "It is better to live alone,' it says. "Let a man walk alone." At his bedside at night, next to his pack of Dunhills or American Spirits, he kept a bundle of sticks with a blue ribbon tied around them. Following the practices described in the ancient *I Ching,* he would toss them and then study their pattern according to *I Ching* hexagrams for advice on dealing with situations in life.

Of course, the one situation in life that everyone faces is death, and even here Zen offers solace. "In Zen one does not feel guilty about dying, or being afraid," Alan Watts wrote. "For in Taoism and Zen, the world is seen as an inseparably interrelated field or continuum, no part of which can actually be separated from the rest or valued above or below the rest." Watts goes on to quote Huineng, the Sixth Patriarch: "Fundamentally not one thing exists." Or, as Harry Dean would say, "You are nothing." No thing.

Yet, at the end, when the silent darkness of death approached Harry Dean, Zen and the writings of Watts, Krishnamurti, Tolle, and the *I Ching* fell short. He was afraid of death. The void that he had told others about for so long frightened him, and he felt that fear up to the moment he entered it.

12

Lucky in the Last Years

My daughter Rachel and I are enjoying Harry Dean tales and photos with his neighbors, actress Mary McCormack, her producer husband, Michael Morris, and two of their three daughters, ten-year-old Rose and six-year-old Lil. We're in their beautiful home just off Mulholland Drive, overlooking Los Angeles's San Fernando Valley. They shared the same driveway with Harry Dean's ranch-style bungalow. They used to watch his midafternoon walks toward his mailbox. For Harry Dean, it was one of his first duties of the day, since he slept until three in the afternoon.

"He looked like a bird. He would haul ass up that driveway with those skinny legs to go get the mail," the actress recalls. "He would go two or three times, too many times, to check the mail, and he would be at a good clip, really fast."

Harry Dean visited his neighbors often, playing and singing with the girls. "They sang a bunch of songs together. He played his harmonica," McCormack said. "Margaret is our oldest, he called her Maggie. Rosie sang 'Desperado' at his funeral. He was like a grandfather. He used to call Rose 'Miami Rose.' She sang for him a lot. We would have him over for Thanksgiving and Christmas, and he would eat just a little tiny bit, drink red wine. One time he came over and we watched *Paris, Texas* together. He would say, 'What did I say?'—his hearing was a little off—or 'That's a good scene.'"

"It was really moving to watch him watch that great, great work," Michael adds. "Sometimes it takes coming back to something to really see it. He was really moved by it."

His wife nods. "He was amazed, too, when I showed him pictures of him on the Internet. He would say, 'How many are there?' He couldn't believe it. There were so many images of him."

When they moved into their home in the early 2000s, the previous owner told them Harry Dean needed a little watching. "He didn't need much looking after," Mary says. "He was in his late seventies."

During one early visit to Harry Dean's house, Michael noted all the trees that crowded the overlook of the valley below. "Harry, you need to cut all these trees down," Michael told him. "You have this view."

"I've seen the view," Harry Dean responded.

Mary grins. "That may be one of the coolest things he said, and he said a lot of cool things."

Harry Dean was a night owl, and he sometimes came home late at night from an evening at Ago and Dan Tana's. "He could not remember the code (to the driveway gate), and he'd be climbing over the gate," Michael says with a chuckle.

However, no one wanted to see Harry Dean behind the wheel of that black Lexus parked in his driveway. The car had been one of his few splurges. He was Ersel's son behind the wheel, and even as a passenger he wanted to break the rules. "I would stop," Mary remembers, "and he would say, 'Why are you stopping?' I said, 'It's a stop sign!'"

They would watch game shows together. "He would get really angry when he got one [answer] wrong," Michael says. "He really liked the seventies game shows, *Jokers Wild, The Newlyweds, Family Feud.*" If he occasionally missed a quiz-show answer, he was rarely stumped by a missing word in a crossword puzzle. "He was nailing those crossword puzzles."

Jamie James gets a laugh whenever he thinks about Harry Dean's crossword puzzles and game shows. "When TV came up with a twenty-four-hour game show network, he was addicted. He loved *Family Feud,* and he liked the ones from the fifties, like *I've Got a Secret* and *What's My Line?* He was so into it. He liked anything that challenged his brain. He loved data. He loved information. He loved answering questions. He loved knowledge on any kind of level. He'd be sitting there, and we'd be watching TV, and he had this pad on his lap and a pretend buzzer on his knee. He would slap his knee when he answered a question, I swear to God! I never made comments on it, but you would not believe it unless you saw it yourself."

When Harry Dean wasn't working his crossword puzzles, watching television game shows, hanging out at Ago and Dan Tana's, and visiting with his neighbors and friends, he was making movies and music in the new century. He made a lot of music, recording his first and only CD and performing with the likes of Willie Nelson and Art Garfunkel. He recited poetry by Charles Bukowksi in a documentary devoted to the underground poet. He made films with young admirers, including Johnny Depp and Sean Penn, and won over a new generation of television fans with an appearance on *Two and a*

Half Men and in the series *Big Love* and *Getting On*. He did a few walk-ons in a handful of forgettable films and as a security guard in the superhero movie *The Avengers,* and then ended his career with one final lead role, essentially playing himself in *Lucky.*

An Oscar would never sit on the living-room mantel at his Mulholland Drive home, but he and his career were feted and praised in two documentaries, a film festival in his hometown of Lexington, Kentucky, and at impromptu, celebrity-packed events in Hollywood.

Still, when Harry Dean came home at night, he generally came home alone. He slept alone and he woke up alone. Sometimes he'd get up in the middle of the night just to smoke a cigarette. The ashtrays were full of butts and ashes, and the house reeked of years of smoking. He never worried that the pack or two or three he smoked every day might lead to cancer. "It is mind over matter," he told Jamie James. "I'm not going to get sick because I love every fuckin' puff." He once told *Esquire* magazine that "I only eat so I can smoke and stay alive." Harry Dean was a thinking man, and smoking is often a thinking man's habit, a thought with each drag, each puff, each moment between drags.

Harry Dean didn't have a pet, but for a while he fed three wild coyotes that would come out of the bushes to visit. "Riley, Socksy, and Tipsy, and they'd come up every day to get food," James said. "Harry would splurge and get big things of chicken. He loved to show off and say, 'It's feeding time.' He'd feed them. I remember Socksy had four white paws. Gorgeous coyotes. I was there—I think it was Riley, he was the oldest—when Harry wanted to show off and hold up this big chicken breast. The coyote came out and snatched it out of his hand! He thought he was going to lose his hand. Scared the shit out of him." That incident, plus the small children next door, convinced Harry Dean finally to stop feeding them.

"I saw him cry when he had to let those coyotes go," James said. "In a lot of ways, he was a lonely guy, a very lonely guy."

Harry Dean spent a lot of time on the phone, particularly during basketball season. Sometimes he'd call home to Kentucky to talk about Wildcats basketball. "We stayed in touch," his cousin Jim Huggins Sr. said. "He was a big Kentucky basketball fan. He had a lot of knowledge about it."

Once in a blue moon he would travel home to Kentucky. "He came back for Christmas, and I go up to the Cincinnati airport, waiting for him to deplane. He comes out like a wild man." This is how Huggins Sr. remembers the subsequent conversation:

"Where can I smoke?"

"Outside the terminal, Harry."

"Let's go."

"No one can smoke in the terminal."

"They need to change that rule."

The second night Harry Dean was in Frankfort, where the Hugginses lived, he got restless.

"Hey, Jimmy, do you go out to any clubs or anything?"

"No. The people at those clubs are the ones I investigate." Huggins Sr., like his son, was an FBI agent at the time.

"I need to go out and do something."

"Talk to my son, Jim."

Recruited to take Harry out on the town, Jim Huggins Jr. found him a popular club called Cooter Brown's. "They go to some redneck bar in Frankfort, and everyone in there recognized him," Senior said. "They had a house band, and Harry played music with them the entire week."

It wasn't long before Junior had had enough.

"I got to get away from Harry," he told his father. "He stays up to two or three in the morning. I can't keep up with him."

Word had gotten around Frankfort, however, that Harry Dean Stanton was in town and playing at Cooter Brown's. "The place was standing room only," Senior said with a laugh. "People everywhere."

More often, Kentucky came to Harry Dean. Sara Stanton, Harry Dean's great-niece, was one of several relatives who moved to California. FBI agent Jim Huggins Jr. had gotten a transfer from Detroit to San Francisco in 1994 and spent a lot of time with Harry Dean in Los Angeles. Chad McKnight, son of Harry Dean's half-brother Stanley Jr., would also move to Los Angeles, work as an actor, and start a casting company.

A student at the University of Louisville at the time, Sara Stanton moved to Los Angeles to continue her studies. Eventually she opened her own casting company, which she still operates today. "I drove out in my pickup truck to Los Angeles to go to school. My girlfriend rode with me. I told her Harry lives off Mulholland Drive and that I should call him and see him. I got on my cell phone and called him." The conversation went something like this:

"Hello, this is Sara Stanton."

"Who?"

"Ralph Junior's kid."

"Oh, okay, can I call you back? I'm on the other line with Marlon Brando."

"Absolutely!"

An hour later Harry Dean calls her back.

"So you're [Ralph's] kid? What do you want?"

"I live in Los Angeles and just wanted you to know that I am here."

"I'm playing at the Mint tonight. I'll reserve you a booth."

When Ralph Jr. and his wife, Sheila, later came to visit their daughter in LA, they also gave Harry Dean a call. "He invited us over," Ralph Jr. remembered. "We just sat down. I had my kids with me. He said, 'What do you want?' I said just to see my uncle. He said, 'You don't want money?' It was like he couldn't believe I didn't want money."

Harry Dean carried some scars from the betrayals he had suffered. Within a few years, however, Sara Stanton and Jim Huggins Jr. would become two of the people closest to him. One of the first assignments Jim Huggins Jr. ever had as an FBI agent was the so-called Unabomber case that led to the capture of Theodore Kaczynski in 1996 for a series of previously unsolved bombings. Harry Dean liked to tell his Hollywood friends, "This is my cousin. He worked on the Unabomber case."

Where Harry Dean met his Hollywood friends was usually at his favorite watering holes. The Mousetrap on Pico, a couple blocks from the Mint, was perfect for a drink and a smoke after performing. "He would come over, him and Dabney [Coleman] and all of them," Mousetrap owner Dawayne Wallace, better known as "Mouse," told me in a November 2018 interview. "It was a bunch of them. They'd drink and have a good time. Harry was a man's man, a real philosopher, a very intelligent man. He didn't pull no punches. He lived the life he loved and loved the life he lived."

Harry Dean's favorite drink at Mouse's place? A Bloody Mary tequila, sometimes chased by a beer. "Everybody loved him," Wallace said. "Nothing bad you could say about him. He did everything you wanted him to do."

A Los Angeles native and former All-American basketball player at UC Berkeley, Mouse got his nickname from his parents after getting into some jars of flour and sugar when he was still a baby. "My parents came back and there I am in my diapers, sugar and flour everywhere. My mother said I looked like a little mouse. You get a nickname in a neighborhood of ten thousand people and you can't get rid of it."

Before Harry Dean got to the Mousetrap or Dan Tana's for his nightcaps, he usually stopped at Ago on Melrose Avenue, an Italian restaurant co-owned by Robert De Niro, Christopher Walken, and a group of other celebrities that included now-disgraced producer Harvey Weinstein. Here, Harry Dean liked a Perfect Manhattan, with Jim Beam and a splash of ginger ale. Bartender Wayne Sable had the drink waiting for him as soon as he walked in the door. "He never liked it in a typical martini glass. Always in a rocks glass, no ice. After that he would move on to Merlot, also in a rocks glass. I guess he had an aversion to stem glasses," said Sable.

As the night wore on and other guests would begin to leave, the staff at Ago would make things comfortable for Harry Dean. "We'd put an ashtray out for Harry and let him smoke," Sable told me in May 2018. "As time passed and smoking rules tightened up, he would smoke at our outside tables, where he pretty much always sat toward the end."

For the Mexican busboys at the restaurant, Sable said, the aging, but ageless, Harry Dean was a phenomenon to behold. "They would look at Harry and this old guy living it up the way he famously did, how he was able to do it night after night. Some of the older busboys would say with a smile, 'Death doesn't want him.' Knowing Harry, he would have smiled at this."

At home in the evening, Harry Dean would be on the phone, whether to relatives back in Kentucky or his friends in the film world, such as neighbor Marlon Brando. In the years before Brando died at age eighty in 2004, he and Harry Dean became close, and they would have long conversations about philosophy, music, Shakespeare, the acting life. Brando "would often call at 3 AM to discuss the *I Ching*, run through *Macbeth*, or just share 'three or four minutes' of absolute silence," Danny Leigh wrote in a 2006 article in *Sight and Sound*. Brando was also a practical joker and sometimes liked to have fun with Harry Dean on the phone. "You want to hear something, Harry?" he'd say. Then, before Harry Dean could answer, click went the phone. Conversation over.

Brando once asked Harry Dean whether his fame had ever affected how they interacted as friends.

"At first," Harry Dean told him.

"What about now?" Brando asked. "What do you think about me now?"

Harry Dean gave him that long, lean look of his and said, "You are nothing."

Around 2005, during filming of the television series *Big Love*, Harry Dean hired twenty-four-year-old actor and future filmmaker Logan Sparks as his personal assistant. The Arizona native would bring him food, accompany him to events and gatherings, check on him several days a week. Sparks used the relationship to connect Harry Dean with a friend, director Brian McGuire, who cast him in small roles in several films during the last years of Harry Dean's life. Sparks also would later cowrite Harry Dean's last film, *Lucky*.

From the Big Screen to the Small Screen

Two years after *Fear and Loathing in Las Vegas*, Harry Dean reconnected with Johnny Depp in English director and screenwriter Sally Potter's moody, beautifully scored *The Man Who Cried* (2000), a tale of World War II Paris and of gypsies and Jews and émigrés and their struggle to survive as Nazi troops approach. The film's all-star cast included Depp as gypsy horse trainer Cesar, Christina Ricci as nightclub singer and Russian émigré Suzie, Cate Blanchett as Russian showgirl Lola, John Turturro as opera singer Dante Dominio, and Harry Dean as theatre company manager Felix Perlman.

Bow-tied and bespectacled, with a French accent, Felix Perlman was a different kind of role for Harry Dean, a character like the others in the film, trying to hold on to the world around him until he's forced to shut his theater company down. "Mussolini certainly has a great sense of theater," he acknowledges at one point. He's Jewish and, like the gypsies and Russians around him, a likely target for the Nazi invaders. The story, however, centers on the love between Cesar and Suzie and the forces that ultimately will separate them.

A year later Harry Dean joined with old buddies Sean Penn, Sam Shepard, Mickey Rourke, and Jack Nicholson in Penn's *The Pledge* (2001), a film that is flawed plotwise, yet still gripping, with elements of both an old-fashioned police procedural and the obsessions and hubris one finds in Shakespearean tragedy. Based on a Friedrich Dürrenmatt novel, the film features Jack Nicholson, who, as retired police detective Jerry Black, can't let go of his last case, the rape and murder of a young girl whose mother forces him to "pledge" to find the murderer.

A mentally challenged Native American is arrested and charged, but Jerry Black doesn't buy it, and his investigation leads him to purchase a rural gas station–store where he can be close to the case and ultimately the true murderer. There he befriends a young mother, Lori, played by Penn's then–real-life wife Robin Wright Penn, and her daughter, whom Black, unknown to her mother, will use as bait to lure the murderer into the open. The murderer dies in a car accident before he shows up where Black planned to expose him. Lori severs her relationship with Black, who ends the film in front of his gas station, muttering incoherently to himself over a bottle of whiskey.

Harry Dean plays Floyd Cage, who sells his gas station to Jerry Black and sees that sale as an escape and a new life both for him and for his daughter. He's seen only very briefly, in a cameo role, but film scholar Deane Williams says that appearance is crucial, writing that "Harry Dean Stanton brings to the film a long history of roles that culminate in a defeated, or least a compliant, eccentric mode of American masculinity as well as an immediately recognizable character actor's face."

As for that face, Williams, in his book *The Cinema of Sean Penn,* quotes another writer, Ian Penman: "The head seems both shrunken and outsize—as if decomposition had set in, but been arrested, and quite possibly this is the case. You try to get an angle on it, but it already contains too many. On paper—enervated but heightened by fax and Xerox—a press shot makes him look like an early photographer's cowboy: one of those gauche, toughing Frontier emulsions. It's a physiog he shares with his buddy Dennis Hopper, and Sam Shepard: ghosts of the uncivil dead." He adds, "Harry Dean has embodied the marginal spirit in every possible guise and period. With Stanton the demarcation 'loser' is never securely circumscribed. Unlike Lee Marvin, he nearly always elicits sympathy: always the stiff, never the pallbearer."

The Pledge, with its somber ending, didn't do well financially, earning roughly $6 million less worldwide than its $35 million budget. "Will you try with your next movie to do one where you're not doomed before you start to having a marginal audience?" Nicholson told Penn with a grin afterward.

Harry Dean and Penn would join up again three years later in a segment titled "Back Off, Mary Poppins" in CBS's popular television series *Two and a Half Men,* which starred Charlie Sheen as Charlie. The two actors, along with musician Elvis Costello, playing themselves, show up at Charlie's place to enjoy scotch and cigars. As what Deane Williams called an "outsider in the Brat Pack era, fifteen years older even than [another outsider, Mickey] Rourke," Harry Dean plays the "eccentric elder statesman" of the group, confessing that he, unlike perhaps the other aging "brats" with him, sometimes doesn't "even get up" at night to pee. Ever the philosopher, Harry Dean opines about human relationships in the show: "Let me tell you something about sharing, kid," he says to Charlie Sheen's character. "Sharing is a two-way street. When you share with another human being you always get back more than you gave. Assuming that you are smart enough to share with someone who has more stuff than you had in the beginning."

Harry Dean Finds Big Love

I couldn't help noticing the wedding ring on lifelong bachelor Harry Dean's finger when I watched Sophie Huber's 2013 documentary on him, *Harry*

Dean Stanton: Partly Fiction. I asked her about it when I interviewed her in August 2018. "That was from *Big Love*," she told me. "He never took it off. You know in *Big Love* he is married to five or six women."

Indeed, in that HBO series about a polygamous Mormon family in modern-day Utah, Harry Dean played Roman Grant, the controlling, conniving patriarch of the Juniper Creek compound, head of a sprawling family that includes the 31 children and 187 grandchildren he has had with his eleven wives. The critically acclaimed and Golden Globe–nominated show featured Bill Paxton as polygamist Bill Hendrickson and Jeanne Tripplehorn, Chloë Sevigny, and Ginnifer Goodwin as Bill's three wives, Barb, Nicki, and Margene, respectively. Created by Mark V. Olsen and Will Scheffer, the series ran from 2006 until 2011 and depicted a family that's relatively normal other than its marital complexity, but with constant struggles not only with a world that condemns polygamy but also with the domineering, cowboy-hat–wearing Roman Grant. Known as the Prophet, Grant happens to be Nicki's father as well as the leader of the Mormon colony that includes Bill's parents. With his innocuous, but misleading, smile, Harry Dean's character sings—"Big Rock Candy Mountain" and "Church in the Wildwood" are a couple of his tunes—but also demands loyalty, and connives and manipulates to keep it.

Even though Harry Dean played what the *Los Angeles Times* called a "particularly creepy, corrupt, and possibly murderous" character, he also brought a complexity to the role that made writers Olsen and Scheffer eventually see his face every time they wrote a line for old Roman. "We didn't write it with him in mind, but with the second episode we were writing for him," Olsen told the *LA Times* shortly before the series' beginning in March 2006. "He is very gifted with dialogue and words. It's a joy to put words in that man's mouth because he savors them."

Scheffer agreed. "There is a kind of sweetness to Harry Dean that we didn't consider part of the character until Harry was saying the words."

The cast of *Big Love* included several actors whose paths Harry Dean had crossed in other films and television shows over his long career—Grace Zabriskie, Bruce Dern, Mary Kay Place. Zabriskie had worked with Harry Dean in several David Lynch films. Dern had played a deputy in *Pat Garrett and Billy the Kid.* Place and Harry Dean both had been in *Mary Hartman, Mary Hartman* back in the 1970s. *Big Love* also came at a good time for Harry Dean financially. Still recovering from financial advisor Bill Wine's embezzlement, Harry Dean needed the cash. "What saved Harry was he got that role in *Big Love*," his cousin Jim Huggins Jr. said. "That put him back on track."

In 2010, the last year he appeared in *Big Love,* Harry Dean also showed up in a segment of the NBC comedy-spy series *Chuck* titled "Chuck Versus the Anniversary." More than a quarter century after *Repo Man,* he once again played a repo man, this time coming to repossess a car partly owned by the main character, Chuck. Played by Zachary Levi, Chuck hasn't made a payment in four months. A year after his *Chuck* appearance, Harry Dean lent his voice to the eyepatch-wearing character Baron Kleberkuh in the Cartoon Network series *Mongo Wrestling Alliance.* The Baron is the patriarch of an old wrestling family, and his grandson Rusty is bound and determined to restore the family's prominence in the cutthroat world of professional wrestling.

Between 2013 and 2015, Harry Dean, now well into his eighties, also appeared in several segments of the HBO series *Getting On,* another project of Will Scheffer and Mark V. Olsen. Based on a series that ran in Great Britain, *Getting On* takes place in the female geriatric wing of a hospital, where doctors, staffers, and patients deal with all the ailments, and occasionally with the surprising pleasures, of aging. Harry Dean played elderly Leonard Butler, whose daughter drops him off at the wing every Thursday. On one visit, lucky Leonard gets a blow job from one of the female patients, Bertie, an occurrence not that unusual in a series that combined some sharp critiques of the US health-care system with strong doses of humor and octogenarian sex.

As he approached ninety, Harry Dean continued to make small appearances in a variety of movies, four alone by Logan Sparks's friend Brian McGuire but in others as well. At this point, just to have Harry Dean's name listed in the cast could help sell a film, but he was wearing down. He was doing people a favor, but "he told me he hated to make those movies," Jim Huggins Jr. said.

Still, he kept making them, and even in a small role he held on to his professional values. McGuire witnessed that professionalism while working with him in his 2012 film *Carlos Spills the Beans.* "It was kind of cool," McGuire told me in February 2019. "He was coming up to me asking me questions about the other characters and their relationship to his. He was awesome. He wanted to know everyone's relationship to his character, the details of the scene."

McGuire saw how Harry Dean could transform on the set from tired old man to engaged actor. "It was a magic transformation. He's old at this point, and he was kind of over making movies, but he kept doing it. He was old. He wanted to watch game shows. He wanted to relax, but when all his buddies were doing it [making movies], he wanted to do it, too. He would come in and wrestle into it. Once the force of the moment came on, he would settle into it, accept it, and it always felt good at the end."

McGuire was at Harry Dean's home once when Harry Dean had to do a phone interview with a reporter from the *London Times*. "The guy was a big fan, but he said the wrong thing," recalled McGuire. "'You're one of my favorite character actors,' he said. Harry didn't hear anything after that. Harry said, 'Hey, I was the lead in *Paris, Texas*. What do you say about that?' He was pushing ninety and still fighting to be the lead man. The guy was a real fan. Harry was an angry Buddha. He was intense. Repo men are always intense."

Harry Dean Gets One More Lead Role

Lucky opens with an announcement on the screen that Harry Dean Stanton *is* Lucky, and there is quickly no doubt. On his dresser is a photo of Harry Dean in his Navy uniform. There's a photograph of Lucky's mom, too, and it's Ersel. Later he will talk about his Aunt Beulah, his favorite, and he'll tell the story of shooting a whippoorwill as a young boy, stifling its song and burning a memory in his brain—"the saddest moment of my whole life." Lucky watches game shows in his underwear and works his crossword puzzles. He does his morning yoga exercise (the first of five every day) before lighting up the first link in the day's long chain of cigarettes. His doctor even confesses to him he's given up telling him to stop smoking. If the cigarettes were going to kill him, they would've done it by now.

Lucky's a lifelong bachelor who sings Mexican songs. He takes long walks at a good stride for a ninety-year-old and usually winds up at his favorite diner or bar, where he inevitably finds buddies nursing their coffees or tequila sunrises. He likes to smoke a joint, and his most likely greeting is "You are nothing."

And, like Harry Dean, Lucky goes to bed alone at night, and that's how he wakes up in the morning.

Logan Sparks, Harry Dean's longtime assistant and cowriter of the *Lucky* script, insisted to *Los Angeles Times* writer Mark Olsen that "it's not a biography. It's not a summarized version of his life at all." However, the film's other writer, Drago Sumonja, had this to say: "Seventy-five percent of it is all Harry. It's all these philosophies that Harry has lived by. They are his mottoes and mantras, and a lot of it is these stories that he has told us over time. It all really stuck with us."

In fact, when Sparks and Sumonja would run low in material as they wrote the film, they'd call Harry Dean and ask him to tell them more stories. Harry Dean is Lucky.

Directed by veteran character actor John Carroll Lynch in his directorial debut and coproduced by Sparks and Sumonja, *Lucky* was Harry Dean's last film, and at eighty-nine he might never have agreed to do it if it hadn't also featured some of the people closest to him over the years: director David Lynch as Howard, mourning the disappearance of his hundred-year-old tortoise, President Roosevelt; Ed Begley Jr. as Lucky's doctor; *Alien* star Tom Skerritt as a fellow World War II veteran. The story takes place in a tiny desert town, a setting very similar to that of *Paris, Texas*. "It's the echoes of *Paris, Texas* that reverberate the loudest" in *Lucky*, wrote David Ehrlich in his eloquent tribute to Harry Dean and the film for *Indiewire*. "*Lucky* is a lot like catching up with Travis Henderson a few decades down the road."

Only now, Travis Henderson/Lucky/Harry Dean Stanton is facing mortality, particularly after a fall that portends more failures of health. His real family now is the collection of friends he's made over the years. They listen as he drops his fatalistic pearls of wisdom throughout the film. "The soul doesn't exist," he tells them. "Nothing is permanent." He remembers a panic attack he had as a child at Aunt Beulah's. "It was all black out there." At the bar called Elaine's, facing his friends, he explains his acceptance of what had scared him as a youth. "It's all going to go away into blackness, the void, and nobody's in charge and you're left with *ungatz*, nothing. That's all there is."

"What do you with that?" someone asks.

"You smile," he says, echoing a war story Tom Skerritt's Fred had told him at the diner. It was about a young Asian girl convinced the Americans were going to kill her. "Maybe seven, she had this beautiful smile, coming from inside, stopped us in our tracks," Skerritt's Fred said. "She's a Buddhist, and she thinks she's going to be killed, and she smiles. They don't give a medal for that kind of bravery."

Yet Lucky, like Harry Dean, was in fact afraid of death. In violation of all the teachings of the Zen masters, Harry Dean feared the void and blackness that he told others awaited them, and he admits it. "I'm scared," Lucky says to a friend as they share a joint and watch Liberace on television. "I know," she says.

It's as if that speech to his friends at Elaine's was more than his final word on the matter, as if he might have added, "If you can tell me different, I'd listen, but you can't."

In the end, Lucky is in the desert, like Travis Henderson, and he smiles into the camera as he walks away. "Beginning as a broad comedy before blossoming into a wry meditation on death and all the things we leave behind," *Lucky* is a "wisp of a movie, blowing across the screen like a tumbleweed," and Harry Dean is its "Rosetta stone, the singular wellspring for all of its laconic energy," David Ehrlich wrote. In the end, Lucky realizes that "being alone might be a lot easier than dying alone," and he's afraid that "knowing nothing lasts might not be a good reason to act like nothing matters." What does matter is the love his friends feel for him because of what he has meant in their lives. Even more than for surviving those Japanese kamikaze attacks back in the war, this is what makes him indeed lucky.

After a premiere showing of *Lucky* at the Harry Dean Stanton Festival in Lexington, Kentucky, shortly after Harry Dean's death in September 2017, director John Carroll Lynch told me he saw Lucky as similar to the character Everyman in the medieval allegory of that name. "This movie was like Everyman, who approached death and the great hereafter, and as he sheds his riches, his belongings, his friends, he's left only with his good deeds." In other words, as one scholar put it when describing *Everyman*, "man can take with him from this world nothing that he has received, only what he has given."

At that same festival, Drago Sumonja told of how he came up with the ending for *Lucky*. "One night I was parked in my car at Bob's Big Boy. It was late, at 1:00 AM. Logan [Sparks] and I had met earlier that day, talking about notes, dressing. One of my favorite movies was *Smokey and the Bandit,* and I don't know, you just sort of go back to tap into what you grew up on. *Smokey and the Bandit* popped in my brain. I remembered the scene when Smokey is trying to outrun the police. He pulls into a back alley, and the car idles. He sees the police [pass him by], and he's gotten away. He looks up at the camera and smiles. I thought that would be interesting. I started thinking how that would translate. What would Harry do? I saw him walking through the desert and just taking out a cigarette and looking up and smile. He looks right into the camera and smiles and walks off into the sunset."

As different as *Smokey and the Bandit* may be from *Lucky,* the smiles in both films are an affirmation of life, and in *Lucky*'s case even in the face of approaching death.

Reviews of the film were mostly positive. Some of them combined review and obituary, many focusing on Harry Dean's career as well as what had become his last role. "Wizened as a dry twig and clearly in fragile health, the ninety-year-old veteran fully inhabits the title character, a chain-smoking old curmudgeon facing up to his own mortality with beatific calm in a backwater desert town," Stephen Dalton wrote in the *Hollywood Reporter*.

"With the unexpected timing of the movie's release just after his death, *Lucky* now stands as a tribute and testament to Harry Dean Stanton as a person, as an artist, and refashions him into something of a national monument," Mark Olsen wrote in the *Los Angeles Times*.

Not everyone was a fan, however. Richard Brody in the *New Yorker*, no fan of *Paris, Texas*, either, said that while *Lucky* was "a generous vehicle for Stanton's presence, it's also a painful trivialization of it. The movie follows the line of the mythologizing of Stanton in *Paris, Texas*—but now the loner with a bleak but blanked-out past is presented as a cute old coot. . . . Like Travis in Wenders' film, Lucky is a blank, a cipher, a symbol, an empty vessel awaiting the delivery of his own over-scripted backstory."

Dalton, in his *Hollywood Reporter* tribute, would have none of this. "Elegaic in tone but full of warmth and humor, *Lucky* feels almost like a planned memorial, a bittersweet lap of honor. Stanton knew what was coming." The film, wrote Dalton, is a fitting final bow for an actor who had "elevated a kind of Zen minimalist performance style into high art. His bittersweet reward for this unshowy approach was a spotty screen career that took decades to blossom, but the huge groundswell of respect and goodwill he accrued served him well in his glorious autumn years. He gambled on the long game, and it finally repaid him handsomely."

Making the film was no easy matter for Harry Dean or for the others. Filming took eighteen days, during which Harry Dean asked tons of questions and fought over lines. At one point, Brian McGuire, Harry Dean's director in several earlier films, filled in for Logan Sparks in both running lines and simply caretaking. Harry Dean quickly fired him when he came up short on knowing the script. Then he turned around and hired him back the next day. "Harry Dean needed justification for his actions [as Lucky]," Sparks later said. "Why Lucky is doing this or that, or not."

For John Carroll Lynch, directing Harry Dean as a freshman director was like "boot camp," he told *Variety* magazine. "He didn't suffer fools. He wanted to know why you wanted everything in the movie. He was meticulous, he was exacting, he was at times infuriating, and he was always inspiring." Added to this was the pressure of working with an actor pushing ninety and knowing he might not live to see the film's premiere. "I personally knew that time wasn't on our side, and that's kind of what the movie is about," Lynch said. "I had a conception that it [Harry Dean dying before completion of the film] might be possible, but what has happened you can't really prepare for. You can conceive of it, but you can't be certain."

"It was a lot of work," Harry Dean said shortly after filming ended. "I'm totally worn out. Great crew. A worthy project. I'm proud of it." Then a parting word from the old curmudgeon: "I've been doing this so long I don't give a fuck anymore."

Harry Dean Faces the Void

Harry Dean didn't live to see the premiere of *Lucky*. Although it was shown at the South by Southwest Festival in Austin, Texas, in March 2017, its Los Angeles premiere and theatrical release weren't until late September that year. Harry Dean's health had already begun to fail by March. Nearly up to that time he was still doing his yoga exercises, pushups, walks. "Logan [Sparks] called and said Harry's having a lot of abdominal pain," Sara Stanton said. "They were driving him to Cedars [Cedars-Sinai Medical Center on Beverly Boulevard]. I met him there. He had an appendix rupture that day."

Harry Dean got through subsequent surgery for his appendix and even the stroke that he suffered during the same period. "I said this guy is a cowboy or either he made some deal with the devil," Sara recalled. "I don't know how he survived."

However, Harry Dean had lost a lot of weight—he was down to a hundred pounds—and was noticeably feeble. He returned to his Mulholland Drive home, but Sara and Jim Huggins Jr. had to secure him home healthcare services to give him round-the-clock care. With both sharing power-of-attorney responsibilities over Harry Dean, they subsequently released Logan Sparks of his duties. "I told him [Harry Dean] we need to let go of Logan," Sara said. "Logan is a personal assistant, not a caregiver. That is not what his job entails."

Sparks, who never responded to efforts to interview him for this book, accepted the severance package that Sara and Jim worked out.

Two weeks after Harry Dean came home, he was seriously ill again, this time with pneumonia. He was transported to Sherman Oaks Hospital on Van Nuys Boulevard because it was closer than Cedars-Sinai. He would spend the next couple of months there in an up-and-down battle that included hallucinations and more struggles with pneumonia. He would spend his birthday in July at Sherman Oaks as friends and family grew increasingly concerned about the care he was getting.

Harry Dean's old flame Rebecca De Mornay grew so incensed that she had confrontations with the staff at Sherman Oaks. "I understand she was frustrated, but you can't be mean to the staff because they take care of Harry," Sara said. De Mornay also didn't respond to my request for an interview.

Eventually Harry Dean was transferred to Barlow Respiratory Hospital on Stadium Way in Elysian Park. Once there, his condition stabilized enough to get him transferred to a Cedars-Sinai–affiliated facility and then, when an infection set in, back to Cedars-Sinai. By then it was August, and Harry Dean had just weeks to live.

Throughout Harry Dean's long hospitalization, friends and colleagues came to visit, including old friends like Jack Nicholson and Kris Kristofferson, with whom Harry Dean at one point felt well enough to sing a few songs. On one of their visits, neighbors Mary McCormack and Michael Morris found that Harry Dean, then with tubes in his mouth and unable to speak, had scribbled a poem for Mary on a writing board with a black marker.

Ther once wuz a man named Harry
Whos neighbor next door wuz Mary
They shared a driveway
In sunny LA
And both acted
To pay for the dairy

"It was so sweet," Michael said. "In the hospital, he would say, 'No fear, Buddha.'"

So many people came to visit Harry Dean—some of whom were friends of friends he barely knew—that Sara and Jim had to impose restrictions. "Everybody wants to have their story, and it is understandable," Sara said. "'Hey, I was there when Harry was dying.' I don't fault them for it, but that wasn't good for Harry, and Harry kept getting infections. He had no immune system, and you are bringing all your germs into the room and you are hugging and kissing him. I told Jimmy, 'You got to do something. They are going to kill him.'"

Harry Dean may have told Michael Morris "No fear, Buddha," but he felt fear, and plenty of it. "He would say, 'I am not ready,'" Sara said. "He wanted to live." Still, he knew the end was close. He told Sara, "I am living my own worst nightmare."

"His philosophy? I always thought it was BS," Sara said. "He truly believed it, but in the end he died thinking about it [what, if anything, might await him after death]."

Harry Dean died on a Friday. Before he died, Sara had asked him whether he wanted to be buried or cremated. "You decide," he told her. She told him that most Buddhists get cremated. "Harry wasn't really a Buddhist, but he did follow some of their ideas. He said okay."

She and Jim made the arrangements, and when she went to the crematorium, she had a strange encounter. "I get there early, and the white hearse was outside. The crematorium is in the middle of a Glendale suburban neighborhood, a city area, not off in a wooded area. This lone coyote is under a tree and staring at me. I took a couple steps forward. He took a few steps off the grass under the tree into the driveway, about a hundred feet away. He walks into the paved area and stares at me, stares at me for like five minutes."

Several memorial services were held. Harry Dean's Hollywood friends gathered at the No Name Bar on Fairfax Avenue. Rebecca De Mornay wore a black dress. Jack Nicholson came. Everyone sang songs and told tales. Sara, Jim, and other family members gathered at Sara's neighbor's home, where they also sang and told stories. Eventually Harry Dean's ashes were brought back to Lexington, where they were interred in a small plot near his mother's grave.

Postscript

FBI agent James Huggins Sr. was in town on business and had some time, so he decided to give his cousin Harry Dean Stanton a call. "Meet me tonight for dinner, and we can catch up," Harry Dean told him. So that evening Huggins went to Dan Tana's in West Hollywood, and inside found his cousin at a table with actor-teacher Martin Landau, Landau's wife, veteran actress Barbara Bain, and a couple other folks. Harry Dean introduced him to everyone, including the bartender, and the conversation turned to the workings of the FBI rather than Hollywood gossip.

When Harry Dean left to go to the restroom, Landau leaned over to Huggins and confided some insider information about Hollywood. "Jim, I don't know how well you know your cousin. He is one of the few people out here who could call any director or producer and get someone a part. He doesn't have a single enemy. He is well respected, treats everybody right, but because of that a lot of people take advantage of him. People have screwed him over."

After Harry Dean's death in September 2017, three men contacted his power-of-attorney and cousin, Jim Huggins Jr., claiming to be his son. Each asked about a will. Huggins, an FBI agent, found none of them credible. "I don't believe Harry Dean had kids, and if he did, he never claimed them."

Yes, Harry Dean suffered some betrayals in life, people seeking to take advantage of him or his name, but those paled in comparison to the deep loyalty friends like Martin Landau felt toward him. He could play—and be—the grumpy curmudgeon, but he was more likely to be the generous softy. After the filming of *Paris, Texas,* production assistant Allison Anders was having a difficult time getting funding for her own first feature film, *Border Radio.* "Harry actually gave her a check for $10,000," Wim Wenders told me. "Harry wasn't rich, and this was an enormous amount of money then, but he gave it to Allison to acknowledge how important she had been for him in the course of our film as his coach and personal assistant. Harry never wanted this to be mentioned, but now, I feel, I have the liberty of bringing it up."

Ed Begley Jr. said that just knowing Harry Dean profoundly changed his life, both as an actor and simply as a human being. Jamie James, Dabney Coleman, Dennis Quaid, Mary McCormack, Michael Morris, Lucy Jones, Jim Huggins Jr., Sara Stanton, Mike Gotovac, Dawayne "Mouse" Wallace all told me the same. Hunter Carson, who played Harry Dean's son in both *Paris, Texas,* and the Rip Van Winkle episode of *Shelley Duvall's Faerie Tale Theatre,* said his make-believe father taught him lessons he'll never forget. "Believe the words you are saying," Harry Dean told him. "You have to mean them. When you say, 'Good night, Dad,' you have to believe that. You have to believe the words. Whatever you are saying, it has to be the truth."

Once, during a break in the filming of "Rip Van Winkle," Harry Dean gave Hunter an impromptu acting lesson. "I weigh a hundred and fifty pounds, but if I want to, I can weigh a thousand pounds," he said to the young boy. Harry Dean slackened his muscles and slouched over Hunter like a massive sack of potatoes. "We wound up on the ground laughing," Carson told me in 2019, smiling at the memory.

Harry Dean never attended an Academy Awards ceremony, much less carried home an Oscar. However, his last years were full of unofficial honors that few actors ever achieve. Documentaries in 2011 and 2013 were devoted to his life and work. He inspired songs by Debbie Harry, Bernie Taupin, Kris Kristofferson, and others. A year before he died, Hollywood came together to celebrate him as he received the Harry Dean Stanton Award at the Theatre in the Ace Hotel in downtown Los Angeles. Under the auspices of the Santa Monica video store turned nonprofit Vidiots, the event featured Ed Begley Jr. as host, with guests including Anjelica Huston, Johnny Depp, Rebecca De Mornay, Danny Huston, David Lynch, Kris Kristofferson, and John Densmore, drummer for the rock group the Doors. Harry Dean was there with tousled hair and an oversized coat, looking every bit of his ninety years. "This is the best night of my life," he told the crowd. "I love all of you. I'll have my people call your people."

Perhaps Harry Dean's biggest honor was the film festival Lucy Jones organized in his honor back in Lexington, Kentucky, in 2011. For Jones, daughter of former Kentucky governor Brereton Jones, the Harry Dean fascination began with a midnight screening of *Repo Man* at Lexington's Kentucky Theater. She was just a teenager at the time but began researching the actor and discovered that he not only was a Kentuckian but also had lived and studied in Lexington. "I was just completely enamored by his screen presence," she told me in May 2017.

After going to a James Dean festival in Fairmount, Indiana, some years later, she began to develop ideas that led to organizing a festival for Harry Dean. "I was blown away by the fact that an entire community could be built around an actor whom everybody relates to," she told the *Huffington Post* in 2015 about the James Dean festival. "I grew up watching movies, but in a very solitary way. So to see people come from all over the world to this tiny town in Indiana to celebrate film and an actor lodged in my subconscious."

Over the years, Kris Kristofferson, Monte Hellman, Hunter Carson, John Carroll Lynch, Alex Cox, and many others have come to participate in the festival and related events. Harry Dean himself came in 2014, accompanied by Michelle Phillips. When he spoke to the crowd, he talked about the blackness and nothingness that awaited them all. "Everyone I've talked to since says that was their favorite part," Jones said.

Sometimes when I think of Harry Dean Stanton, I see him back at his little bungalow on Mulholland Drive, in the wee hours, a time when his friends have gone home and the fans are far away and back in their homes, too, with their loved ones. What did Harry Dean think about on those nights as he stubbed his last cigarette of the day into the crowded ashtray by his bed? Did he start to turn out the light but then let it burn just a little bit longer? Did he look at the picture of Ersel on the dresser? Did he wonder whether he really did have a son somewhere out there, his own blood? Did he once more go over regrets from the "Wall of Shame" of missed opportunities he joked about with his buddies—that promised recording gig with Bob Dylan, that promised get-together with Eric Clapton? Did he brood about missing a question on *Family Feud* that day? Did he ponder the familiar emptiness next to him in his bed, or maybe think about the nothingness awaiting him in the great beyond?

Sure, he thought about all those things. At one time or another. And I know what he did about it. He smiled, and then he muttered into the silence surrounding him, "Maybe one more cigarette."

Acknowledgments

So many people were important in my effort to tell the story of Harry Dean Stanton that it is impossible to list them all. However, I would like especially to thank Patrick McGilligan, whose persistence in urging me to take on this project made it happen and thus opened the door to a world of new experiences for me. Anne Dean Dotson of the University Press of Kentucky was there at the beginning and throughout, advising and encouraging. Others with the press, including David L. Cobb, Natalie B. O'Neal, and Tori Robinson, were so helpful. So was Donna Bouvier, whose close copyediting was masterful. Also of great help were my wife, Suzanne, and my daughter, Rachel, who became my personal chauffeur from one end of Los Angeles to the other. This book wouldn't exist without the help of Lucy Jones of the Harry Dean Stanton Fest. Jamie James, Jim Huggins Jr., Sara Stanton, Ralph Stanton Jr., all of the McKnights, as well as Patsy Wallace were of great assistance. Jerry Eltzroth was my tour guide to Irvine, Kentucky, and the Stanton ancestry. I also want to thank Yvonne Harrison of the Estill County (Kentucky) Historical Society and Museum. Ned Comstock at the University of Southern California's Cinematic Arts Library, Faye Thompson and Rachel Bernstein at the Academy of Motion Picture Arts and Sciences Margaret Herrick Library, Ross Clark at the Pasadena Playhouse, and Judy Sackett and Kathryn Caton at the University of Kentucky opened their archives to me. Writers Susan Compo, Robert "Bob" Crane, and Ace Atkins helped make crucial contacts. Many thanks, too, to Tom Thurman, Ellen Hisako, Keiko Olivia Tominaga, Mary McCormack, Michael Morris, Sophie Huber, Richard Howorth, and the University of Mississippi and its School of Journalism and New Media.

Notes

Prologue

2 "She was a very free spirit": Joy Spicer, interview by author, Irvine, KY, July 17, 2018.

2 "He was just like her": Etta Clay Moberly Hamilton, telephone interview by author, July 9, 2018.

2 "I asked Jim Huggins Jr. once": Jim Huggins Jr., interview by author, Lexington, KY, September 28, 2017.

3 "He turned that part into his own story": Wim Wenders, commentary, *Paris, Texas* (Road Movies Film Produktion GMBH & Argos Films SA, 1984, DVD Netflix distribution).

4 "I have in fact loved to work with actors": Wim Wenders, email interview by author, October 3, 2019. Unless otherwise noted, all quotations from Wim Wenders in this chapter are drawn from this interview.

4 "Not gorgeous enough to be stars": Melissa Holbrook Pierson and Luc Sante, eds., *O.K. You Mugs: Writers on Movie Actors* (New York: Pantheon Books, 1999), xii.

4 "I told him I wanted to play something of some beauty": Steve Oney, "Harry Dean Stanton Was Too Big for His Niche," *Stacks,* September 18, 2017 (article originally appeared in *New York Times Magazine*, November 16, 1986), https://thestacks.deadspin.com/harry-dean-stanton-was-too-big-for-his -niche-1817176718.

4 "His face is a story": Sophie Huber, *Harry Dean Stanton: Partly Fiction*, 2013, documentary film (Hugofilm, Schweizer Radio und Fernsehen/SRG SSR with Isotope Films, Adopt Films distribution, DVD).

4 "These sort of characters don't exist in Europe": Sophie Huber, telephone interview by author, August 2, 2018.

5 "My own Harry Dean Stanton act": Harry Dean Stanton biography, IMDb, http:// www.imdb.com/name/nm0001765/bio.

5 "I don't think they had a good wedding night": Sean O'Hagan, "Harry Dean Stanton: 'Life? It's One Big Phantasmagoria,'" *Guardian*, November 23, 2013, https://www.theguardian.com/film/2013/nov/23/harry-dean-stanton -interview.

5 "Go straight ahead till you hit something": James Hughes, "Tramps, Drifters, and Cockfighters: A Visit to the Fifth Annual Harry Dean Stanton Festival in Kentucky," *Grantland,* June 8, 2015, http://grantland.com/hollywood -prospectus/tramps-drifters.

5 "I think she resented me as a kid": O'Hagan, "Harry Dean Stanton: 'Life? It's One Big Phantasmagoria.'"

6 "I felt rage against adults": Harry Dean Stanton biography, IMDb.

7 "A film with great character actors": Frank Darabont, comments, television broad-cast of *Cool Hand Luke* (Turner Classic Movies, January 3, 2017).

7 "A gritty new realism and ethnicity": Peter Biskind, *Easy Riders, Raging Bulls: How the Sex-Drugs-and-Rock 'n' Roll Generation Saved Hollywood* (New York: Simon & Schuster, 1998), 16, 17.

8 "It's my favorite film that I was in": O'Hagan, "Harry Dean Stanton: 'Life? It's One Big Phantasmagoria.'"

8 "It's frightening, terrifying, but joyous, too": Steven Rosen, "Lexington's Harry Dean Stanton Fest Is a Model for Other Actor-Themed Film Festivals," *Huffington Post,* May 27, 2015, http://www.huffingtonpost.com/steven-rosen/lexingtons -harry-dean-sta_b_7441656.html.

9 "A kind of lone drifter in Hollywood": O'Hagan, "Harry Dean Stanton: 'Life? It's One Big Phantasmagoria.'"

9 "Supporting players worked hard, if not harder than leading stars": Cynthia Brideson and Sara Brideson, *Also Starring . . . : Forty Biographical Essays on the Greatest Character Actors of Hollywood's Golden Era, 1930–1965* (Duncan, OK: BearManor Media, 2012), 12.

9 "A lost art": William Friedkin, commentary, *The Narrow Margin* (RKP Productions, 1952, DVD Netflix distribution).

10 "His lean face and hungry eyes": Roger Ebert, *Paris, Texas,* review, December 8, 2002, www.rogerebert.com/reviews/great-movie-paris-texas-1984.

10 "Stanton has made silence and stillness": O'Hagan, "Harry Dean Stanton: 'Life? It's One Big Phantasmagoria.'"

10 "I've always felt like an outsider": Harry Dean Stanton biography, IMDb.

1. "Something Went Wrong"

11 "Not about him but the music": Sophie Huber, telephone interview by author, August 2, 2018.

11 "A struggle going on there": *WTF with Marc Maron,* podcast, Harry Dean Stanton, from 2014 (episode 464, reposted September 16, 2017), https://www .youtube.com/watch?v=RFejvPkRyXU.

11 "Mind must free itself": Jiddu Krishnamurti, *Total Freedom: The Essential Krishnamurti* (San Francisco: HarperSanFrancisco, 1996), 10.

11 "You can't change your roots": Tom Thurman, *Harry Dean Stanton: Crossing Mulholland,* 2011, documentary film, http://www.ket.org/episode/KMUSE %20000402/.

Notes

12 "The most self-consciously Southern of states": Michael Barone and Grant Ujifusa, *The Almanac of American Politics, 1982* (Washington, DC: Barone & Co., 1981), 413.

13 "Irvine became a railroad town": *200 Years in Pictures: Estill County, Kentucky, 1808–2008* (Morley, MO: Acclaim Press, 2009), 7.

13 "An intensity of care and a refinement of skill": Wendell Berry, *Sex, Economy, Freedom and Community* (New York: Pantheon Books, 1993), 54.

13 "Night riders, singing church hymns and waving their Bibles": John van Willigen and Susan C. Eastwood, *Tobacco Culture: Farming Kentucky's Burley Belt* (Lexington: University Press of Kentucky, 1998), 45.

14 "There have always been people who disliked it": Berry, *Sex, Economy, Freedom and Community*, 56.

15 "And he meant it, too": Joy Spicer, interview by author, Irvine, KY, July 17, 2018. All quotations from Joy Spicer in this chapter are drawn from this interview.

15 "An outgoing, fun-loving lady": Jim Huggins Sr., telephone interview by author, January 2, 2018. All quotations from Jim Huggins Sr. in this chapter are drawn from this interview.

15 "One day I just got up and started singing": Sean O'Hagan, "Harry Dean Stanton: 'Life? It's One Big Phantasmagoria,'" *The Guardian,* November 23, 2013, https://www.theguardian.com/film/2013/nov/23/harry-dean-stanton-interview.

16 "Climb up on a kitchen stool and sing songs": Steve Oney, "Harry Dean Stanton Was Too Big for His Niche," *The Stacks,* September 18, 2017 (article originally appeared in *New York Times Magazine*, November 16, 1986), https://thestacks.deadspin.com/harry-dean-stanton-was-too-big-for-his-niche-1817176718.

16 "They made me sit in this tub till I got it right": Jamie James, interview by author, Los Angeles, March 17, 2018.

16 "His parents began to argue more and more": Mark Matousek, "Harry Dean Stanton on *Paris, Texas*: For the First Time, I Got the Girl," *Interview,* May 5, 2018 (article originally appeared in 1985), https://interviewmagazine.com/culture/harry-dean-stanton-mark-matousek-interview.

16 "All the Stantons were all meaner, tougher, and smarter than the other one": Ralph Stanton Jr., telephone interview by author, January 1, 2018. All quotations from Ralph Stanton Jr. in this chapter are drawn from this interview.

16 "Do you accept Jesus Christ as your Lord and Savior?": Stanley McKnight Jr., telephone interview by author, November 8, 2018. All quotations from Stanley McKnight Jr. in this chapter are drawn from this interview.

16 "Thinking I was Humphrey Bogart": Martin Chilton, "Why America Misses Its Icon Harry Dean Stanton," *Independent,* September 13, 2018, https://www.independent.co.uk/arts-entertainment/films/featres/harry-dean-stanton-death-career-lucky-twin-peaks-alien-paris-texas-a853691.html.

16 "I lived up in the hills": Tom Thurman, *Harry Dean Stanton: Crossing Mulholland,* 2011, documentary film, http://www.ket.org/episode/KMUSE%20000402/.

17 "If he did nothing, he'd still be in a rocking chair in Kentucky": Sophie Huber, *Harry Dean Stanton: Partly Fiction*, 2013, documentary film (Hugofilm, Schweizer Radio Und Fernsehen/SRG SSR with Isotope Films, Adopt Films distribution, DVD).

17 "'Briar,' and it's not a complimentary term": Jerry Eltzroth, interview by author, Irvine, KY, July 17, 2018. Also cited are stories provided and written by Eltzroth for the Irving, KY, *Citizen Voice & Times* on Stanton in 2017 and 2018.

17 "Supply and demand into harmony": Pete Daniel, *Breaking the Land: The Transformation of Cotton, Tobacco, and Rice Cultures since 1880* (Urbana: University of Illinois Press, 1986), 110–111.

18 "I killed a mockingbird": Thurman, *Harry Dean Stanton: Crossing Mulholland*.

18 "He said it was the saddest moment of his whole life": Chilton, "Why America Misses Its Icon Harry Dean Stanton," *Independent*, September 13, 2018.

19 "There is one part I really want to play": Oney, "Harry Dean Stanton Was Too Big for His Niche."

19 "uppity pro-slavery Bluegrass region to the north": Barone and Ujifusa, *The Almanac of American Politics 1982*, 417.

20 "We'd hang it in the barn, let it dry out": *WTF with Marc Maron*, podcast.

20 "Cutting tobacco is strenuous work": van Willigen and Eastwood, *Tobacco Culture*, 123.

20 "Each laborer must be able to keep his balance": Ibid., 135.

20 "It is a dangerous thing": Ibid., 136.

21 "Cut twelve hundred to sixteen hundred sticks a day": Ibid., 123.

21 "We were just kids running and playing in the yard": Etta Clay Moberly Hamilton, telephone interview by author, July 9, 2018.

21 "Sheridan and she would go on the road to carnivals": McKnight Jr., phone interview, November 8, 2018.

22 "It's all based on fear": *WTF with Marc Maron*, podcast.

22 "She was closest to Arch": McKnight Jr., phone interview, November 8, 2018.

22 "I was there the night it happened": Matousek, "Harry Dean Stanton on *Paris, Texas*."

22 "Marie Dozier, like her sister, died a premature death": Jerry Eltzroth, "Harry Dean Stanton Home Identified," Irvine, KY, *Citizen Voice & Times*, January 12, 2018, http://www.cvt-news.com/news/?p=12289.

23 "Lillian, who turned sixteen in 1940": Jerry Eltzroth, "Just a Closer Walk with Thee," Irvine, KY, *Citizen Voice & Times*, October 26, 2017 (copy sent by Eltzroth via email to author).

23 "He had an older sister named Lillian": Paul Sturgill, telephone interview by author, August 21, 2018. All quotations from Paul Sturgill in this chapter are drawn from this interview.

24 "One of those guys who just kind of hung around": Richard "Dick" Derrickson, telephone interview by author, August 20, 2018. All quotations from Richard Derrickson in this chapter are drawn from this interview.

24 "I've always been a singer": Chilton, "Why America Misses Its Icon Harry Dean Stanton."
25 "People would smoke in his chair": *WTF with Marc Maron,* podcast.
25 "Ersel would leave her children": Whitney Fishburn, telephone interview by author, November 14, 2018. All quotations from Whitney Fishburn in this chapter are drawn from this interview.
26 "Now I have to be nice to him all the time": Spicer, interview, July 17, 2018.
26 "I was fourteen and I was terrified": Huber, *Harry Dean Stanton: Partly Fiction.*
26 "I sent her a heart, a ceramic heart": *WTF with Marc Maron,* podcast.
26 "What's the hurry?": Eltzroth, "Just a Closer Walk with Thee."

2. "Riding a Stick of Dynamite"

27 "I was damn lucky I didn't get blown up or killed": Martin Chilton, "Why America Misses Its Icon Harry Dean Stanton," *Independent,* September 13, 2018, https://www.independent.co.uk/arts-entertainment/films/featres/harry-dean-stanton-death-career-lucky-twin-peaks-alien-paris-texas-a853691.html.
27 "Five ammunition-loaded LSTs blew up in a single day": Jerry L. Rogers, *So Long for Now: A Sailor's Letters from the USS Franklin* (Norman: University of Oklahoma Press, 2017), 94.
27 "Kamikaze attacks were sinking at least one US ship every day": *D-Days in the Pacific: The Path to Victory; From Guadalcanal to Okinawa,* 2005, documentary film (Lou Reda Productions for History, A&E Television Networks, DVD).
28 "I was originally assigned to what they call a Kaiser's coffin": Jeff Corey with Emily Corey, *Improvising Out Loud: My Life Teaching Hollywood How to Act* (Lexington: University Press of Kentucky, 2017), 34.
28 "I had another dream": Ibid., 37.
28 "They put you where they wanted to put you": Paul Sturgill, telephone interview by author, August 21, 2018.
28 "The draft was lawful and rational": Rogers, *So Long for Now,* 61.
29 "The 'Dogfaces' of the Army and the 'Leathernecks' of the Marine Corps": Ibid., 62.
29 "The Navy issued him a Bible and a Bluejacket's Manual": *Navy Knowledge: World War II Navy Boot Camps,* http://astralpublishing.com/wwii-navy-boot-camps.html.
29 "Climb up a rope ladder": Rogers, *So Long for Now,* 66.
29 "You didn't have to know a lot": *WTF with Marc Maron,* podcast, Harry Dean Stanton, from 2014 (episode 464, reposted September 16, 2017), https://www.youtube.com/watch?v=RFejvPkRyXU.
29 "The Nansei stretch as far south as Taiwan": *Operation Iceberg: The Assault on Okinawa; The Last Battle of World War II* (Part 1) April–June 1945, http://historyofwar.org/articles/battles_okinawa1.html.

29 "I don't like the ocean": *WTF with Marc Maron,* podcast.

30 "Earl somehow got Harry Dean a job in the kitchen": Jim Huggins Sr., telephone interview by author, January 2, 2018.

30 "The chow line, perhaps because it was a break from serious work": Rogers, *So Long for Now,* 127.

30 "After months at sea": Ibid., 102.

30 "Knocked back a slug": Ibid., 31.

31 "Never volunteer for anything": Ibid., 314.

31 "Wide-paced, swaying": Ibid., 157.

31 "Too much to fight the last war": Rogers, *So Long for Now,* 4.

31 "Something out of *Frankenstein*": *D-Days in the Pacific.*

3. From the Lexington Stage to a New York Park Bench

32 "Pressure groups, black marketers, used-car shysters": Bill Mauldin, *Back Home* (New York: William Sloane Associates, 1947), back cover.

32 "How's things outside, boys": Ibid., 101.

32 "Several thousand young uniformed punks": Ibid., 55.

34 "A magnificent job of failing": Ibid., 56.

34 "The result was that many thousands of soldiers": Ibid., 57–58.

34 "He never talked about his military experience": Lois Pemble, telephone interview by author, December 6, 2017. All quotations from Lois Pemble in this chapter are drawn from this interview.

34 "I changed majors every year": Tom Thurman, *Harry Dean Stanton: Crossing Mulholland,* 2011, documentary film, http://www.ket.org/episode/KMUSE %20000402/.

34 "He was marvelous": Ed Faulkner, interview by author, Tunica, MS, June 8, 2017.

35 "A firmly divided family": Ralph Stanton Jr., telephone interview by author, January 1, 2018. All quotations from Ralph Stanton Jr. in this chapter are drawn from this interview.

35 "In second gear the whole way": Joy Spicer, interview by author, Irvine, KY, July 17, 2018. All quotations from Joy Spicer in this chapter are drawn from this interview.

35 "One time they made their delivery": Jim Huggins Sr., telephone interview by author, January 2, 2018. All quotations from Jim Huggins Sr. in this chapter are drawn from this interview.

36 "I learned a lot of bad habits": Roger Leasor, interviewed by Jeanne Ontko Suchanek, September 16, 2003, Oral History Collection, University of Kentucky College of Fine Arts, *History of the Guignol Theater Oral History Project,* Lexington, Kentucky.

37 "I was pretty good": Alex Simon, "Harry Dean Stanton: American Character," *The Hollywood Interview,* September 15, 2017 (article originally appeared in *Venice Magazine,* August 1997), http://thehollywoodinterview.blogspot .com/2008/02/harry-dean.

37 "Theater allows you to examine alternate possibilities for yourself": Leasor, interviewed by Suchanek, September 16, 2003.

37 "I was at home on the stage": Thurman, *Harry Dean Stanton: Crossing Mulholland.*

37 "I had to decide if I wanted to be a singer or an actor": Jerry Eltzroth, undated story on Stanton from the Irvine, KY, *Citizen Voice & Times,* provided by Eltzroth via email on June 27, 2018.

37 "You have the potential to be a great actor": Thurman, *Harry Dean Stanton: Crossing Mulholland.*

37 "I made it a point not to graduate": Steve Oney, "Harry Dean Stanton Was Too Big for His Niche," *The Stacks,* September 18, 2017 (article originally appeared in *New York Times Magazine,* November 16, 1986), https://thestacks.deadspin .com/harry-dean-stanton-was-too-big-for-his-niche-1817176718.

37 "Had my fill of pompous little men": Mauldin, *Back Home,* 67.

38 "A temple of the arts": Carl Rollyson, *Hollywood Enigma: Dana Andrews* (Jackson, MS: University Press of Mississippi, 2012), 78.

38 "Reflections of an arts movement": Ibid., 70.

39 "He knew how to raise money": Ross Clark, telephone interview by author, September 18, 2018. All quotations from Ross Clark in this chapter are drawn from this interview.

39 "Find themselves and stand on their own feet": Marion Castleberry, *Blessed Assurance: The Life and Art of Horton Foote* (Macon, GA: Mercer University Press, 2014), 71.

39 "All thirty-seven of Shakespeare's plays": "The Founding," Pasadena Playhouse, https://pasadenaplayhouse.org/about.

39 "They seemed to be doing really very little": Castleberry, *Blessed Assurance,* 58.

39 "A veritable talent funnel": "The Founding," Pasadena Playhouse.

40 "Hollywood agents scouted theater productions": Judy O'Sullivan, *The Pasadena Playhouse: A Celebration of One of the Oldest Theatrical Producing Organizations in America* (Pasadena, CA: Pasadena Playhouse, 1992), 41.

40 "From early morn till late at night": Rollyson, *Hollywood Enigma,* 77.

40 "was greeted by his Aunt Mag": Castleberry, *Blessed Assurance,* 48.

40 "The need to tap into yourself and get truthful behavior": Nehemiah Persoff, interview by author, Cambria, CA, June 16, 2016.

42 "My hair stood on end": Nehemiah Persoff, email interview by author, December 3, 2016.

42 "To reveal the human condition": Jeff Corey with Emily Corey, *Improvising Out Loud: My Life Teaching Hollywood How to Act* (Lexington: University Press of Kentucky, 2017), 84.

42 "You must be serious": E. Vakhtangov, "Preparing for the Role" in *Acting: A Handbook of the Stanislavski Method,* compiled by Toby Cole (New York: Crown Publishers, 1955), 120.

43 "The greatness of a man's acting": Corey with Corey, *Improvising Out Loud,* 175.

43 "You will have to forget everything": Castleberry, *Blessed Assurance,* 73.

43 "I should've gone to New York": Simon, "Harry Dean Stanton: American Character."

44 "This Baptist preacher who wanted to spread the word of God through song": Ibid.

44 "Twenty-four guys on a bus": Sean O'Hagan, "Harry Dean Stanton: 'Life? It's One Big Phantasmagoria,'" *The Guardian,* November 23, 2013, https://www.theguardian.com/film/2013/nov/23/harry-dean-stanton-interview.

44 "When Elvis Presley entered Sam Phillips's Sun Records Studio": Pete Daniel, *Lost Revolutions: The South in the 1950s* (Chapel Hill: University of North Carolina Press, 2000), 135.

44 "Mitch Miller hated rock 'n' roll": Peter Guralnick, *Last Train to Memphis: The Rise of Elvis Presley* (Boston: Little, Brown and Co., 1994), 202.

44 "Miller had America singing": Bruce Eder, "Mitch Miller," https://allmusic.com/artist/mitch-miller-mm0000577261.

45 "Difference between the 'hip' and the 'square'": Norman Mailer, *Advertisements for Myself* (1959; New York: G. P. Putnam's Sons, 1970), 389–390.

45 "Film production would shift toward Hollywood": Nat Segaloff, *Stirling Silliphant: The Fingers of God* (Duncan, OK: BearManor Media, 2013), 29.

45 "The dark corners of the human heart": Castleberry, *Blessed Assurance*, 155.

46 "The best actors, writers, and directors are in New York": *The Collected Works of Paddy Chayefsky: The Television Plays* (New York: Applause Books, 1995), 134.

46 "Live TV made demands on the actors": Persoff, interview by author, June 16, 2016.

46 "Not so much a religion as a technique": Mailer, *Advertisements for Myself*, 391.

46 "A chance discovery of a used book": Simon, "Harry Dean Stanton: American Character."

47 "Existentialism, the collective unconscious, Zen Buddhism": Patrick McGilligan, *Jack's Life: A Biography of Jack Nicholson* (New York: W. W. Norton & Co., 2015, 1994), 29, 108–109.

47 "Brilliant corners": title of an LP and track recording by Thelonious Monk, Riverside Records, 1957.

47 "They really didn't like it": Bob Dylan, *Chronicles: Volume One* (New York: Simon & Schuster, 2004), 48.

48 "The New York folk scene had shattered": Joe Klein, *Woody Guthrie: A Life* (1980; repr., New York: Dell Publishing, 1999), 400.

48 "A classic account of Appalachian music and culture": John Szwed, *Alan Lomax: The Man Who Recorded the World* (New York: Viking, 2010), 246.

48 "The Village upheld the tenets of his personal faith": Susan Compo, *Warren Oates: A Wild Life* (Lexington: University Press of Kentucky, 2010), 37.

48 "The chicks were wilder and the pace was faster": Ibid.

49 "A coldwater flat at Tenth and Bleecker Streets": Ibid., 39.

49 "He got on a bus and went to New York": Steve Moberly, telephone interview by author, August 22, 2017.

49 "Stuck doing another miserable road tour": Simon, "Harry Dean Stanton: American Character."

50 "Acting jobs were fleeing to the West Coast": Compo, *Warren Oates*, 49–50.
50 "If all the work is in California": Ibid., 50.
50 "Television's center of gravity was shifting": Ibid.

4. Early Days in Hollywood

51 "Here is a leading man in a character actor's body": Lois Pemble, telephone interview by author, December 6, 2017.
51 "He was not the best-looking guy in Hollywood": Paul Sturgill, telephone interview by author, August 21, 2018.
51 "Harry Dean and I were doing the heavies": L. Q. Jones, telephone interview by author, February 1, 2018.
52 "A transforming world": Susan Compo, *Warren Oates: A Wild Life* (Lexington: University Press of Kentucky, 2010), 52.
52 "He was convinced that within a couple of years he'd become a star": Steve Oney, "Harry Dean Stanton Was Too Big for His Niche," *The Stacks,* September 18, 2017 (article originally appeared in *New York Times Magazine*, November 16, 1986), https://thestacks.deadspin.com/harry-dean-stanton-was-too-big -for-his-niche-1817176718.
52 "An early gig for a US Air Force documentary": *WTF with Marc Maron,* podcast, Harry Dean Stanton, from 2014 (episode 464, reposted September 16, 2017), https://www.youtube.com/watch?v=RFejvPkRyXU.
52 "Those people were trained here": Ross Clark, telephone interview by author, September 18, 2018.
52 "Hollywood had been going through major changes": Anthony R. Fellow, *American Media History*, 3rd ed. (Boston: Wadsworth, 2013 [orig. pub. 2005]), 229.
52-53 "The vertical integration of the studios": Alex Cox, *Introduction to Film: A Director's Perspective* (Harpenden, Herts, UK: 2016), 117–118.
53 "They were mysteriously closed to me": William S. Hart, *My Life East and West: The Life Story of William S. Hart* (1929; repr., Landisville, PA: Yurchak Printing, 2013), 48, 198–199, 343, 345.
53 "I fought cleanly, without rancor or malevolence": Ibid., 351.
53 "The collapse of the studio system": Glenn Frankel, *High Noon: The Hollywood Blacklist and the Making of an American Classic* (New York: Bloomsbury, 2017), 291.
54 "It was about economics": Fellows, *American Media History*, 233.
55 "On the verge of the industry's grimmest phase": Paul Buhle and Dave Wagner, *Radical Hollywood: The Untold Story behind America's Favorite Movies* (New York: New Press, 2002), 323.
55 "They were mean-spirited and out only for themselves": Jeff Corey with Emily Corey, *Improvising Out Loud: My Life Teaching Hollywood How to Act* (Lexington: University Press of Kentucky, 2017), 147.

55 "The Hollywood Ten hearings of 1947": Frankel, *High Noon*, 87.

55 "More than one out of every three homes featuring a television set": Michael Emery and Edwin Emery, *The Press and America: An Interpretive History of Mass Media*, 7th ed. (Englewood Cliffs, NJ: Prentice-Hall, 1992 [orig. pub. 1954]), 367–368.

56 "Television was one way of filling the gaps of both time and money": Patrick McGilligan, *Jack's Life: A Biography of Jack Nicholson* (New York: W. W. Norton & Co., 2015, 1994), 171.

56 "One of the bleakest films in the history of the cinema": Alain Silver and Elizabeth Ward, eds., *Film Noir: An Encyclopedic Reference to the American Style*, 3rd ed. (Woodstock, NY: Overlook Press, 1992 [orig. pub. 1979]), 319.

56 "Alfred Hitchcock was an asshole": Joseph B. Atkins, "Nehemiah Persoff: Intensity In-Depth," in *Noir City Annual Nine: The Best of Noir City E-magazine 2016* (San Francisco: Film Noir Foundation, 2017), 180.

56 "Hitchcock 'trusted the actors'": Tom Thurman, *Harry Dean Stanton: Crossing Mulholland*, 2011, documentary film, http://www.ket.org/episode/KMUSE %20000402/.

57 "Tepidly routine . . . mundane and minor in every way": *Tomahawk Trail* (1957), IMDb, reviews, https://www.imdb.com/title/tt0165990.

57 "Part of a Western movie factory line": *Revolt at Fort Laramie* (1957), IMDb, reviews, https://www.imdb.com/title/tt0050895.

59 "The series made a hero out of a notorious gunslinger": Douglas Brode, *Shooting Stars of the Small Screen* (Austin: University of Texas Press, 2009), 67–68.

59 "Always on the lookout for the role": Ibid., 51–52.

60 "Part of a Western block": Ibid., 224.

60 "Always played the outsider" Frankel, *High Noon*, 21.

60 "We were the first adult Western": Hugh O'Brian, interview by author, Olive Branch, MS, June 1, 2012.

60 "An alternative definition": Brode, *Shooting Stars of the Small Screen*, 244.

61 "A proto-feminist progression": Ibid., 41.

61 "Peckinpah was fascinated by the perverse vitality": Compo, *Warren Oates*, 61.

5. Zelig in La La Land

63 "He is like Zelig": Whitney Fishburn, telephone interview by author, November 14, 2018. All quotations from Whitney Fishburn in this chapter are drawn from this interview.

64 "A gentleman's gentleman who hopped around lighting his cigars": *A Time for Killing*, press book, Columbia Pictures Corporation, 1967. Clipping files, Cinematic Arts Library, University of Southern California.

64 "No movie featuring either Harry Dean Stanton or M. Emmet Walsh in a supporting role can be altogether bad": Harry Dean Stanton biography, IMDb, http://www.imdb.com/name/nm0001765/bio?ref_=nm_ov_bio_sm.

Notes

64 "Audience's memory bank": William Friedkin, commentary, *The Narrow Margin* (RKP Productions, 1952, DVD Netflix distribution).

65 "Waiting, waiting, waiting for the gravy train": George Geary, "A Look Back: LA's Schwab's Pharmacy Was More Than a Drugstore," *Food Republic,* October 10, 2016, https://www.foodrepublic.com/2016/10/10/a-look-back -1-a-s-schwabs-pharmacy-was-more-than-a-drugstore.

65 "He had some guys that back in the '60s": Jamie James, interview by author, Los Angeles, March 17, 2018. All quotations from Jamie James in this chapter are drawn from this interview.

65 "Have to select more carefully what it is you're playing": Jeff Corey with Emily Corey, *Improvising Out Loud: My Life Teaching Hollywood How to Act* (Lexington: University Press of Kentucky, 2017), 176.

66 "My purpose was to help them find some essential aspect of the scene": Ibid., 84.

66 "The greatness of a man's acting": Ibid., 175.

66 "Within the framework of a conflict": Ibid., 231.

66 "An organic connection to anger": Ibid., 186.

66 "One of Hollywood's most organic actors": Sophie Huber, *Harry Dean Stanton: Partly Fiction,* 2013, documentary film (Hugofilm, Schweizer Radio Und Fernsehen/SRG SSR with Isotope Films, Adopt Films distribution, DVD).

67 "Landau wanted his students to 'physicalize' their inner emotions and tensions": Patrick McGilligan, *Jack's Life: A Biography of Jack Nicholson* (New York: W. W. Norton & Co., 2015, 1994), 128.

67 "A bed, a desk, and a record player": Ibid., 181.

67 "All those good-looking guys had the jobs": Susan Compo, *Warren Oates: A Wild Life* (Lexington: University Press of Kentucky, 2010), 69.

67 "It was the era of the pretty guys": McGilligan, *Jack's Life*, 131.

67 "It was the tail end of the Rock Hudson–Tab Hunter school": Robert Crane and Christopher Fryer, *Jack Nicholson: The Early Years* (Lexington: University Press of Kentucky, 2012), 30.

68 "In-Between Generation, coming of age": McGilligan, *Jack's Life*, 107–108.

68 "A good fit for actors who were constantly worried about winning their next part": Alan Watts, *This Is It and Other Essays on Zen and Spiritual Experience* (New York: Vintage Books, 1973 [orig. pub. 1958]), 101.

68 "I never did it for fun": Alex Stapleton, *Corman's World: Exploits of a Hollywood Rebel,* documentary film, 2011 (A&E IndieFilms, New York, NY).

68 "Falling back into a pile": Compo, *Warren Oates*, 327.

69 "As *The Dharma Bums* made plain": Watts, *This Is It and Other Essays*, 101.

69 "Burgeoning Laurel Canyon rock aristocracy": Sean O'Hagan, "Harry Dean Stanton: 'Life? It's One Big Phantasmagoria,'" *The Guardian,* November 23, 2013, https://www.theguardian.com/film/2013/nov/23/harry-dean-stanton -interview.

69 "One of the cycle of misunderstood teenager flicks": McGilligan, *Jack's Life*, 103.

69 "University of Corman": Stapleton, *Corman's World*.

69 "The whole world is so different": Ibid.

70 "Cement the bond between Nicholson and Monte Hellman": McGilligan, *Jack's Life*, 124.

70 "Monte got me over the line of being exclusively an actor": Crane and Fryer, *Jack Nicholson*, 167.

70 "Only nature, survival, a little greed": Michael Atkinson, commentary, *The Shooting/Ride in the Whirlwind: Two Films by Monte Hellman* (Criterion Collection, DVD).

70 "A B Western with some A nuances": McGilligan, *Jack's Life*, 165.

70 "There's no Indians": Ibid., 174.

70 "One film became two films, and both were shot back to back": Brad Stevens, *Monte Hellman: His Life and Films* (Jefferson, NC: McFarland & Co., 2003), 58–59.

71 "Part of Roger Corman's stock company": McGilligan, *Jack's Life*, 93.

71 "They tried to keep within a tight budget": Monte Hellman, commentary, *The Shooting/Ride in the Whirlwind: Two Films by Monte Hellman* (Criterion Collection, DVD).

72 "Here we enter the altar space of American totemology": Michael Atkinson, "We Can Bring a Good Bit of Rope," essay, *The Shooting/Ride in the Whirlwind: Two Films by Monte Hellman* (Criterion Collection, DVD).

72 "Early on the whole point of acting": Jerry Eltzroth, interview by author, Irvine, KY, July 17, 2018. Also cited are stories provided and written by Eltzroth for the Irvine, KY, *Citizen Voice & Times* on Stanton in 2017 and 2018.

73 "Used to be the anti-hero was a bad guy we secretly liked": Roger Ebert, *Cool Hand Luke,* review, December 3, 1967, https://rogerebert.com/reviews/cool-hand-luke-1967.

74 "He wanted real sweat and real exhaustion": Samantha Wells, "Behind the Scenes Secrets of *Cool Hand Luke* Revealed," *Noteably,* June 7, 2018, http://noteably.com/culture/secrets-cool-hand-luke-yh.

75 "Our mother, she was a little bit crazy": Stanley McKnight Jr., telephone interview by author, November 8, 2018.

76 "He cut every kid's hair in Lexington": Ralph Stanton Jr., telephone interview by author, January 1, 2018. All quotations from Ralph Stanton Jr. in this chapter are drawn from this interview.

6. Harry Dean and the New Hollywood

77 "I basically made movies unconsciously": Monte Hellman, interview by author, Los Angeles, March 15, 2018. All quotations from Monte Hellman in this chapter are drawn from this interview.

78 "Stevens gives special thanks to Hellman": Brad Stevens, *Monte Hellman: His Life and Films* (Jefferson, NC: McFarland & Co., 2003), vii.

78 "The perennial outsider in Hollywood": Patrick McGilligan, *Jack's Life: A Biography of Jack Nicholson* (New York: W. W. Norton & Co., 2015, 1994), 200.

78 "Existential modernity": Michael Atkinson, "We Can Bring a Good Bit of Rope," essay, *The Shooting/Ride in the Whirlwind: Two Films by Monte Hellman* (Criterion Collection, DVD).

78 "A body of risky, high-quality work": Peter Biskind, *Easy Riders, Raging Bulls: How the Sex-Drugs-and-Rock 'n' Roll Generation Saved Hollywood* (New York: Simon & Schuster, 1998), 17.

79 "Society within the shell of the old": Patrick Renshaw, *The Wobblies: The Story of Syndicalism in the United States* (Garden City, NY: Anchor Books, 1968), Illustration 1.

79 "Hollywood discovered his gentleness and range": Ian Nathan, "Actor, Singer, Drinker, Philosopher, Poet, Fallen Angel, Icon," *Empire*, November 2017, 87.

79 "He fit perfectly alongside the individualists and weirdos of New Hollywood": Zach Vasquez, "Harry Dean Stanton Dissolves into Thin Air," *Crooked Marquee*, September 18, 2017, https://crookedmarquee.com/harry-dean-stanton-dissolves-into.

80 "It's a continual problem when you don't have the lead": Frederic Forrest biography, IMDb, http://www.imdb.com/name/nm0002078/bio?ref_=nm_ov_bio_sm.

80 "It is a kind of kiss of death": Thomas McGuane, telephone interview by author, March 20, 2019. Unless otherwise indicated, all quotations from Thomas McGuane in this chapter are drawn from this interview.

80 "Next time, I'd like to get the girl instead of the horse": Frederic Forrest biography, IMDb.

81 "The most evocative of the private detective movies": Roger Ebert, *Farewell, My Lovely*, review, January 1, 1975, https://www.rogerebert.com/reviews/farewell-my-lovely-1975.

82 "When I worked with Hitchcock and Kazan": Robert Crane and Christopher Fryer, *Jack Nicholson: The Early Years* (Lexington: University Press of Kentucky, 2012), 67.

82 "Dennis left the show because he wanted to prove his versatility on the stage and in movies": James Arness with James E. Wise Jr., *James Arness: An Autobiography* (Jefferson, NC: McFarland & Co., 2001), 105.

83 "Big Wombassa": McGilligan, *Jack's Life*, 274.

83 "The careers of the surrogate family": Ibid., 273.

83 "Shoestring, independent films for scale": Ibid., 337.

84 "I'm wearing the same boots I wore in the film": Kris Kristofferson, comments at screening of *Pat Garrett and Billy the Kid*, Harry Dean Stanton Fest, Lexington, KY, May 23, 2017.

84 "The greatest collection of character actors assembled in one film": Tom Thurman, *Harry Dean Stanton: Crossing Mulholland*, 2011, documentary film, http://www.ket.org/episode/KMUSE%20000402/.

84 "Working with Sam Peckinpah was a wild ride": Kristofferson, comments at screening of *Pat Garrett and Billy the Kid*.

84 "Violence-drenched 'masterpiece'" *The Wild Bunch*, review by Roger Ebert, https://www.rogerebert.com/reviews/great-movie-the-wild-bunch-1969.

84 "A fascist work of art": Leonard Engel, ed., *Sam Peckinpah's West: New Perspectives* (Salt Lake City: University of Utah Press, 2003), 11.

85 "A rather ugly stench of ruthless business ethics": Jan Aghed, "Pat Garrett and Billy the Kid," in *Sam Peckinpah Interviews,* ed. Kevin J. Hayes (Jackson: University Press of Mississippi, 2008), 123–124. (Orig. pub. *Sight and Sound* 42, Spring 1973.)

86 "Nothing like it had been made before": Tom Thurman, *Sam Peckinpah's West: Legacy of a Hollywood Renegade,* 2004, documentary film, https://youtube /gkAJuxUyzwo.

86 "Harry and I went to his bedroom": Thurman, *Harry Dean Stanton: Crossing Mulholland.*

86 "You ruined the scene!": Sophie Huber, *Harry Dean Stanton: Partly Fiction,* 2013, documentary film (Hugofilm, Schweizer Radio Und Fernsehen/SRG SSR with Isotope Films, Adopt Films distribution, DVD).

86 "The man was crazy": L. Q. Jones, telephone interview by author, February 1, 2018.

87 "There were days when he couldn't raise himself from his chair": Roger Ebert, *A Kiss Is Still a Kiss* (Kansas City: Andrews, McMeel & Parker, 1984), 163.

88 "A passionate, mad artist and poet": Thurman, *Sam Peckinpah's West.*

88 "All of them said something to me that had an impact": Thurman, *Harry Dean Stanton: Crossing Mulholland.*

88 "Almost entirely on one note—a low, melancholy one": Roger Ebert, *Pat Garrett and Billy the Kid,* a review, May 23, 1973, https://www.rogerebert.com /reviews/pat-garrett-and-billy-the-kid-1973.

88 "This film is so rich, sensual, and lyrical": Gabrielle Murray, *This Wounded Cinema, This Wounded Life: Violence and Utopia in the Films of Sam Peckinpah* (Westport, CT: Praeger, 2004), 74.

88 "The thing I remember most about that shoot is becoming friends with Bob Dylan": Alex Simon, "Harry Dean Stanton: American Character," *The Hollywood Interview,* September 15, 2017 (article originally appeared in *Venice Magazine,* August 1997), http://thehollywoodinterview.blogspot .com/2008/02/harry-d:ean.

89 "If you don't fix the plumbing": McGuane, telephone interview by author.

89 "Brando is already in a financial bind": Peter Thompson, *Jack Nicholson: The Life and Times of an Actor on the Edge* (Secaucus, NJ: Carol Publishing Group, 1997), 142–147.

90 "I foresaw *The Missouri Breaks* as a kind of modest, moderate-budget movie": Susan Compo, *Warren Oates: A Wild Life* (Lexington: University Press of Kentucky, 2010), 335.

90 "It's something that could only happen in Hollywood": Claire Clouzot, "Interview with Arthur Penn," in *Arthur Penn Interviews,* ed. Michael Chaiken and Paul Cronin (Jackson: University Press of Mississippi, 2008), 104–109. (Originally appeared in *Ecran,* December 15, 1976.)

91 "He would later sell Kastner 5 percent of his royalties for $1 million": *The Missouri Breaks,* AFI Catalogue of Feature Films 1893–1993, https://catalog.afi.com /Catalog/moviedetails/55285.

91 "Nobody disputes that, instantly, the star": McGilligan, *Jack's Life*, 320.

91 "There was no actor who was not inspired by Brando": Nehemiah Persoff, email interview by author, December 3, 2016.

92 "I don't think he's that bright": McGilligan, *Jack's Life*, 329.

93 "Brando was right in thinking of Clayton as a man without a center": Clouzot, "Interview with Arthur Penn," 106.

93 "He couldn't wait to get into this great calico dress": Richard Combs, "Arthur Penn," in *Arthur Penn Interviews*, 143–144. (Unpublished seminar from the National Film Theatre, British Film Institute, August 15, 1981.)

93 "Before filming the scene, Stanton jumped Brando": McGilligan, *Jack's Life*, 325.

93 "Why does the greatest actor in the world need cue cards": Thompson, *Jack Nicholson*, 146.

93 "To be fair to Nicholson": McGilligan, *Jack's Life*, 325.

93 "Penn diplomatically praised Brando's performance": Jean-Pierre Coursodon, "Arthur Penn," in *Arthur Penn Interviews,* 116. (Originally appeared in *Cinéma*, May 1977.)

94 "We had a terrific time making the film": Combs, "Arthur Penn," 143–144.

94 "There were lots of exciting things about the flamboyant stuff Brando brought to it": Compo, *Warren Oates*, 335.

94 "A period when they were carving up Montana": Combs, "Arthur Penn," 144.

94 "A mirror up to the American people": Clouzot, "Interview with Arthur Penn," 108.

94 "Time has been kind to *The Missouri Breaks*": Lee Pfeiffer, "Review: *The Missouri Breaks*," Cinema Retro, May 19, 2015, http://cinemaretro.com/index.php /archives/8606-Review-The-Missouri-Breaks-1976-Starring-Marlon -Brando-and-Jack-Nicholson;-Blu-Ray-Release-from-Kino-Lorber -Studio-Classics.html.

7. The Passing and the Passing Through

96 "Did they let her keep smoking weed?": The details of this conversation between Harry Dean Stanton and Stanley McKnight Jr., Ersel McKnight's funeral service, and all quotations from Stanley McKnight Jr. in this chapter are drawn from telephone interviews I had with Stanley McKnight Jr. on November 8, 2018, and March 26, 2019.

98 "I'm going to go fishing": Whitney Fishburn, telephone interview by author, November 14, 2018. All quotations from Whitney Fishburn in this chapter are drawn from this interview.

98 "Get that fuckin' piece of shit out of my driveway": McKnight Jr., telephone interview by author, March 26, 2019.

98 "What the hell is your problem?": Fishburn, telephone interview by author, November 14, 2018.

99 "She was very kind to me": Patsy Wallace, telephone interview by author, January 23, 2019.

Notes

100 "I am playing an FBI agent": Jim Huggins Sr., telephone interview by author, January 2, 2018. All quotations from Jim Huggins Sr. in this chapter are drawn from this interview.

100 "She would always dress with like the glamour beat smile": Chad McKnight, telephone interview by author, November 23, 2018.

100 "I sure wish I'd matured earlier": Steve Oney, "Harry Dean Stanton Was Too Big for His Niche," *The Stacks,* September 18, 2017 (article originally appeared in *New York Times Magazine,* November 16, 1986), https:// thestacks.deadspin.com/harry-dean-stanton-was-too-big-for-his-niche -1817176718.

100 "To live completely, fully, in the moment": Jiddu Krishnamurti, *Total Freedom: The Essential Krishnamurti* (San Francisco: HarperSanFrancisco, 1996), 122–123.

101 "I've only started getting good parts": Oney, "Harry Dean Stanton Was Too Big for His Niche."

101 "The participants seem to be saying whatever comes into their heads": Pauline Kael, "The Current Cinema: The Calvary Gig," *New Yorker,* February 13, 1978, 107–111.

101 "The very, very worst thing ever made": *Renaldo and Clara,* Rotten Tomatoes, https://www.rottentomatoes.com/m/renaldo_and_clara.

101 "A failed attempt": Gail Williams, "Flatbed Annie and Sweetiepie: Lady Truckers," television review, *Hollywood Reporter,* February 9, 1979.

101 "Postmodern before postmodern had a name": Brandon Nowalk, "*Mary Hartman, Mary Hartman* Combined Soap Opera, Satire, and Nightmare," *AV Club,* December 9, 2013, https://tv.avclub.com/mary-hartman-mary -hartman-combined-soap-opera-satire-1798242393.

102 "We didn't hit it off immediately": Dabney Coleman, telephone interview by author, January 14, 2018.

102 "Harry Dean Stanton or M. Emmet Walsh": Steve Almasy, "Harry Dean Stanton, Longtime Character Actor, Dies at 91," *CNN,* September 16, 2017.

102 "The film 'is beautifully acted'": Vincent Canby, "*Straight Time* a Film of Grim Wit," *New York Times,* March 18, 1978, https://nytimes.com/1978/03/18 /archives/straight-time-a-film-of-grim-wit.html.

102 "He has a personality that's very much like what you see": Dustin Hoffman, commentary, *Straight Time* (First Artists, Warner Bros. DVD).

103 "I had seen him in some Westerns": Bertrand Tavernier, telephone interview by author, August 27, 2018. All quotations from Bertrand Tavernier in this chapter are drawn from this interview.

103 "Ninety percent of a director's job": Stuart Klawans, "Faith and Faithfulness in John Huston's *Wise Blood,*" *The Moviegoer,* Library of America, August 10, 2016, https://loa.org/news-and-views/1184-faith-and-faithfulness.

104 "Preoccupation with belief and with death": Lewis A. Lawson, *Another Generation: Southern Fiction since World War II* (Jackson: University Press of Mississippi, 1984), 32.

104 "Where the blind don't see": Flannery O'Connor, *3 by Flannery O'Connor: The Violent Bear It Away, Everything That Rises Must Converge, Wise Blood* (New York: Penguin Books, 1983 [orig. pub. 1949]), 60.

104 "From tree to tree in the back of his mind": Ibid., 16.

104 "He thought at the end Hazel Motes has some kind of existential rebellion": Brad Dourif, interview, *Wise Blood* (Criterion Collection, Janus Films, DVD).

104 "Jesus wins": Francine Prose, "A Matter of Life and Death," essay, *Wise Blood* (Criterion Collection, Janus Films, DVD), 8.

105 "The director had made a film about a Christian in spite of himself": Ibid., 8.

105 "He sang 'El Revolucionario'": Lawrence Grobel, *The Hustons: The Life and Times of a Hollywood Dynasty* (New York: Cooper Square Press, 2000, 1989), 40.

105 "One of the most memorable scenes": Janet Maslin, "Film: Bette Midler in 'The Rose': Music-World Portrait," *New York Times,* November 7, 1979, https://www.nytimes.com/1979/11/07/archives/film-bette-midler-in-the -rosemusicworld-portrait.html.

105 "How 'tough' Harry Dean could be": Bette Midler, interview from 2015, June 19 post by Aaron West, https://criterionclosup.com/tag/harry-dean-stanton, blog archives.

105 "The same kind of upheavals": Nat Segaloff, *Stirling Silliphant: The Fingers of God* (Duncan, OK: BearManor Media, 2013), 155.

106 "Talks like Robert Mitchum's mean kid brother": Roger Ebert, *The Black Marble,* review, January 7, 1980, https://www.rogerebert.com/reviews/the-black -marble-1980.

106 "I don't like sci-fi or monster movies": David McIntee, *Beautiful Monsters: The Unofficial and Unauthorized Guide to the Alien and Predator Films* (Tolworth, Surrey, UK: Telos Publishing, 2005), 29.

106 "I don't either, but I like this one": "*Alien* (1979): Harry Dean Stanton Interviewed," *Scraps from the Loft,* October 27, 2017 (Orig. pub.: "*Alien,*" the *Officially Authorized Magazine of the Movie,* December 1979), https:// scrapsfromtheloft.com/2017/10/27/alien-1979-harry-dean-stanton -interviewed.

106 "I wasn't attracted to it at all": Ibid.

107 "I had some funny lines": Ibid.

107 "*Alien* may be the death knell for Stanton's anonymity": Ibid.

107 "He was way too earthbound": Ian Nathan, "Actor, Singer, Drinker, Philosopher, Poet, Fallen Angel, Icon," *Empire,* November 2017, 87.

108 "The 'cheap scare' of villains": John Carpenter, Biography, IMDb, https://www .imdb.com/name/nm0000118/bio.

108 "I could've been much more famous and richer": *WTF with Marc Maron,* podcast, Harry Dean Stanton, from 2014 (episode 464, reposted September 16, 2017), https://www.youtube.com/watch?v=RFejvPkRyXU.

108 "Brain is 'emotionally unreliable'": Vincent Canby, *Escape from New York,* review, *New York Times,* July 10, 1981, https://www.nytimes.com/1981/07/10/movies /escape-from-new-york.html.

108 "I remember it being a lot better": Maryann Johanson, *Escape from New York,* review, *flickfilosopher,* October 1, 2001, https://flickfilosopher.com/2001/10 /escape-from-new-york.

109 "Knew nothing about Harry Dean's career prior to *Escape*": Adrienne Barbeau, email interview by author, August 31, 2019.

109 "Pretty shop worn" *Christine,* reviews, Rotten Tomatoes, https://rottentomatoes .com/m/christine.

109 "Disheveled humanity and wiry wit": Nathan, "Actor, Singer, Drinker, Philosopher, Poet, Fallen Angel, Icon."

109 "A small, delicate porcelain figure of a film": Peter Biskind, *Easy Riders, Raging Bulls: How the Sex-Drugs-and-Rock 'n' Roll Generation Saved Hollywood* (New York: Simon & Schuster, 1998), 418.

110 "A petri dish of creative talent": Ibid., 417.

110 "From the blizzard of coke": Ibid., 409–410.

110 "By locking himself away": Frederic Forrest biography, IMDb, http://www .imdb.com/name/nm0002078/bio?ref_=nm_ov_bio_sm.

110 "Coppola's megalomania": Biskind, *Easy Riders, Raging Bulls,* 418.

110 "Small pleasures": Roger Ebert, *One from the Heart,* review, January 1, 1982, https://www.rogerebert.com/reviews/one-from-the-heart-1982.

111 "For a 'big time' director, really wonderful": Alex Simon, "Harry Dean Stanton: American Character," *The Hollywood Interview,* September 15, 2017 (article originally appeared in *Venice Magazine,* August 1997), http:// thehollywoodinterview.blogspot.com/2008/02/harry-dean.

111 "I met Harry Dean when I first came out to LA": Rebecca De Mornay, comments, First Harry Dean Stanton Awards Ceremony, Los Angeles, October 23, 2016. YouTube, https://www.youtube.com/watch?v=6QrJoI8jCcU.

112 "The closest he had come to permanence": Nathan, "Actor, Singer, Drinker, Philosopher, Poet, Fallen Angel, Icon."

112 "I got her in the movie with Tom Cruise": Sophie Huber, *Harry Dean Stanton: Partly Fiction,* 2013, documentary film (Hugofilm, Schweizer Radio Und Fernsehen/SRG SSR with Isotope Films, Adopt Films distribution, DVD).

112 "The champagne is for Harvey": Tavernier, telephone interview by author, August 27, 2018.

114 "Harry, can we have another revolutionary song": Ibid.

116 "European directors tend to work more collaboratively": Marshall Fine, *Harvey Keitel: The Art of Darkness* (New York: Fromm International, 2000, 1998), 35.

116 "That were never or barely released in the United States": Ibid., 140.

8. A Repo Man and His "Tense Situations"

117 "Refusal to learn one's lines": Alex Cox, *X Films: True Confessions of a Radical Filmmaker* (Brooklyn: Soft Skull Press, 2008), 49.

117 "Cox said no": Ibid., 53.

118 "They let me do whatever the fuck I want": Ibid., 50.

118 "Harry Dean Stanton only uses REAL baseball bats": Ibid., 55.

118 "Arthur Penn didn't get a great performance": Ibid., 50.

118 "The quintessential cult film": Dante A. Ciampaglia, "15 Atomic Truths about *Repo Man*," *Mental Floss,* August 21, 2015, http://mentalfloss.com/article /67675/15-atomic-truths-about-repo-man.

119 "I think it is a great American film": Michael Nesmith, telephone interview by author, October 30, 2018. All quotations from Michael Nesmith in this chapter are drawn from this interview.

119 "Yes, Alex Cox": Harry Dean Stanton, interview by Peter McCarthy, *Repo Man,* Focus Features (Criterion Collection, DVD).

119 "A 'nut' and an 'egomaniac'": Sean O'Hagan, "Harry Dean Stanton: 'Life? It's One Big Phantasmagoria,'" *The Guardian,* November 23, 2013, https://www .theguardian.com/film/2013/nov/23/harry-dean-stanton-interview.

119 "I don't like hanging around people who are rude": Alex Cox, telephone interview by author, November 12, 2018.

119 "All of them 'assholes'": Cox, *X Films,* 30.

119 "Who elected, sometimes through no fault of their own": "A Repo Man Speaks Out," Mark Lewis, interview, booklet, 60, *Repo Man,* Focus Features (Criterion Collection, DVD).

119 "A particularly world-weary, exhausted, saddened face": Cox, *X Films,* 16.

119 "When he smiled": Ibid., 40.

120 "I don't know that anyone can say that they were close to him": Bertrand Tavernier, telephone interview by author, August 27, 2018.

120 "A brutal, misogynist lunk with no patience": Sam McPheeters, "A Lattice of Coincidence," *Repo Man* booklet, 13, *Repo Man,* Focus Features (Criterion Collection, DVD).

120 "Otto is a blank page": Alex Cox, commentary, *Repo Man,* Focus Features (Criterion Collection, DVD).

121 "I'd planned to draw the whole script": Cox, *X Films,* 31.

121 "The original art form of the twentieth century": Ibid., 2.

121 "Things that don't go away": Cox, telephone interview by author, November 12, 2018.

121 "Independent filmmakers are apt to be political, angry, and scornful": Cox, *X Films,* 35–36.

122 "Its 'unsympathetic' characters": Ibid., 36.

122 "I didn't want more money": Ibid., 37.

123 "So my first professional directing gig": Ibid., 39.

124 "Harry Dean was authentic and sincere": Cox, telephone interview by author, November 12, 2018.

124 "Whom he identified at the Harry Dean Stanton fest": Alex Cox, comments after screening of *Repo Man,* Harry Dean Stanton Fest, Lexington, KY, July 14, 2019.

124 "This was an eye-opener": Cox, *X Films,* 40.

124 "Kelly remained his agent": John Kelly, email interview with author, January 17, 2019.

124 "A 'small film'": Ciampaglia, "15 Atomic Truths about *Repo Man.*"

125 "The thing is I couldn't tell Harry": Cox, telephone interview by author, November 12, 2018.

125 "It was never an easy relationship": Ibid.

125 "What is wrong with you people": Nesmith, telephone interview by author, October 30, 2018.

126 "Is there a movie to go with this?": Cox, *X Films,* 75.

126 "It is too good of an opportunity not to do it": Cox, telephone interview by author, November 12, 2018.

126 "I went over for the opening" Cox, *X Films,* 76.

127 "I thought *Repo Man* was a brilliant satire": Alex Simon, "Harry Dean Stanton: American Character," *The Hollywood Interview,* September 15, 2017 (article originally appeared in *Venice Magazine,* August 1997), http://thehollywoodinterview.blogspot.com/2008/02/harry-dean.

9. To Paris, Texas, and Beyond

128 "The most transcendent piece in all American music": Jas Obrecht, liner notes, *Blind Willie Johnson: Dark Was the Night* (Mojo Workin' Blues for the Next Generation, Columbia, Sony Music Entertainment Inc., CD, 1998).

128 "One of those interplanetary world musicians": Ibid.

128 "It never crossed my mind for a second": Wim Wenders, email interview by author, October 3, 2019.

129 "Seems somehow to have burned itself into the landscape": Nick Roddick, "On the Road Again," essay, *Paris, Texas,* Janus Films (Criterion Collection, DVD).

129 "Ry Cooder was so much in harmony": Wim Wenders, commentary, *Paris, Texas,* Janus Films (Criterion Collection, DVD).

129 "If he doesn't talk, convert that into melody": Ry Cooder, commentary, *Paris, Texas,* Janus Films (Criterion Collection, DVD).

129 "A 'smashed suitcase'": Sam Shepard, *Motel Chronicles* (San Francisco: City Lights Books, 1982), 104.

130 "There was an alchemy between Sam and myself": Wenders, commentary, *Paris, Texas,* Janus Films.

130 "For two weeks I sat in the hotel": Ibid.

130 "No script, only an itinerary": Wim Wenders, commentary, *Kings of the Road, The Road Trilogy,* Janus Films (Criterion Collection, DVD).

131 "We declare our intention": "The Oberhausen Manifesto" (February 28, 1962), in *West German Filmmakers on Film: Visions and Voices,* ed. Eric Rentschler (New York: Holmes & Meier, 1988), 2.

132 "Prowled the lot": Peter Biskind, *Easy Riders, Raging Bulls: How the Sex-Drugs-and-Rock 'n' Roll Generation Saved Hollywood* (New York: Simon & Schuster, 1998), 417.

132 "At once minimal and romantic": Michael Almereyda, "Between Me and the World," booklet, 9. *Kings of the Road, The Road Trilogy,* Janus Films (Criterion Collection, DVD).

132 "A road movie for me is a way of life": Wim Wenders, interview by Roger Willemsen, *Paris, Texas,* Janus Films (Criterion Collection, DVD).

133 "The studio only saw that he'd never made a screenplay": Wenders, commentary, *Paris, Texas,* Janus Films.

133 "I hadn't done what I wanted to do": Wenders, interview by Roger Willemsen, *Paris, Texas,* Janus Films.

133 "Wenders knew of the movie I made": Monte Hellman, interview by author, Los Angeles, March 15, 2018.

133 "Difficult to get there": Wenders, commentary, *Paris, Texas,* Janus Films.

134 "Landscape . . . [that] is essentially an interior one": Brad Stevens, *Monte Hellman: His Life and Films* (Jefferson, NC: McFarland & Co., 2003), 126–127.

134 "His face is the story": Sophie Huber, *Harry Dean Stanton: Partly Fiction,* 2013, documentary film (Hugofilm, Schweizer Radio Und Fernsehen/SRG SSR with Isotope Films, Adopt Films distribution, DVD).

134 "I want to play something of some beauty or sensitivity": Ian Nathan, "Actor, Singer, Drinker, Philosopher, Poet, Fallen Angel, Icon," *Empire,* November 2017, 87.

135 "When he didn't have to do anything": Huber, *Harry Dean Stanton: Partly Fiction.*

135 "The worst movies with Harry were always good": Wenders, commentary, *Paris, Texas,* Janus Films.

135 "Every actor who ever sees him admires": Huber, *Harry Dean Stanton: Partly Fiction.*

135 "Why aren't you doing it": Steve Oney, "Harry Dean Stanton Was Too Big for His Niche," *The Stacks,* September 18, 2017 (article originally appeared in *New York Times Magazine,* November 16, 1986), https://thestacks.deadspin.com/harry-dean-stanton-was-too-big-for-his-niche-1817176718.

135 "You have to have an eye who is going to be good on screen": Werner Herzog, comments following screening of *The Wild Blue Yonder* (2005), Rhodes College, Memphis, TN, September 14, 2017.

136 "I finally got the part I wanted to play": Sean O'Hagan, "Harry Dean Stanton: 'Life? It's One Big Phantasmagoria,'" *The Guardian,* November 23, 2013, https://www.theguardian.com/film/2013/nov/23/harry-dean-stanton-interview.

136 "Pestilence personified": Herzog, comments following screening of *The Wild Blue Yonder* (2005), Rhodes College, Memphis, TN, September 14, 2017.

136 "Over Kinski hovers the fearful cloud": David Jenkins, "Nastassja Kinski Interview: 'I've Had Such Low Self-Esteem,'" *The Telegraph,* February 6, 2015 (article originally appeared in *The Daily Telegraph* in January 2001), https://telegraph.co.uk/culture/films/11394696/Nastassja-Kinski.

136 "Kinski 'reinvented herself'": Wenders, interview by Roger Willemsen, *Paris, Texas,* Janus Films.

137 "Hunter himself came up with the idea": Wenders, commentary, *Paris, Texas,* Janus Films.

137 "We would dream it up a little bit": Ryan Gilbey, "Robby Müller Obituary," *The Guardian,* July 5, 2018, modified July 22, 2018, https://theguardian.com /film/2018/jul/05/robby-muller-obituary.

138 "Some kind of Dutch interior painter": Ibid.

138 "He doesn't really light from the outside in like most people": Mark Mordue, "Asphalt Jungle Jim," in *Jim Jarmusch Interviews,* ed. Ludvig Hertzberg (Jackson: University Press of Mississippi, 2001), 81. (Article originally appeared in *Cinema Studies,* January 1988.)

138 "Müller at his most entrancingly poetic": Gilbey, "Robby Müller Obituary."

138 "The magic of the Polaroid filter": Wenders, commentary, *Paris, Texas,* Janus Films.

138 "I never had the impression": Robby Müller, interview by Paul Joyce for Lucida Productions, *Paris, Texas,* Janus Films (Criterion Collection, DVD).

138 "The music is never added to a film": "Wim Wenders' Hollywood April '84," *Cinéma cinémas, Paris, Texas,* Janus Films (Criterion Collection, DVD).

138 "I dreamed of working with him": Ibid.

138 "He calls me and says, 'I'm making a movie'": Müller, interview by Paul Joyce for Lucida Productions, *Paris, Texas,* Janus Films.

139 "They didn't blow the whistle on us": Wenders, email interview by author, October 3, 2019.

139 "I'll never forget watching Wim": Allison Anders, interview by Kent Jones, *Paris, Texas,* Janus Films (Criterion Collection, DVD).

140 "I was a young assistant": Allison Anders, "A Girl's Story," essay, *The Road Trilogy,* Janus Films (Criterion Collection, DVD).

140 "It was crucial for Harry to shoot this in chronological order": Wenders, commentary, *Paris, Texas,* Janus Films.

140 "Let them do the scene first": Ibid.

140 "Harry was in the trailer": Anders, interview by Kent Jones, *Paris, Texas,* Janus Films.

141 "It was shocking for Harry Dean": Claire Denis, commentary, *Paris, Texas,* Janus Films (Criterion Collection, DVD).

141 "Nastassya had forty-eight hours": Wenders, interview by Roger Willemsen, *Paris, Texas,* Janus Films.

141 "I can never learn this in a matter of days": Wenders, email interview by author, October 3, 2019.

141 "He brought the kid in": Harry Dean Stanton, interview by Paul Joyce for Lucida Productions, *Paris, Texas,* Janus Films.

141 "When Wim said you're not going back": Ibid.

142 "Harry felt that Travis had deserved this family": Wenders, email interview by author, October 3, 2019.

142 "At the very end of the shoot": Ibid.

142 "Harry Dean 'sat at the opposite end of the table'": Sara Stanton, telephone interview by author, March 2, 2018.

142 "It was a strange and awkward dinner": Jim Huggins Jr., telephone interview by author, December 16, 2017.

142 "Under Eddie Albert's casual performance": Paddy Chayefsky, *The Collected Works of Paddy Chayefsky: The Television Plays* (New York: Applause Books, 1995), 275.

143 "His lean face and hungry eyes": Roger Ebert, *Paris, Texas,* review, December 8, 2002, www.rogerebert.com/reviews/great-movie-paris-texas-1984.

143 "As the years tugged at Mr. Stanton's face": Manohla Dargis, "Harry Dean Stanton: Fully Inhabiting Scenes, Not Stealing Them," *New York Times,* September 17, 2017, https://www.nytimes.com/2017/09/17/movies/harry-dean-stanton.

143 "When you learn to be still and quiet": George Hatzis, telephone interview by author, June 18, 2019.

143 "I think everybody talks too much": Stanton, interview by Paul Joyce for Lucida Productions, *Paris, Texas,* Janus Films.

143 "It was so good to finally hear Harry Dean speak": Wenders, commentary, *Paris, Texas,* Janus Films.

144 "Harry Dean was scared of heights": Ibid.

144 "The bared American soul": Nathan, "Actor, Singer, Drinker, Philosopher, Poet, Fallen Angel, Icon."

145 "People become so impatient today": Wenders, commentary, *Paris, Texas,* Janus Films.

145 "In their trips through the looking-glass": Lotte H. Eisner, *The Haunted Screen: Expressionism in the German Cinema and the Influence of Max Reinhardt,* rev. ed. (Berkeley: University of California Press, 1965 [orig. pub. 1952]), 130.

145 "You have enabled us to find a link": Werner Herzog, "Tribute to Lotte Eisner," in *West German Filmmakers on Film: Visions and Voices,* ed. Eric Rentschler (New York: Holmes & Meier, 1988), 116.

145 "The darker corners of American noir": Ebert, *Paris, Texas,* review, December 8, 2002.

146 "The film had such a grace": Denis, interview by Kent Jones, *Paris, Texas,* Janus Films.

146 "Sold Harry Dean Stanton short": Richard Brody, "How 'Paris, Texas' Sold Harry Dean Stanton Short," *New Yorker,* September 28, 2017, https://newyorker.com/culture/richard-brody/how-paris-texas-sold-harry-dean-stanton-short.

147 "Americans don't like others showing them themselves": Wenders, interview by Roger Willemsen, *Paris, Texas,* Janus Films.

147 "People would have too much to say about it": Anders, interview by Kent Jones, *Paris, Texas,* Janus Films (Criterion Collection, DVD).

147 "The movie lacks any of the gimmicks": Ebert, *Paris, Texas,* review, December 8, 2002.

147 "A love letter to America": Roddick, "On the Road Again," essay, *Paris, Texas,* Janus Films.

147 "I was able to do everything I've been wanting to do": Wenders, commentary, *Paris, Texas,* Janus Films.

147 "*Paris, Texas* and *Repo Man* are the beginnings of the American independent film movement": Anders, interview by Kent Jones, *Paris, Texas,* Janus Films (Criterion Collection, DVD).

10. Harry Dean the Punk Icon

148 "Like a roller-skating Studio 54": Richard T. Kelly, *Sean Penn: His Life and Times* (New York: Canongate U.S., 2004), 67–68.

148 "So I sat and talked to Harry": Ibid., 138.

148 "He told me he'd been a big fan of mine": Ibid., 139.

149 "Maybe you should find somewhere else to stay": Ibid.

149 "The position of punk icon": Steve Oney, "Harry Dean Stanton Was Too Big for His Niche," *The Stacks,* September 18, 2017 (article originally appeared in *New York Times Magazine,* November 16, 1986), https://thestacks.deadspin .com/harry-dean-stanton-was-too-big-for-his-niche-1817176718.

149 "The patron saint of the edgy set": Ian Nathan, "Actor, Singer, Drinker, Philosopher, Poet, Fallen Angel, Icon," *Empire,* November 2017, 86.

150 "Party central": Patrick McGilligan, *Jack's Life: A Biography of Jack Nicholson* (New York: W. W. Norton & Co., 2015, 1994), 187.

150 "De Niro was bopping around town": Shawn Levy, "The Night Belushi Died," *Hollywood Reporter,* April 24, 2019 (excerpt from Shawn Levy, *The Castle on Sunset,* Doubleday, 2019), https://hollywoodreporter.com/features/night -john-belushi-died.

150 "In a fetal position in his bed": Bob Woodward, *Wired: The Short Life and Fast Times of John Belushi* (New York: Pocket Books, 1984), 462.

151 "The food is the best consistently of any restaurant": Dabney Coleman, telephone interview by author, January 14, 2018.

152 "I remember one situation that was so funny": Mike Gotovac, telephone interview by author, March 22, 2017.

152 "We'd be sitting there, and Buck Henry would walk in": Ed Begley Jr., telephone interview by author, August 4, 2018.

152 "There were three 'old guys' there": Kelly, *Sean Penn,* 158.

152 "Someone had arranged for about twenty-five Playboy Bunnies": Ibid., 159.

153 "A Fellini movie": Ibid., 160.

153 "Behind that rugged old cowboy face": Oney, "Harry Dean Stanton Was Too Big for His Niche."

153 "Harry Dean has got a rebelliousness in him": Ibid.

153 "I find younger people less conditioned": Peter Travers, "The Coolest Dude in the Room," *Rolling Stone,* September 16, 2017, https://www.rollingstone.com

/movies/news/peter-travers-on-harry-dean-stanton-coolest-dude-in-the
-room-w503569.

153 "I know he's lonely sometimes": Oney, "Harry Dean Stanton Was Too Big for His
Niche."

153 "Harry always had so much hostility and resentment": Ibid.

154 "The role for Harry Dean really is still out there": Ibid.

154 "The big 'official' youth picture": Alex Cox, *X Films: True Confessions of a Radical
Filmmaker* (Brooklyn: Soft Skull Press, 2008), 76.

155 "Arguably his [Harry Dean's] most accomplished comic role": Peter Stack, "Crazy
Characters Are a Delight in 'UFOria,'" *San Francisco Chronicle,* September
18, 1985, p. 61.

155 "A 'tactical miscalculation'": Roger Ebert, *One More Christmas,* review, November
22, 1985, https://www.rogerebert.com/reviews/one-magic-christmas-1985.

155 "We feel we might be looking at the characters in a story by William Faulkner":
Roger Ebert, *Fool for Love,* review, December 18, 1985, https://www
.rogerebert.com/reviews/fool-for-love-1985.

156 "I think Harry Dean's a victim": Oney, "Harry Dean Stanton Was Too Big for His
Niche."

156 "I represented both Harry and Randy Quaid in that film": John S. Kelly, email
interview by author, August 1, 2019.

157 "His most iconic mainstream performance": Zach Vasquez, "Harry Dean Stanton
Dissolves into Thin Air," *Crooked Marquee,* September 18, 2017, https://
crookedmarquee.com/harry-dean-stanton-dissolves-into.

157 "Having the chance to work with Harry Dean": Molly Ringwald, comments,
Harry Dean Stanton: Appreciation of Nothing, Facebook page, October 19,
2017 (posted), https://www.facebook.com/search/top/?q=harry%20dean
%20stanton%3A%20appreciation%20of%20%27nothing%27%20molly%
20ringwald&epa=SEARCH_BOX

158 "I'm more interested in impressionistic films": Stephen Farber, "Francis Coppola
Sallies into TV on a Fairie Tale," *New York Times,* December 27, 1984,
https://nytimes.com/1984/12/27/arts/francis-coppola-sallies-into-TV-on
-a-fairie-tale.

158 "The 'black sheep' of the series": "A fairly good adaption of the great American
classic", Rkerekes, 20 June 2008, user reviews, https://www.imdb.com/title
/tt0278438/reviews?ref_=tt_urv.

158 "Definitely not leading man material": Julien Houle, "*Rip Van Winkle* in *Fairie
Tale Theatre,*" review, *Pop Culture Thoughts,* November 18, 2018, https://
popculturethoughts.com/2018/11/18/fairie-tale-theatre-rip-van-winkle.

158 "Stanton and Coppola really give their all": Mark Curtis, "Francis Ford Coppola's
Fairie Tale Theatre: 'Rip Van Winkle' Episode," *Directors Series,* May 31,
2017, https://directorssieries.net/2017/05/31/francis-ford-coppola-fairie
-tale-theatre.

158 "Wayne Wang was in a little over his head maybe": John Doe, comments
after screening of *Slam Dance,* Harry Dean Stanton Fest, Lexington, KY,
September 30, 2017.

159 "*Slam Dance* is like junk food": "Slam Dance," Variety Staff, *Variety*, December 31, 1986, https://variety.com/1986/film/reviews/slam-dance-1200427119/.

159 "Compete confusion, a movie without any identity whatsoever": Vincent Canby, *Slam Dance*, review, *New York Times*, November 8, 1987, https://www.nytimes.com/1987/11/06/movies/film-slamdance-with-tom-hulce.html.

159 "I called Bob Mitchum": Lawrence Grobel, *The Hustons: The Life and Times of a Hollywood Dynasty* (New York: Cooper Square Press, 2000, 1989), 28.

160 "Slow-moving": Roger Ebert, *Mr. North*, review, August 19, 1988, https://rogerebert.com/reviews/mr-north-1988.

160 "Reassuring evidence that the Huston dynasty lives on": Grobel, *The Hustons*, 781.

160 "The film is 'indeed technically blasphemous'": Roger Ebert, *The Last Temptation of Christ,* October 29, 2008, https://rogerebert.com/reviews/the-last-temptation-of-christ-1988.

161 "Do you know that centuries will pass": Fyodor Dostoevsky, *Notes from Underground/The Grand Inquisitor* (London: Penguin Group, 2003, 1960), 133–134.

162 "He's got this innocence": Sophie Huber, *Harry Dean Stanton: Partly Fiction*, 2013, documentary film (Hugofilm, Schweizer Radio Und Fernsehen/SRG SSR with Isotope Films, Adopt Films distribution, DVD).

163 "The sublime, the uncanny, the abject": Dennis Lim, *David Lynch: The Man from Another Place* (New York: Amazon Publishing, 2015), 7.

163 "I'd always been impressed with David's films": David Lynch and Kristine McKenna, *Room to Dream* (New York: Random House, 2018), 245.

163 "I could sit next to him for hours": Ibid., 270.

164 "I didn't want to go on that violent trip": Ibid., 208.

164 "I think I was afraid of it": Alex Simon, "Harry Dean Stanton: American Character," *The Hollywood Interview,* September 15, 2017 (article originally appeared in *Venice Magazine,* August 1997), http://thehollywoodinterview.blogspot.com/2008/02/harry-dean.

164 "I have to play Frank because I am Frank": Lim, *David Lynch*, 69.

164 "Dennis and I have laughed about it before": Simon, "Harry Dean Stanton: American Character."

165 "A triumph of startling images": Peter Travers, *Wild at Heart,* review, *Rolling Stone,* August 17, 1990, https://www.rollingstone.com/movies/movie-reviews/wild-at-heart-120043.

165 "A cinematic act of self-mutilation": Roger Ebert, "David Lynch Gives Filmgoers All They Can Handle," May 27, 1990, https://rogerebert.com/festivals-and-awards/david-lynch-gives-filmgoers-all-they-can-handle.

165 "Gets shot in the head and his brains splatter against the wall": Lynch and Kristine McKenna, *Room to Dream*, 291.

165 "Didn't break the rules of dramatic television": Lim, *David Lynch*, 96.

166 "To go back into the world before it started": Ibid., 114.

166 "It's not the worst movie ever made": Ibid., 119.

166 "David Lynch has disappeared so far up his own ass": Ibid.

166 "Few movies have undergone so complete a rehabilitation": Ibid., 120.

167 "The most experimental film I've made": Lynch and Kristine McKenna, *Room to Dream*, 405–406.

167 "Pure David Lynch": Chris Rodley, ed., *Lynch on Lynch*, rev. ed. (New York: Farrar, Straus and Giroux, 2005 [orig. pub. 1997]), 146, 245.

167 "A tear-jerking, sentimental side of Lynch": Lim, *David Lynch*, 118.

167 "Tenderness can be just as abstract as insanity": Ibid., 119.

168 "The word 'natural' is them": Lynch and Kristine McKenna, *Room to Dream*, 405.

168 "A while back Sean Penn gave me a copy of a speech": Ibid., 397.

168 "David's sets are very relaxed": Ibid.

168 "I was lying there, thinking how it was going to feel": John Johnson and Efrain Hernandez Jr., "Actor Harry Dean Stanton Hurt in Home Robbery," *Los Angeles Times,* January 22, 1996, http://articles.latimes.com/1996–01–22 /local/me-27417_1_actor.

169 "It was something of an inside job": Begley Jr., telephone interview by author, August 4, 2018.

169 "It was someone who knew him": Mary McCormack, interview by author, Los Angeles, March 18, 2018.

169 "Harry Dean's trusting nature": Jim Huggins Jr., telephone interview by author, December 16, 2017.

169 "They cheated him over a period of two and a half years": Jamie James, interview by author, Los Angeles, March 17, 2018.

169 "Harry Dean 'trusted people'": Huggins Jr., telephone interview by author, December 16, 2017.

170 "I think I'm blessed with a pretty tough psyche": Johnson and Hernandez Jr., "Actor Harry Dean Stanton Hurt in Home Robbery."

11. The Musician and Philosopher

171 "Shook hands with me and moved me on": *WTF with Marc Maron,* podcast, Harry Dean Stanton from 2014 (episode 464, reposted September 16, 2017), https://www.youtube.com/watch?v=RFejvPkRyXU.

171 "Bertrand, do you think we can verbalize the concept of Christ": Bertrand Tavernier, telephone interview by author, August 27, 2018.

172 "Deep down I think he was saying a lot of stuff": Ralph Stanton Jr., telephone interview by author, January 1, 2018. All quotations from Ralph Stanton Jr. in this chapter are drawn from this interview.

172 "There was nothing out there": Sophie Huber, *Harry Dean Stanton: Partly Fiction,* 2013, documentary film (Hugofilm, Schweizer Radio Und Fernsehen/SRG SSR with Isotope Films, Adopt Films distribution, DVD).

172 "It's all going to go away": Ibid.

172 "He did think he would be a leading man": "Conversation with Sophie Huber," *WTF with Marc Maron,* podcast, Harry Dean Stanton from 2014 (episode

464, reposted September 16, 2017), https://www.youtube.com/watch?v
=RFejvPkRyXU.

172 "Let's not think of it as a documentary": Sophie Huber, telephone interview by
author, August 2, 2018.

172 "He loves to bring that wounded beast to the table": Tom Thurman, *Harry Dean
Stanton: Crossing Mulholland*, 2011, documentary film, http://www
.ket.org/episode/KMUSE%20000402/.

173 "A jacket 'with a sheen on it'": Jamie James, interview by author, Los Angeles,
March 17, 2018. All quotations from Jamie James in this chapter are drawn
from this interview.

174 "I love all kinds of music": Harry Dean Stanton, comments, *Harry Dean Stanton:
Appreciation of Nothing*, Facebook page, October 23, 2017 (posted), https://
www.facebook.com/Harry-Dean-Stanton-Appreciation-of-Nothing
-13174008655/?__tn__=%2Cd%2CP-R&eid=ARAuryYMyYKVlQN14
IVdowQwLc_jQHqY01tgQlfdTzsOZCPSY9PwADk8DRpvurETyQtZkw9i
NnQas3_i

177 "Some of the first people": George Hatzis, telephone interview by author,
June 18, 2019. All quotations from George Hatzis in this chapter are drawn
from this phone interview.

177 "When things fall apart": Philip Toshio Sudo, *Zen Guitar* (New York: Simon &
Schuster, 1998), 54.

177 "Play what you are meant to play": Ibid., 73.

178 "I was at the Pasadena Playhouse": Alex Simon, "Harry Dean Stanton: American
Character," *The Hollywood Interview*, September 15, 2017 (article originally
appeared in *Venice Magazine*, August 1997), http://thehollywoodinterview
.blogspot.com/2008/02/harry-dean.

178 "These roses under my window": Harald Sack, "Ralph Waldo Emerson (1803–
1882)," *Ralph Waldo Emerson and the Transcendentalism Movement*, May
25, 2019, http://scihi.org/ralph-waldo-emerson-transcendentalism.

178 "The present moment holds the key to liberation": Eckhart Tolle, *Practicing the
Power of Now: Essential Teachings, Meditations and Exercises from the Power
of Now* (Mumbai, India: YogiImpressions, 2002), 27, 34.

179 "The '60s were great": Simon, "Harry Dean Stanton: American Character."

179 "I can't relate to the Judaic-Christian concept at all": Ibid.

180 "He and the late Italian tenor Enrico Caruso": Irving Shulman, *Valentino* (New
York: Trident Press, 1967), 434.

180 "This was before Oprah got hold of him": Chad McKnight, telephone interview
by author, November 13, 2018. All quotations from Chad McKnight in this
chapter are drawn from this interview.

181 "A confused 'mishmash' of Buddhism and Calvanism": Alex Cox, telephone
interview by author, November 12, 2018.

181 "Changed my life in some meaningful ways": Ed Begley Jr., telephone interview
by author, August 4, 2018. All quotations from Ed Begley Jr. in this chapter
are drawn from this interview.

181 "He was such a rebel": Jim Huggins Sr., telephone interview by author, January 2, 2018.

182 "The actor's life is one of the hardest lives": Dennis Lim, *David Lynch: The Man from Another Place* (New York: Amazon Publishing, 2015), 156.

182 "Where there is silence, one finds peace": Lao Tzu, *Tao Te Ching* (New York: Penguin Group, 2001), 48.

182 "The silence is not that of the desert": D. T. Suzuki, *An Introduction to Zen Buddhism* (New York: Grove Press, 1964), 35.

182 "You can see something clearly only when your mind is silent": Jiddu Krishnamurti, *Total Freedom: The Essential Krishnamurti* (San Francisco: HarperSanFrancisco, 1996), 316.

182 "Silence is very powerful": Huber, *Harry Dean Stanton: Partly Fiction*.

182 "Beat Zen is a complex phenomenon": Alan Watts, *This Is It and Other Essays on Zen and Spiritual Experience* (New York: Vintage Books, 1973 [orig. pub. 1958]), 89–92.

182 "There's a fine line between Buddhism and fuck it": "Conversation with Sophie Huber," *WTF with Marc Maron*, podcast.

183 "There is no self": *Harry Dean Stanton, Personal Quotes*, IMDb, https://www.imdb.com/name/nm0001765/bio?ref_=nm_ov_bio_sm.

183 "I didn't have the title until the last week of the edit": Sophie Huber, telephone interview by author, August 2, 2018.

183 "He said he wasn't anything": Huber, *Harry Dean Stanton: Partly Fiction*.

183 "All forms are unreal": "The Dhammapada," selections, in *A Treasury of Asian Literature,* ed. John A. Yohannan (New York: New American Library, 1964 [orig. pub. 1958]), 382.

183 "It is better to live alone": Ibid., 383.

183 "In Zen one does not feel guilty about dying": Watts, *This Is It and Other Essays on Zen and Spiritual Experience*, 89.

183 "Fundamentally not one thing exists": Ibid., 91.

12. Lucky in the Last Years

184 "He looked like a bird": Mary McCormack, interview by author, Los Angeles, March 18, 2018. All quotations from Mary McCormack in this chapter are drawn from this interview.

184 "It was really moving to watch him": Michael Morris, interview by author, Los Angeles, March 18, 2018. All quotations from Michael Morris in this chapter are drawn from this interview.

185 "When TV came up with a twenty-four-hour game show network": Jamie James, interview by author, Los Angeles, March 17, 2018. All quotations from Jamie James in this chapter are drawn from this interview.

186 "It is mind over matter": Ibid.

186 "I only eat so I can smoke and stay alive": Alec Nevala-Lee, "Musings of a Cigarette Smoking Man," Nevala-Lee (blog), September 22, 2017, https:// nevalalee.wordpress.com/tag/harry-dean-stanton.

186 "We stayed in touch": Jim Huggins Sr., telephone interview by author, January 2, 2018. All quotations from Jim Huggins Sr. in this chapter are drawn from this interview.

187 "I got to get away from Harry": Ibid.

187 "I drove out in my pickup truck to Los Angeles": Sara Stanton, telephone interview by author, March 2, 2018. All quotations from Sara Stanton in this chapter are drawn from this interview.

188 "He invited us over": Ralph Stanton Jr., telephone interview by author, January 1, 2018.

188 "This is my cousin": Jim Huggins Jr., telephone interview by author, December 16, 2017. All quotations from Jim Huggins Jr. in this chapter are drawn from this interview.

188 "He would come over, him and Dabney": Dawayne Wallace, telephone interview by author, November 14, 2018. All quotations from Dawayne Wallace in this chapter are drawn from this interview.

189 "He never liked it in a typical martini glass": Wayne Sable, email interview by author, May 23, 2018. All quotations from Wayne Sable in this chapter are drawn from this interview.

189 "Brando 'would often call at 3 AM'": Deane Williams, *The Cinema of Sean Penn: In and Out of Place* (New York: Wallflower Press, 2016), 92.

189 "You want to hear something, Harry?": James, interview by author, Los Angeles, March 17, 2018.

189 "What about now": Ibid.

191 "Harry Dean Stanton brings to the film a long history of roles": Williams, *The Cinema of Sean Penn*, 92.

191 "The head seems both shrunken and outsize": Ibid.

191 "Harry Dean has embodied the marginal spirit": Ibid., 94.

191 "Will you try with your next movie": Patrick McGilligan, *Jack's Life: A Biography of Jack Nicholson* (New York: W. W. Norton & Co., 2015, 1994), 500.

191 "Outsider in the Brat Pack era": Williams, *The Cinema of Sean Penn*, 92–93.

192 "That was from *Big Love*": Sophie Huber, telephone interview by author, August 2, 2018.

192 "A particularly creepy, corrupt, and possibly murderous": Susan King, "Softening the Edges of a Hard-Charging Sect Patriarch," *Los Angeles Times,* February 26, 2006, sec. E, p. 17.

193 "It was kind of cool": Brian McGuire, telephone interview by author, February 13, 2019. All quotations from Brian McGuire in this chapter are drawn from this interview.

194 "It's not a biography": Mark Olsen, "'Lucky' Is a Tribute Tailor-Made for Actor Harry Dean Stanton," *Los Angeles Times,* September 28, 2017, http://latimes .com/entertainment/movies/la-et-mn-lucky.

194 "Seventy-five percent of it is all Harry": Ibid.

195 "It's the echoes of *Paris, Texas*": David Ehrlich, "'Lucky' Review: 90-Year-Old Harry Dean Stanton Gives a Performance for the Ages in Wry Comedy Co-Starring David Lynch—SXSW 2017," *Indiewire,* March 11, 2017, http://www.indiewire.com/2017/03/lucky-review-john-carroll-lynch-harry-dean-stanton-sxsw-2017–1201792467.

196 "Beginning as a broad comedy": Ibid.

196 "The movie was like Everyman": John Carroll Lynch, comments, Harry Dean Stanton Fest, Lexington, KY, September 28, 2017.

196 "Man can take with him from this world nothing": "Everyman" in *The Norton Anthology of English Literature,* vol. 1, ed. M. H. Abrams (New York: W. W. Norton & Co., 1962), 282.

196 "One night I was parked in my car": Drago Sumonja, comments, Harry Dean Stanton Fest, Lexington, KY, September 28, 2017.

196 "Wizened as a dry twig": Stephen Dalton, "Critic's Notebook: Harry Dean Stanton, a Zen Cowboy Who Said Everything by Saying Nothing," *Hollywood Reporter,* September 16, 2017, http://www.hollywoodreporter.com/news/critics-notebook-harry-dean-stanton-a-zen-cowboy-who-said-everything-by-saying-nothing-1039865.

197 "With the unexpected timing of the movie's release": Olsen, "'Lucky' Is a Tribute Tailor-Made for Actor Harry Dean Stanton."

197 "A generous vehicle for Stanton's presence": Richard Brody, "How 'Paris, Texas' Sold Harry Dean Stanton Short," *New Yorker,* September 28, 2017, https://newyorker.com/culture/richard-brody/how-paris-texas-sold-harry-dean-stanton-short.

197 "Elegaic in tone but full of warmth": Dalton, "Critic's Notebook: Harry Dean Stanton, a Zen Cowboy Who Said Everything by Saying Nothing."

197 "Harry Dean needed justification for his actions": Interview with Writers/Producers Logan Sparks and Drago Sumonja, *Lucky,* 2016 (Magnolia Home Entertainment, DVD).

197 "He didn't suffer fools": Rebecca Rubin, "Harry Dean Stanton: 'Lucky' Director, Cast Share Memories of Working with Late Actor," *Variety,* September 27, 2017, https://variety.com/2017/scene/news/harry-dean-stanton-lucky-1202574148.

197 "I personally knew that time wasn't on our side": Olsen, "'Lucky' Is a Tribute Tailor-Made for Actor Harry Dean Stanton."

198 "It was a lot of work": Harry Dean Stanton, comments, *Lucky* (Magnolia Home Entertainment, DVD).

Postscript

201 "Meet me tonight for dinner": Jim Huggins Sr., telephone interview by author, January 2, 2018. All quotations from Jim Huggins Sr. in this chapter are drawn from this interview.

Notes

201 "I don't believe Harry Dean had kids": Jim Huggins Jr., email interview by author, October 4, 2019.

201 "Harry actually gave her a check for $10,000": Wim Wenders, email interview by author, October 3, 2019.

202 "Believe the words you are saying": Hunter Carson, interview by author, Lexington, KY, July 13, 2019.

202 "This is the best night of my life": Lauren Modery, "Harry Dean Stanton: Celebrating 90 Years of Awesomeness," Hipstercrite (blog), October 25, 2016, https://bullshit.ist/harry-dean-stanton-celebrating-90-years-of -awesomeness.

203 "I was just completely enamored": Lucy Jones, interview by author, Lexington, KY, May 22, 2017.

203 "I was blown away by the fact": Steven Rosen, "Lexington's Harry Dean Stanton Fest Is a Model for Other Actor-Themed Film Festivals," Huffington Post (blog), May 27, 2015, http://www.huffingtonpost.com/steven-rosen /lexingtons-harry-dean-sta_b_7441656.html.

203 "Everyone I've talked to since says that was their favorite part": Ibid.

Index

Note: The abbreviation HDS stands for Harry Dean Stanton.

Index

Index

Index

Index

Index

Index

Index

Index

Index

Virginian, The, 63
Vitarelli, Joseph, 152
Viva Zapata!, 91
Vogler, Rüdiger, 131, 136
Voyage of the Damned, 73

Wagner, Dave, 55
Waiting for Godot, 70
Walken, Christopher, 153, 188
Walker, 121, 127
Walker, Tracey, 118
Wallace, David Foster, 163
Wallace, Dawayne, 188, 202
Wallace, Patty, 99
Walsh, M. Emmet, 64, 102
Walter Winchell File, The, 57
Wang, Wayne, 158–59
Wanted: Dead or Alive, 60
Ward, Elizabeth, 56
Ward, Fred, 155
Warhol, Andy, 153
Warner, Jack, 78
Watts, Alan, 68, 69, 100, 179, 181, 182, 183
Wayne, John, 34, 54
Weaver, Dennis, 82
Weavers, 48
Webb, Andy, 57
Webb-Pomerene Act (1918), 53
Weddle, David, 61
Wegener, Paul, 145
Weinstein, Harvey, 188
Welles, Orson, 64
Wenders, Wim: casting for Paris, Texas, 134–37; critical reception of Paris, Texas, 146–47; direction of Hammett, 80, 110, 111, 132–33; filming Paris, Texas, 139–42; from German New Cinema, 8, 105, 131–32; on HDS's acting, 143–44; on HDS's generosity, 201–2; and Monte Hellman, 133–34; influenced by German Expressionist film, 145–46; preference for character actors, 3–4, 80, 111, 135; story

development for Paris, Texas, 129–31, 141–42; work with Ry Cooder, 128–29; work with Robbie Müller, 123, 137–38
Westerns, 57–62, 70–72, 94
Wexley, John: The Last Mile, 43
White Christmas, 57
White Rock, North Carolina, 17–18
Wicki, Bernard, 137
Wild at Heart, 162, 164–65
Wild Bunch, The, 84, 86
Wilder, Billy, 64–65, 131
Wilder, Thornton, 159
Wild Ride, The, 69–70
Wild Wild West, The, 63
Williams, Cindy, 155
Williams, Clarence, 25
Williams, Deane, 190–91
Williams, Gail, 101
Williams, Hank, 48
Williams, Red, 25
Williams, Robin, 150, 157
Williamson, Bruce, 160
Wills, Chill, 84
Wilson, Glenn, 11
Wilson, Owen, 2, 180
Wine, Bill, 169, 192
Winner, Derek, 57
Winter's Tale, 41
Wise, Ray, 166
Wise Blood, 7, 79, 99, 103–5
Witt, Albert, 15
Wolff, Art, 152
Woodward, Bob, 150
Woodward, Joanne, 74
Woodward, Morgan, 7, 73
Wool, Abbe, 122
Worden, Hank, 80, 111
World War II, 27–32
Wright, Robin, 163, 190
Wrong Man, The, 6, 55, 56
Wrong Move, 130, 132, 136
Wurlitzer, Rudolph, 85, 126–27
WUSA, 73

Index

Screen Classics

Screen Classics is a series of critical biographies, film histories, and analytical studies focusing on neglected filmmakers and important screen artists and subjects, from the era of silent cinema through the golden age of Hollywood to the international generation of today. Books in the Screen Classics series are intended for scholars and general readers alike. The contributing authors are established figures in their respective fields. This series also serves the purpose of advancing scholarship on film personalities and themes with ties to Kentucky.

Series Editor

Patrick McGilligan

Books in the Series

Olivia de Havilland: Lady Triumphant
Victoria Amador

Mae Murray: The Girl with the Bee-Stung Lips
Michael G. Ankerich

Harry Dean Stanton: Hollywood's Zen Rebel
Joseph B. Atkins

Hedy Lamarr: The Most Beautiful Woman in Film
Ruth Barton

Rex Ingram: Visionary Director of the Silent Screen
Ruth Barton

Conversations with Classic Film Stars: Interviews from Hollywood's Golden Era
James Bawden and Ron Miller

Conversations with Legendary Television Stars: Interviews from the First Fifty Years
James Bawden and Ron Miller

You Ain't Heard Nothin' Yet: Interviews with Stars from Hollywood's Golden Era
James Bawden and Ron Miller

Von Sternberg
John Baxter

Hitchcock's Partner in Suspense: The Life of Screenwriter Charles Bennett
Charles Bennett, edited by John Charles Bennett

Hitchcock and the Censors
John Billheimer

A Uniquely American Epic: Intimacy and Action, Tenderness and Violence in Sam Peckinpah's The Wild Bunch
Edited by Michael Bliss

My Life in Focus: A Photographer's Journey with Elizabeth Taylor and the Hollywood Jet Set
Gianni Bozzacchi with Joey Tayler

Hollywood Divided: The 1950 Screen Directors Guild Meeting and the Impact of the Blacklist
Kevin Brianton

He's Got Rhythm: The Life and Career of Gene Kelly
Cynthia Brideson and Sara Brideson

Ziegfeld and His Follies: A Biography of Broadway's Greatest Producer
Cynthia Brideson and Sara Brideson

The Marxist and the Movies: A Biography of Paul Jarrico
Larry Ceplair

Dalton Trumbo: Blacklisted Hollywood Radical
Larry Ceplair and Christopher Trumbo

Warren Oates: A Wild Life
Susan Compo

Improvising Out Loud: My Life Teaching Hollywood How to Act
Jeff Corey with Emily Corey

Crane: Sex, Celebrity, and My Father's Unsolved Murder
Robert Crane and Christopher Fryer

Jack Nicholson: The Early Years
Robert Crane and Christopher Fryer

Anne Bancroft: A Life
Douglass K. Daniel

Being Hal Ashby: Life of a Hollywood Rebel
Nick Dawson

Bruce Dern: A Memoir
Bruce Dern with Christopher Fryer and Robert Crane

Intrepid Laughter: Preston Sturges and the Movies
Andrew Dickos

Charles Walters: The Director Who Made Hollywood Dance
Brent Phillips

Some Like It Wilder: The Life and Controversial Films of Billy Wilder
Gene D. Phillips

Ann Dvorak: Hollywood's Forgotten Rebel
Christina Rice

Lewis Milestone: Life and Films
Harlow Robinson

Michael Curtiz: A Life in Film
Alan K. Rode

Arthur Penn: American Director
Nat Segaloff

Film's First Family: The Untold Story of the Costellos
Terry Chester Shulman

Claude Rains: An Actor's Voice
David J. Skal with Jessica Rains

Barbara La Marr: The Girl Who Was Too Beautiful for Hollywood
Sherri Snyder

Buzz: The Life and Art of Busby Berkeley
Jeffrey Spivak

Victor Fleming: An American Movie Master
Michael Sragow

Hollywood Presents Jules Verne: The Father of Science Fiction on Screen
Brian Taves

Thomas Ince: Hollywood's Independent Pioneer
Brian Taves

Picturing Peter Bogdanovich: My Conversations with the New Hollywood Director
Peter Tonguette

Carl Theodor Dreyer and Ordet: My Summer with the Danish Filmmaker
Jan Wahl

Clarence Brown: Hollywood's Forgotten Master
Gwenda Young